SEW
FAST, FASTER,
FASTEST

SEW FAST, FASTER, FASTEST

Timesaving Techniques and Shortcuts for Busy Sewers

Sue Hausmann

Rodale Press, Inc.
Emmaus, Pennsylvania

The author and editors who compiled this book
have tried to make all of the contents as accurate
and as correct as possible. Illustrations, photographs, and text have all been carefully checked
and cross-checked. However, due to the variability
of personal skill and materials, neither the author
nor Rodale Press assumes any responsibility for
any injuries suffered or for damages or other losses
incurred that result from the material presented
herein. All instructions should be carefully studied
and clearly understood before beginning a project.

Stitch lengths in this book are given as a number,
such as 2.5, which refers to the length of the stitch
in millimeters. This is the stitch-length system found
on the majority of sewing machines currently sold in
North America. Some sewing machines still in use
are calibrated in stitches per inch (spi). However,
the following guidelines may be useful in inter-
preting the millimeter stitch settings in terms of
stitches per inch: 2.5 is an average stitch length
roughly equivalent to 10 spi; 4 is a long stitch length
roughly equivalent to 6 spi; and 1.5 is a short stitch
length roughly equivalent to 18 spi.

Editor: Toni D. Toomey
Technical Assistant: Susan Nester
Interior Designers: Carol Angstadt,
    Christopher Rhoads
Layout Designer: Susan P. Eugster
How-to Illustrator: John Kocon Illustration
Fashion Illustrator: Sandy Haight
Digital Imaging Specialist: Dale Mack
Interior Photographer: John Hamel
Photo Stylist: Pam Simpson
Cover Designer: Christopher Rhoads
Cover Photographer: Mitch Mandel
Back Cover Designer: Marta Mitchell Strait
Photography Editor: Jim Gallucci
Copy Editors: Nancy N. Bailey, Patricia A. Sinnott
Manufacturing Coordinator: Patrick T. Smith
Indexer: Nan Badgett
Editorial Assistance: Jodi Guiducci, Susan L. Nickol

Rodale Home and Garden Books
Vice President and Editorial Director:
    Margaret J. Lydic
Managing Editor, Sewing Books: Cheryl Winters-Tetreau
Director of Design and Production: Michael Ward
Associate Art Director: Carol Angstadt
Production Manager: Robert V. Anderson Jr.
Studio Manager: Leslie M. Keefe
Copy Director: Dolores Plikaitis
Manufacturing Manager: Mark Krahforst
Office Manager: Karen Earl-Braymer

Library of Congress Cataloging-in-Publication Data

Hausmann, Sue.
    Sew fast, faster, fastest : timesaving techniques and
shortcuts for busy sewers / Sue Hausmann.
        p.   cm.
    Includes index.
    ISBN 0–87596–793–0   (hardcover : acid-free paper)
    1. Machine sewing.   I. Title.
TT713 .H37 1998
646.2'044—ddc21   98–25324

Printed in the United States of America on
acid-free ∞, recycled ♲ paper

Distributed in the book trade by St. Martin's Press

2 4 6 8 10 9 7 5 3 1   hardcover

With gratitude to

my Heavenly Father,

who has blessed me

with sewing skills

and the ability

to share them,

I dedicate this book

to everyone who

loves to sew and

to my husband,

Herb, for his constant

encouragement

and support.

CONTENTS

Sue's Favorite Fast Cover-Up Garments   44

Construction Techniques   76

Garment Details   112

Several years ago the first "America Sews with Sue Hausmann" television program was born out of my feeling that there was a need for a way to demonstrate sewing techniques that would make sewing faster and more fun. Home sewing has really changed over the last decade. Today, thanks to new techniques and tools and to a new attitude that there is no one right way to sew, many garments can be completed in hours instead of days! I truly believe that there is no one right way to do things. We must use the techniques that work

for us. I am privileged to have so many people sharing new techniques with me. And I am pleased to have the opportunity—actually, the mission—to share them with others.

Many viewers of "America Sews" have asked for more step-by-step instructions that give speed-sewing options as alternatives to the pattern instructions. For this reason, when the sewing editors at Rodale Press suggested this book after attending my program titled "Fast, Faster, Fastest Sewing," I jumped at the opportunity to share some of my favorite sewing techniques with you.

Over the last 30 years I have sewn for my family, my home, and my job. As my sewing time has become more and more limited due to hours on airplanes and at the computer, I have often substituted quicker methods than those suggested in the pattern instructions.

Today a variety of sewing techniques are not only accepted but encouraged by sewing enthusiasts all over the world. They choose sewing techniques based upon the sewing equipment they have available to them, the amount of sewing time they can devote, and the purpose of the project. For example, a pair of pajamas for the grandchildren, a T-shirt for gardening, or a costume for Halloween can be constructed quickly on the serger with no finishing details. A suit or dress for the office will have a professional look with a few more construction details and finishing techniques. Sewers the world over will labor joyously and painstakingly for months on a wedding dress or christening outfit that will become a family heirloom. The key is to know what technique to use and when to use it.

Sew Fast, Faster, Fastest is designed to help you with technique choices. Before beginning a sewing project, read through the pattern instructions. When your pattern calls for a time-consuming technique or one that you do not understand (or enjoy sewing), simply look up the technique in the index of this book and select a faster or easier way!

Throughout the book you'll find my shortcuts in boxes called "Sue's Snippets," "On the Fast Track," "Here's What I Do," and "Sue's Favorite Fast Accessories." Be sure to check them out and integrate these sewing tips and techniques into the construction steps of every project. They are guaranteed to save you time without sacrificing the quality of your sewing.

Sue Hausmann

GETTING READY TO SEW

Each day we make choices about every aspect of our lives. Many of the choices relate to ordinary matters, such as what to cook for dinner tonight, while other choices actually determine our life direction. As I travel across the country visiting with sewers of all ages and lifestyles, I find one thing we all have in common is that we are busy people, yet we choose to spend as much time as we can sewing. This chapter is about some choices we can make to get the most out of our sewing time.

WHY SEW?

Today many people ask me why I still sew. The answer is simple—I enjoy the process. I truly enjoy turning a piece of cloth into a one-of-a-kind garment, and I find that most sewers feel the same way. It is amazing to see a flat piece of cloth evolve into a wonderful garment for me to wear or to give to someone I love. Because I sew them myself, my garments are special and unlike anything that can be purchased "off the rack." They also fit better and hold up longer than ready-to-wear because I have taken care to construct them to last. And, of course, the garments I make are often a lot less costly than comparable ready-to-wear, and I get to choose the color!

My sewing time is limited, so I make choices at the beginning of a project that determine how long it will take and how hard or easy the sewing will be. I am always looking for new techniques that will save me time, but never at the expense of the final quality and appearance of the garment!

CHOOSING WHAT TO SEW

The need, or more often than not the desire, for something new is what usually motivates me to sew. Often I want to create something special for a vacation, party, or special event. I also try to sew two new suits each season to wear to the office and on my television show "America Sews."

To help decide what to sew, look for ideas anywhere they are to be found. Look through

When I began teaching others to sew over 30 years ago, I would start my class by listing the reasons I sewed. I needed to save money, and I wanted clothes with a better fit and better workmanship than I could afford to buy. Plus, I wanted the special pleasure I got from sewing and from wearing garments I had made.

I was inspired to make this silk dinner suit when I saw a newspaper ad for the ready-to-wear version. I saved $188 by making it myself.

catalogs, newspapers, and magazines for inspiration. Take notes on what you like, then go to your local fabric store and look for similar patterns. Be prepared to spend time poring over the pattern books. Some stores will loan out or sell pattern books after their current date expires.

I subscribe to all the sewing magazines and get many ideas from them. They feature only the most current pattern styles, so I'm not overwhelmed with too many choices.

The inspiration for my pink dinner suit shown in the photo above came from a department store newspaper ad picturing a similar suit that cost $240. I took the ad with me to the fabric store and selected a pattern with the same princess lines, then purchased raw silk for the suit and a scalloped lace for the sleeves and insert. I used the sleeve pattern piece to determine the lace yardage since there was none given in the pattern, and I wanted the hemline to be placed along the scalloped border. The small lace insert at the V-neck ties in with the lace sleeves and keeps the neckline modest. The actual cost to make this suit was $52, with $12 of that spent on the rhinestone buttons. I bought these buttons at a fabric store, but many of my special buttons are those that I have cut off garments I was discarding. You can also find great buttons in button boxes and on garments at resale shops.

Copy Ready-to-Wear

Designer clothing is well worth the time and effort to recreate on your sewing machine. Shop at the best stores and try on garments to see what's in style and, more important, what looks good on you. Pattern companies stay on top of current fashions, so if you find a garment you like in ready-to-wear, you will most likely find a pattern to sew in a similar style. The best part is you can sew it to fit your exact size in the fabric and color of your choice!

My silky jacket, blouse, and skirt shown in the photo below were inspired by an international designer who specializes in mixing prints. I admired a friend's ensemble, and because the design concept was so striking, I had planned to buy one of the suits or dresses. When I learned they sell for $400 to $500 and are made from polyester, not silk, I decided to make one myself. My copy cost less than $80.

The combination of colorful prints is what makes this designer ensemble so striking. When I chose the prints for the jacket, I selected one main print with two strong colors, black and royal blue, plus green, pink, and purple as accent colors. I then chose complementary fabrics in a variety of prints, each with a different size and scale. The common colors help to blend the different fabrics together. Blocks of fabric were stitched together to make a piece large enough to cut

A similar skirt, blouse, and jacket ensemble from a designer who specializes in mixing prints cost over $400 and was made of polyester. My copy cost less than $80.

out each pattern piece. I placed large horizontal pieces across the shoulder line and darker colors at the sides to create a slimmer look. I made a matching Career Change Blouse (see page 28) out of one of the prints and a solid and a skirt out of solid blue fabric.

Mix and Match with Ready-to-Wear

If you don't have time to make a jacket, purchase one instead, and sew several sets of coordinates to go with it. The mainstay of my wardrobe is career clothing, but I don't want to dress like everyone else. And because my sewing time is more limited than it used to be, I don't make as many tailored jackets as I used to. I like to go to the name-brand outlets that sell quality ready-to-wear at affordable prices. Many times the clothing needs alterations

I purchase an occasional ready-to-wear wardrobe staple, like this blazer, then make quick skirts and blouses that mix and match.

or repairs, but that isn't a problem for anyone who sews!

I purchased the fuchsia blazer, shown in the photo at right, out of season, came home and selected coordinating fabrics that I already had in my fabric collection, and hung them on a hanger with the jacket. As the fall season approached, I made two blouses and skirts so I had two outfits to go with the store-bought jacket. These easy mix-and-match separates come from my favorite fast garments,

on the
FAST TRACK...

to Tailored Jackets

When I sew tailored suits, I often make two at one time. I cut out two suits from the same pattern, along with lining and interfacing, in fabrics that can be sewn with the same color thread.

To save time, I cut and construct two jackets at a time. This collarless silk tweed jacket was quick to make, and it's the perfect match for many of my quick skirts and blouses.

Often I make one solid and one tweed in the same color tones. You can usually double the interfacing and lining so you cut the pieces for both suits at one time.

The real time-saver is not having to read the directions or think through the construction steps on the second suit! Sew the suits simultaneously, repeating each step for both suits. It seems a little tedious while sewing, but I always remind myself that in the end I will have two new suits!

I save even more sewing and tailoring time by choosing a jacket pattern with no lapels or collar. This collarless jacket in a multicolor raw silk sewed up quickly and has been a favorite of mine for several years. Team it with a silk Career Change Blouse (see page 28), and it can be worn in any season.

which you will find in "Sue's Favorite Fast Garments" on page 20.

Let the Fabric Be Your Guide

Often a beautiful fabric is the inspiration for a garment. I fell in love with an elegant fabric painted with beautiful flowers when I was in Hawaii recently with my husband, Herb, as part of a Husqvarna Viking Sewing Machine group.

Take one painted silk piece of fabric. Add a serger and one determined sewer (that's me!). Put them all in the same room for an afternoon, and *voilà*—a quick and easy belted jacket.

Hand-painted silk garments are featured in many of the more exclusive shops on the island of Maui, and I soon had my heart set on one. But I just couldn't buy it, because I knew I could make it for less. Herb and I decided to find out if the silks were hand painted on Maui, and if so, where.

It did not take us long searching the Yellow Pages to find a boutique that sold painted silk garments. Perhaps someone there could tell me where I could find the fabric. At the shop, as I closely studied the beautiful handmade garments, the owner asked me if I sewed. I replied yes, thinking that now I was in trouble. She invited Herb and me to see her studio, led us to a room full of paint, silk, and creativity, and asked if I would like to buy yardage! I chose the silk charmeuse fabric for my purple and

fuchsia jacket shown in the photo at left. The fabric actually had the shape of the jacket and belt pieces hand painted on it, so all I had to do was cut on the lines. I was able to serge up the garment in our hotel room that afternoon and wear it to dinner that night. (Yes, I do take my sewing machine and sometimes my serger on many of my trips!)

BEFORE YOU SEW— KNOW YOUR MACHINE

We all have our favorite sewing tools and notions, but it is always fun to look for what's new on the market. Those of us who love to sew are lucky that today the home-sewing industry is tireless in trying to keep up with our demand for better equipment and new materials to sew with.

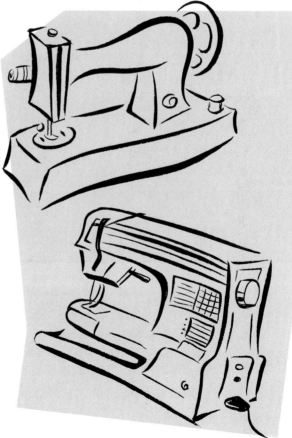

You and Your Machine

If you are still sewing on a basic model without many of the new features available today, you might consider a new machine. I feel more sewers are deterred by poor-quality machines than by any other factor. When a sewing machine constantly jams up or the tension is always poor, it is more than a little discouraging. My advice is to spend as much as you can afford on a new sewing machine and to buy it from a local sewing machine retailer that has a strong interest in education. It is an investment in your sewing future and pleasure.

If you already love to sew, consider upgrading to a computerized model. Today the computer in the sewing machine takes away the guesswork of where and how to set the stitches and saves you time for the fun of sewing.

Something Old, Something New

When I was growing up, my father did a great deal of the sewing in our home—mostly drapes, bedspreads, dust ruffles, and curtains—all on the treadle sewing machine that had belonged to my grandmother. Daddy had taken it out of the cabinet and added a motor. The machine sewed only one speed—very fast. My mom said the speed was why she did not sew much.

When I showed interest in sewing in our local 4-H club, my dad invested in a top-of-the-line sewing machine. The year was 1953, the price tag was $383, and this machine sewed only a straight stitch! At the time, my finishing techniques were nil, but because the machine was an excellent-quality one, my sewing skills blossomed.

When Herb and I were first married, my aunt gave me an old black machine to use. It was a total frustration, and Herb decided we were going to invest in a new machine. We bought the top-of-the-line model in a nice cabinet. We had been married for several years, and this was the

SUE'S SNIPPETS
A LIFELONG AFFAIR

I love to tell the story about one of my childhood sewing mentors, Carol Christensen, a neighbor for whom I used to baby-sit. When I first met Carol, she had no sewing machine and sewed complete garments for herself and her young family by hand. What a thrill when her husband bought her a machine. She cut out garments on the bed, and I remember one time she cut through too many layers, resulting in a chenille bedspread cut into the dress pattern. Carol made the chenille "dress" into a robe for herself. Today, almost 50 years later, she still lives down the road from me and still loves to sew.

most expensive purchase we had made except for our house and car. I remember crying on the way home from the store, saying "We should have bought a television for the family."

My new sewing machine did it all, at least for the 1960s. To be able to finish seams with a zigzag (I didn't even know a three-step zigzag would keep the edges neater and flatter) and to make buttonholes without putting on that huge attachment—I was in sewing heaven!

Getting the Most from My Machine

One technique was a mystery. When I bought the machine, the salesperson told me it would hem. I read the instruction book and tried to figure out the illustrations, but the technique eluded me. At my first lesson on the machine, I asked about the blindhem technique, and the teacher demonstrated the folding and sewing. It was as though a light bulb went on in my head. I got it and have been blind hemming ever since.

Then came the days when our family was young—I was doing alterations and custom sewing at home, and time was short for my own sewing. I sewed hems by machine, I avoided

HERE'S WHAT **I DO**...

to Leave the Serger at Home

Because I travel so much and sew in hotel rooms along the way, I carry my machine with me, but it is often impossible to carry my serger too. To get a garment ready to sew while I'm away, I cut out and underline all the pieces, then I finish the edges on the serger while I'm still at home. Then into a bag the pieces go with everything I need to finish the garment. Whether you sew on the road or at home, this technique saves time and results in quality finished garments.

patterns with buttons and buttonholes, and I had a closet full of skirts without skirt hooks and eyes.

After a few years of using safety pins to close waistbands, I was determined to learn to do the finishing faster. My sewing machine was the answer. I had just never learned to use it well. Sewing buttons and snaps was an eye-opener, too. Who would have ever thought my sewing machine would sew them on quicker and much stronger than I could ever do it by hand?

Then there were other finishing techniques that I began to notice in fine ready-to-wear. There were the details like binding and piping that set one garment apart from another. I was determined to learn to add those details to my garments. For years I had followed the pattern instructions to the letter. Now it was time to use the instructions as a guide. Then I could use my own finishing technique, which I could do many times faster and easier. Some of my first attempts were learning experiences—I would try a technique, then rip it out.

The finishing techniques often make the difference between the handmade and homemade look! Today I sew all these finishing details with

my sewing machine in a fraction of the time. And now my rule is to never consider a skirt wearable until the skirt hooks and eyes have been stitched in place (by machine, of course)!

BEFORE YOU SEW— FABRICS AND PATTERNS

I must confess that I love beautiful fabrics. Silks, cottons, wools, rayons, prints, solids, plaids—I collect them all. When you see a fabric you love, add it to your collection and don't feel guilty. My husband would tell you not to bother entering the "she-who-dies-with-the-most-fabric-wins" contest, because I've already won. He wants to insulate our house with my collection!

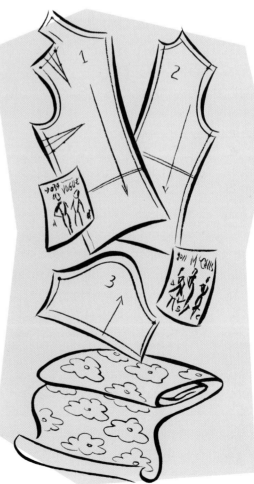

Go for Quality

My advice on fabric is to buy the best you can afford; natural fibers and prints are actually easier to sew because they are so forgiving of mistakes and they press and mold to the shape of your pattern. Synthetic fabrics, especially permanent press, are "trained" and frequently coated, so that they return to their original flat state on the bolt rather than conform to the shape of your garment. Because I sew for pleasure, I want to enjoy the process, and working with beautiful, quality fabrics is part of that experience. I think of natural-fiber fabrics as a long-term investment in my wardrobe; quality fabrics made into classic patterns will be worn year after year.

Consider the Characteristics of the Fabric

When shopping for fabric, the weight, the drape, and the "hand" of a fabric are really the most important considerations. The type of fiber has nothing to do with the hand of a fabric. Wools, cottons, linens, and silks can all be heavyweight and stiff or lightweight and drapable. No sewer should go fabric shopping without touching everything! Most fabric-store owners encourage it and do it themselves because they understand that this is the only way really to know about the hand of a fabric—whether it wrinkles and, most important, how it will feel when you wear it. I think this is the success of the new washed silks, rayons, and microfibers. I know once I touch them, I can't leave the store without them.

Heavier weaves and weights tailor into jackets and straight skirts, while lighter weights are suitable for fuller styles with more fabric gathers. You can change the weight and hand of a light- or medium-weight fabric by under-

lining it with fusible interfacing, lining fabric, or both. A full skirt and fitted jacket can be made from the same lightweight fabric just by underlining the jacket with fusible knit interfacing. I like to fuse the entire piece of fashion fabric before cutting out the pattern pieces.

If you buy only a small amount, it's easier to splurge on special fabrics like the patchwork silk used in this vest.

Once you have chosen your fabric, how do you know how much yardage to purchase if you don't have your pattern in hand? This is a question I'm often asked. If you have a style or garment type in mind, it's quite easy to calculate the yardage needed by adding the lengths of the main pattern pieces. Be prepared and always bring a tape measure to measure the approximate length of the garment you want to make. For example, if you are making a jacket and the fabric is 60 inches (152.4 cm) wide, the amount you'll need is the length of the jacket plus the length of the sleeve. When the fabric is 45 inches (114.3 cm) wide, you will usually need two jacket lengths plus a sleeve length.

You will get really good at this with practice, but if you miscalculate or find a wonderful remnant that just isn't quite long enough, don't worry. You always have the option of making the jacket slightly shorter or with short sleeves instead of long. We sewers are the mothers of invention!

It's easier to splurge on beautiful natural fibers and handwovens when you're only buying ⅝ to ¾ yard (0.6 to 0.7 m) of fabric. A simple vest is a quick project that can update an outfit, either casual or formal, in any season. I purchased the patchwork silk for the vest shown in the photo on the opposite page already pieced because I wanted to be able to spend my time embellishing it with machine embroidery. I often make a vest to try out new machine art and embellishment techniques.

The silk charmeuse printed with miniature quilt blocks shown in the photo below was so pricey that I bought only enough for a square scarf (or so I thought). It matched a jewel-blue raw-silk remnant I already had, so a coordinating jacket and dress was in order. This was quite a challenge from 1¼ yards (1.1 m) of fabric remnants! The jacket was lined with the *Fast* technique in "Lining and Underlining" on page 82, and the dress was underlined with the *Faster* technique on page 83.

I thought I had bought only enough of this pricey silk print to make a scarf. However, I was able to "stretch" the fabric far enough to make this jacket instead by shortening the hem on the jacket pattern.

Which Comes First— The Pattern or the Fabric?

The inspiration for most of my sewing projects begins with a piece of fabric. This is backward according to most sewing rules, which say you're supposed to look for the pattern first and then buy the fabric. Which you do can change from project to project. But choosing a pattern from all the ones that are available today can be overwhelming.

I prefer basic styles with clean lines and just a few pattern pieces. Working with fewer pattern pieces really does save sewing time. If the pattern you choose has too many pieces to allow for quick construction, you can reduce the number of pieces by making simple pattern modifications. For example, the center back seamline in a vest or jacket can often be positioned on the folded edge of the fabric. On a blouse pattern, you can lap the front facing over the front pattern piece, matching up the seamlines. This will give you a blouse front and fold-back facing in one pattern piece. Be careful not to make any modifications that would eliminate style and design lines or any vertical lines that have a slimming effect.

I have found that many sewers choose a pattern based on the way it looks in the pattern book. They like the color or type of fabric used in the sketch or photograph. Style is such a personal statement that we do not need to let ourselves be dictated to by trends or designers. Creative sewers have the freedom to make any garment they desire. Choose patterns that suit your body type and your lifestyle, then update your look with embellishment details and accessories.

Save every pattern you sew—and those you have never sewn, if you have the space. Often you can combine parts of an old pattern with parts of a new one. (I make notes on the pattern

tissue and envelope for future projects.) Favorite patterns can be made several times. You know exactly what you are sewing, and by using different fabrics, lengths, and buttons, the garments will look entirely different.

Once you have selected a pattern, choose a fabric that is suitable for the style. Here again, shopping ready-to-wear can be a great guide to what fabrics give you the results you expect from the pattern. Check the labels and feel the hand of the fabric on ready-to-wear garments that you admire to get an idea of the fabric that was used, then look for similar fabrics to purchase. Always check the fabric recommendations on the pattern envelope, as well.

BEFORE YOU SEW—SHOPPING SHORTCUTS

When I am in the middle of a sewing project, I do not want to disrupt my sewing time to make an emergency shopping trip. To avoid emergency runs, stock up on the basics, and store them in clear plastic boxes with labels. Buy quantities of your sewing essentials, like interfacing, elastic, and thread, on sale so you always have what you need on hand.

For me there are two types of fabric-store shopping trips. One I make when I have a specific project in mind; the other is more for inspiration. I make many of both.

SUE'S SNIPPETS
THE BUDDY SYSTEM

To save time fabric shopping, I usually take my husband, Herb, or a friend along to stand in line and have fabric cut while I shop. On one occasion, I had to make a dress in a specific teal color for a television appearance and had very little shopping and sewing time. Herb and I both have T-shirts in the teal color I was looking for, so we wore them into the fabric store. We went in different directions in the store to look for fabrics that matched our T-shirts and met back at the cutting table with several bolts. I chose the fabric I wanted, then while Herb had the fabric cut, I shopped for notions. I rushed home and sewed a teal silk-noil dress that afternoon.

When shopping for a project, I make a list at home with as many of the specifics as possible. If I already have the fashion fabric, I always tape a small piece of it to the list so I can match the lining, thread, and zippers.

Stocking Up Saves Time

Shopping trips for specific materials cut into my sewing time, so I keep these trips to a minimum by stocking up in advance. Not everyone has the space or desire to stock up on supplies as I do. But if you can, buy quantities of what you use the most, and make special trips to the fabric store only when needed. If you do your shopping with an independent dealer, let the dealer know what types of sewing you do and what types of notions and fabrics you are looking for. It's easier for dealers to serve their customers if they know what their customers are looking for and can be sure to have those items in stock.

Interfacing

Purchase your favorite fusible interfacings in 5-yard (4.6-m) pieces. It is more economical to work with larger pieces since you can avoid the unusable leftover ends you get from shorter lengths purchased for individual projects. Serge or stitch storage bags from the plastic instruction sheets that come with the interfacings. I make two for each type and keep yardage in one and scraps in the other. When I'm running low, I take my instruction "bag" to the store to be sure I find my favorites in the maze of interfacings.

To make things faster and easier, I stock up on three basic fusible interfacings in light and dark colors. For tailored garments requiring more shaping, I use a weft-insertion interfacing sold under brand names such as Suit-Shape and Armo Weft by Handler Textile Corporation (HTC). I use this on coat and suit fabrics such as wool, linen, denim, double knit, and synthetic suede. Fusible tricot interfacing is available in two weights and meets virtually all my other interfacing needs for light- to medium-weight fabrics that do not require a defined shaping. Fusible tricot is sold under the names Fusi-Knit and So-Sheer, a very light sheer version, and can also be used to underline. Al-

HERE'S WHAT **I DO**...
to Interface

Follow the lead of ready-to-wear manufacturers, and fuse the interfacing to the garment, not the facing piece, so the shape and stability is where you need it. On many tailored garments, you may interface both. Try different weights, such as weft-insertion interfacing on the undercollar and knit tricot interfacing on the upper collar for a soft yet stable collar.

ways test the interfacing first on a scrap of fabric. The list of new fusible interfacings available to the home sewer continues to grow. HTC offers a convenient test kit containing ten samples of different interfacings. (See "Sources" on page 203.)

Thread

Most of us have thread on hand that is way past its prime. If your machine is balking at this thread, get rid of it and invest in quality thread in an assortment of colors. It can save time and headaches later. If you have a serger, buy cone thread in all the basic colors. Many times you can use gray for light fabrics and navy or black for darks. To sew the seam in the fashion color, thread the left needle with a standard spool of thread in a color that matches the fabric.

Zippers

Keep a supply of zippers on hand in the colors you sew the most. (I still have invisible zippers I stocked up on at a sale some years ago.) Zippers are much easier to put in when the pull extends above the placket, so buy long zippers and cut them to size after you insert them. (Be sure the pull is at the bottom before cutting!)

on the
FAST TRACK...
to Cutting Interfacing

If you plan to make more than one garment from a pattern, stack two layers of fusible interfacings, and cut an extra set for a pattern you plan to make again. Store the extra interfacing pieces in the pattern envelope and save time the next time you make the garment.

Elastic

Survey the notions wall at your fabric store to see the choices available for waistband elastic. I prefer 1-inch (2.5-cm) nonroll elastic for my waistbands. For more mileage out of your elastic, buy it in odd-numbered amounts such as 3, 5, 7, or 9 yards (2.7, 4.6, 6.4, or 8.2 m). Most people can cut one waistband from 1 yard (0.9 m) and four waistbands from 3 yards (2.7 m). Eliminate those short leftover pieces!

Many people are not familiar with clear elastic. It is sold in packages and by the yard in most fabric stores. I like it for fixes and for lingerie because it is soft against the body, can be sewn through easily, and is see-through so it can be stitched in visible applications. It is not meant to replace quality waistband and swimwear elastic.

Buttons

I buy buttons whenever I see them, so I almost always have just the right buttons on hand. Store them by color in plastic bags in a large clear plastic box. The number of buttons to buy is always the hard part. My rule of thumb is one very large decorative button for a one-button jacket; three buttons for a short jacket or five for a long jacket with two additional ones for the sleeves; seven to nine for a blouse; and ten or more for a button-down dress. You can usually adjust the button placement on your garment to accommodate the number of buttons you have.

Fasteners

I keep a good supply of skirt hooks, snaps, and hooks and eyes on hand in a variety of sizes. I store them in a box in their own packaging so they're right at my fingertips. I keep the box in a drawer of my sewing machine cabinet because I sew them on by machine. If you are a hand sewer, keep a few needles already threaded with basic colors in a strawberry pincushion to save having to thread the needle first thing!

Shoulder Pads

I have a box full of both new and used shoulder pads in a variety of shapes and sizes. I often cut ones in good condition out of garments before I give the garments away and save the shoulder pads for another project.

BEFORE YOU SEW— NOTIONS I CANNOT LIVE WITHOUT

I buy most of my supplies from the nearest independent sewing machine dealer or from the suppliers listed in "Sources" on page 203. I have two basic lists of notions that I cannot live without. The first list includes the notions I take with me on the road. (You might be surprised at how many sewers carry their projects, including their sewing machines and notions, with them when away from home!) The second list includes the other sewing tools and notions that I use at home.

On the Road

As I travel, I often sew in a hotel room, so my sewing supplies are limited to what I can carry in my suitcase. You can sew just about anything with these supplies—maybe not as easily as if you had all your equipment from home, but you can do it. (Ask me how I know that!) Here's what I take with me.

Good-Quality Sewing Machine If you read "You and Your Machine" on page 6, you know how I feel about having the best machine you can afford. No matter how much or how little you sew, consider a serger for your next sewing

sew with the poor irons provided in hotel rooms. And I can't press without my Titan soleplate, because nothing ever sticks to it and the soleplate heats so evenly that it prevents scorching and shine.

June Tailor Cut and Press Board This is a dual-purpose rotary-cutting mat on one side and padded pressing board on the other. It comes in a variety of sizes. I travel with a 12-by-12-inch (30.5-by-30.5-cm) mat, which fits conveniently in my suitcase.

Rotary Cutter This is one of the biggest time-savers in sewing, especially for cutting straight lines. I also carry a rotary pinking blade for trimming seam allowances.

Rotary Cutter Ruler The fastest way to cut straight pieces of fabric is to use a rotary cutter, cutting mat, and plastic ruler made to be used with a rotary cutter. If you haven't already added these tools to your collection of sewing notions, consider doing so. You will wonder how you ever got along without them! These plastic rulers have inch markings and fractions-of-inch markings, making it very quick and easy to cut straight lines accurately.

Eight-Inch Gingher Bent-Handle Dressmaker's Shears There are some places, such as curves and seam clippings, where only a good pair of shears will do. I can't cut without my good pair of Ginghers.

investment. As for bringing the serger on the road, I often do all the serging before leaving home so I can carry only the machine.

Schmetz Sewing Machine Needles The two most important needles that I'm never without are size 80 Universal and size 90 Stretch needles. Have you ever been in a hotel room (or at home for that matter) at night and broken your last needle? Since I travel so much, I always keep a pack of size 80s in my purse. You never know when you or a friend might need a sewing machine needle!

Rowenta Sew and Press Iron with Titan Soleplate I have the larger Rowenta at home, as listed on page 15, but I travel with the Sew and Press model because it is smaller. I just can't

SUE'S SNIPPETS
ON TRAVELING WITH RULERS

I used to travel with a plastic gridded rotary-cutting ruler, even though it was always a little too long for my suitcase. Then on one trip it broke in two, which was great. Now I carry half of the ruler, and it's just the right size.

Lightweight Fiskars Pinking Shears In sewing situations where pinking is called for but a rotary pinking blade is impractical, I rely on Fiskars pinking shears because I like the long cutting blades. The blades stay sharp and are easy to cut with.

Six-Inch Trimming Scissors I keep a pair of plastic-handle scissors at the machine, which I use to cut anything that's in my way. It's too much work to protect every pair of scissors, so I keep this one unprotected pair on hand so I don't have to worry what I cut with it.

Bamboo Point Turner I've found that I can press over this point turner. You press points all the time in sewing, and you can also use the back of the turner as a seam opener as you're pressing.

Grabbit and Long Plastic-Head Pins I never leave home without my Grabbit. How did we ever survive without these magnetized pin holders! I like being able to toss a pin at the magnet from a few inches away and know that

HERE'S WHAT **I DO**...
to Take Care of Good Scissors

When my children were little, I used to put a red ribbon on my good scissors. The ribbon signaled to the kids that these scissors were off-limits! No matter where in the house the scissors might be, the kids knew they were not to be touched. Some of my scissors still have their red ribbons.

To this day as I travel and teach classes, my scissors are marked with grosgrain ribbons. But now I use the embroidery function on my sewing machine to embroider my name on the ribbons.

it will hit its mark. (Be aware that not all pins stick to a magnet. When you buy pins, even if they are stainless steel, be sure to test them on a Grabbit to see if they stick.)

Tape Measure My favorite tape measure has inches marked on both sides.

Six-Inch Needle-Nose Pliers I carry these along for putting needles in my serger. They have come in handy for other things too, such as fixing the screw in my glasses!

Fabric Markers I carry a purple air-soluble marking pen, a blue water-soluble marking pen, and white chalk. These three markers cover just about anything I need to mark.

In addition to the notions listed above, I carry the following basic supplies.

Black and White Fusible Tricot Interfacing Clear Elastic, ½ Yard (0.5 M) of Each I use this for quick fixes, such as gaps in necklines and armholes and ribbing that has lost its stretch.

One-Inch (2.5-Cm) Elastic You never know when you might want to make a skirt!

At Home

Here are some notions and supplies that I can't live without at home but that are too big for my suitcase!

High-Quality Serger About 20 years ago when I first began sewing on sergers, they were so hard to use that I had no desire for one. Then the sewing machine companies began to make them easier and easier to use and made them do more and more! Today I don't know how I ever sewed without a serger. I want everything I make to have the professional (and fast) edge finishes that a serger makes. Best of all is sewing knit garments—sergers and knits were made for each other!

Sew/Fit Table This is a big fold-up cardboard table with a large cutting surface (for use with scissors only!). If you do not have a large table, this sturdy cardboard table, which comes in two heights (for short and average-height people), is one of the best investments you will make for your sewing room. For convenience, you can fold the table flat and slide it under the bed when you have company once a year.

Sew/Fit Cutting Mat This 30-by-53-inch white rotary-cutting mat marked with an overall 1-inch grid fits exactly on the Sew/Fit table. The marked grid on the mat simplifies many measuring chores, and you can pin directly into the mat, as well. The cutting mat can be slipped under the bed with the table for storage.

Rowenta Professional Iron with Titan Soleplate This is the larger, home-size version of the iron I travel with. The professional steam and burst of steam are fantastic. It has a removable tank, which is easy to carry to the sink for a water refill. When even a tiny drop of water or steam can ruin a project, you can remove the water tank from the iron and eliminate any danger of water accidents.

Tailor's Ham Using a tailor's ham is the best way to press darts and other curved areas. As you press, it allows you to mold curves into the garment to match the shape of your curved body. Pressing a dart on a flat surface gives you a flat garment, which defeats the purpose of the dart.

Seam Roll I use a seam roll mostly for pressing seams open. It helps prevent pressing an impression of the seam allowance edge through to the right side.

BEFORE YOU SEW— CUTTING OUT

I find it interesting that many sewers hate the cutting-out process when they begin a project, because I really enjoy this part. In the early years of my sewing, I cut out many garments

on the
FAST
TRACK...
to Double the Cutting

When possible, I cut double. If the fabric widths allow, sometimes I cut two garments together, or I cut the lining and the fashion fabric stacked. This can be tricky because the more layers and different fabric weights there are, the less accurate the cutting is. Try it with lightweight fabrics, and if the fabrics are different weights, work with the lighter weight one on top.

on the floor or the bed, but today this is pretty hard on my back, so I need to use a table. I recommend the Sew/Fit table and cutting mat mentioned on page 15. If you have a table, consider protecting it with a folding cardboard mat, also for use only with scissors, not rotary cutters, and available at most fabric stores.

With the folding cardboard mat or the Sew/Fit table, I can preshrink dry-clean–only fabrics by laying them out on either of these surfaces and steaming them well with my iron.

Get the Pattern Ready

I never cut the pattern tissue pieces carefully on the cutting lines. Instead, I highlight the piece numbers on the pattern instructions for the view I am making and then cut around each piece to separate it from the others as quickly as possible. I have heard all kinds of theories about the tissue paper dulling my good shears and about lack of accuracy, but I feel cutting out the pattern pieces quickly really saves time! It is easy to lay the pieces to be used in one pile and the others in another

to fold and immediately put back into the pattern envelope to avoid confusion. The excess tissue outside the cutting edge allows me to make alterations on the tissue, and this is the time to make such changes.

I recommend that every sewer take a good fitting class to become aware of what alterations are needed to the pattern pieces to make the garment fit their body. Once I know what alterations to make on the pattern, I simply adjust every pattern before cutting it out.

You can get a good clue for what needs to be adjusted by the way ready-to-wear garments fit. For example, one of the major reasons I began to sew was that I am very long-waisted and ready-made garments do not fit, so I add 1½ inches (3.8 cm) to the waist length of every garment. I am also full-busted and swaybacked, and I have a very full tummy—all these adjustments are easy to make on the pattern tissue before I begin to cut out a garment.

I do take the time to press each tissue pattern piece and actually find that the pressing gives the tissue some static electricity, which helps the pieces cling to the fabric.

Survey the Fabric

The first cutting step is to lay out the fabric on the cutting surface and take time to mark any fabric flaws, making mental note of special cutting circumstances such as placement of print, one-way patterns, or nap. I am often asked if you should fold the fabric with the right sides on the inside or outside. I say whichever works better and is easier. Just stay consistent on the garment.

One great tip for cutting lightweight and slippery fabrics is to lay them out on and pin them to a piece of tissue paper. When you cut through the paper, the pattern tissue on top and tissue paper on the underside stabilize the fabric.

Although I usually have the yardage required and look at the cutting layout on the pattern instructions (as a check for what pieces are needed and what is cut single, double, on the fold, and so on), it is almost a game for me to see how little fabric I can use. I have many fabric remnants left over that are really too small to make anything, but I still have this motivation to beat the pattern layout!

Easy on the Pins

When I teach sewing, I notice that cutting seems to be very awkward and tedious for new sewers. One thing that makes it difficult for the new sewer is the pinning, but it doesn't need to be so difficult. Place enough pins to hold the pattern tissue in place. But don't go overboard, because each pin makes a little tuck in the fabric. These tucks can cause a slight shifting of layers, resulting in pieces that are not accurately cut. I like to place a pin in the seam allowance at each corner of the piece and one or two between. If the fabric and pattern tissue have been well pressed, this should be sufficient.

Now Cut!

Quality bent-handle cutting shears and a sharp rotary cutter are the keys to accurate cutting. If you are struggling to cut, have your shears sharpened or invest in a new pair. Take along fabric scraps to test the scissors before buying new ones.

I am right-handed, so as I cut, I hold the pattern to the fabric with my left hand flat against the tissue. I move the shears along with my right hand, which is cutting with the actual bent blade of the shears gliding against the cutting surface. Left-handed sewers would reverse this.

Many people today do most of their cutting with a rotary cutter. For me, it is a matter of

what I am used to. I prefer to cut the actual garment with bent shears except for the pieces with straight edges, such as waistbands and cuffs. On these edges the rotary cutter and a plastic cutting ruler to cut along are much faster and very accurate.

Make Your Mark

One big time-saver is to mark as you cut. Too many sewers do not mark dots and notches at all. Sewing without markings is a sure way to have finished garments that scream homemade. I've checked fine ready-to-wear and seen snip markings to guide even the most professional sewers. As I cut, I snip straight into the seam allowance about ¼ inch (0.6 cm) for seamline dots, and I cut notches outside the seam allowance to avoid the fraying and possible little holes at the seamline later.

Many people do not know that the single notch is the front of the sleeve and the double notch is the back of the sleeve and that most companies number the notches so that notches with the same number are to be matched. I also snip the top and bottom of any straight line marking, such as the center front, and find it easy to fold using these snips as a guide to press mark it later.

on the
FAST
TRACK. . .
to Quick Marking

Use your iron to mark by pressing creases in the fabric whenever possible. While the pattern tissue is still pinned on, fold the fabric along the center front, back, tucks, design lines, and so on, and press to make creases.

HERE'S WHAT I DO...
to Plan Ahead

When I plan to sew a garment from a new pattern, I put the instruction sheet in my briefcase to read over on an airplane, in the car (while Herb drives!), or when waiting somewhere. I highlight the pattern pieces that will be needed for the view I am making and jot down changes I plan to make while sewing the garment. Many times this is the last time I look at the instructions because I generally sew with the *Fast, Faster, Fastest* techniques in this book.

Once my pieces are cut out and marked, I remove all the pins and fold the pieces with the tissue pattern piece inside or leave one pin in smaller pieces. For me this saves time because the pieces are ready to pick up and sew.

When fabrics do not have a definite right and wrong side, I take time to mark one lower corner of the wrong side with a water-soluble marking pen or chalk, marking an X, a CF for center front, CB for center back, and so on.

BEFORE YOU SEW— INTERFACE

Interfacing is the key to a quality finished garment. It determines the shape and many times the actual style of the garment. Do you remember when we interfaced with an extra layer of the fashion fabric? This is the way I was taught, and in those days the interfacings available to the home sewer were limited mostly to the stiff sew-in nonwoven type.

Times have changed, and today many of the interfacings used by the designers are available

to the home sewer. Fusible interfacings, for example, are used by the top designers, and many of the same fusible interfacings are stocked at better fabric shops.

There are four basic types of interfacing. A woven interfacing is woven with lengthwise and crosswise fibers, is stable in length and width, and stretches on the bias like a woven fabric.

Nonwoven interfacing is made by bonding or felting synthetic fibers together. It can have stretch in every direction or crosswise stretch and lengthwise stability.

Tricot-knit interfacing has stretch in the width and some give in the length. Weft-insertion interfacing is also a knit that is stable in width and has some give in the length.

A temporary-fuse interfacing is perfect for silks and other fabrics that cannot take the heat of the wool iron setting or that tend to reveal the fusible resins after fusing. Try the HTC light-weight woven rayon interfacing known as Touch O'Gold. A light temporary bond fuses at the silk iron setting and holds the interfacing during construction, then the interfacing separates from the fashion fabric after sewing.

Cut fusible interfacings with pinking shears. This eliminates bulk and the hard line that can press through to the right side of the garment. Pin the pattern pieces on with the pins inside the seamlines. Slide your pinking shears under the edge of the pattern piece and cut out the interfacing along the seamline. This eliminates bulk in the seam allowance, and the pinked edge is barely caught in the seam.

TIME TO SEW!

The rest of this book is full of ideas for making your sewing faster and more fun. In "Sue's Favorite Fast Garments" on page 20 and "Sue's Favorite Fast Cover-Up Garments" on page

44, I've shared with you instructions for some of my favorite fast garments. These are the staples of my wardrobe. They are quick and easy to make, and they allow me to extend my wardrobe to fill a special need or just to take advantage of some fun fabric I come across. "Construction Techniques" on page 76 is a collection of my garment construction techniques. They are presented roughly in the order that you would do them when constructing a garment. "Garment Details" on page 112 shows you details such as collars, pockets, and sleeves. "Finishing Techniques" on page 144 offers you choices for techniques such as buttonholes and hems.

And finally, even the most skilled and experienced sewer would not be altogether candid without admitting to the occasional sewing disaster. We all have them, and "Sue's Fast Fixes for Sewing Slipups" on page 180 shows you

ways out of a sewing disaster once you've fallen into one.

Our sewing is an extension of who we are. It reflects our love for textiles and creativity. Use it for joy in everyday life, and share the sewing life skill with others. Teach someone you love to sew. You will be planting the seeds for a lifetime of creativity and job skill.

Through the years I have had the opportunity to share with many sewers. Many sew for pleasure, some to save money, and others to make money. The sewing life skill can meet needs at every stage of life. Whatever the reason you sew, the skill is the same. We take fabric, cut it, stitch it, embellish it, and turn it into a garment that reflects who we are to all who see it. This is why I love to sew. I hope you do, too.

Now, let's get sewing!

Fast Faster Fastest

SUE'S FAVORITE
FAST GARMENTS

My closet is full, but I love to make
new clothes! Every season I pore
over pattern books and magazines,
planning several garments to make.
But these new patterns are almost always supplemented with my quick
and easy favorites, which I can
make from my personal collection of
fabrics and notions that I always
have on hand. I hope this chapter
will inspire you to create your own
fast garments.

SUE'S NO-PATTERN QUICK SKIRTS

These Quick Skirts are some of my favorite sewing projects because they are so inexpensive and fast to make. Each skirt takes only one length of a wide fabric and one hour or less to make. One thing that makes these skirts so quick is that you do not need patterns for them.

QUICK LIST

60-inch (152.4-cm)-wide fabric
You will need one skirt length plus 6 inches (15.2 cm). One fabric width fits hips 46 inches (116.8 cm) or smaller. Larger sizes may need two lengths. The ideal fabric for the Quick Skirt is a rayon or wool challis or any other lightweight, drapey fabric.

1-inch (2.5-cm)-wide nonroll elastic
You will need your waist measurement plus 5 inches (12.7 cm).

¼ yard (0.2 m) lining or self-fabric for the pocket
I always cut the pocket on the crosswise grain of the fabric so it will fit on a ¼-yard (0.2-m) piece of fabric.

Cut and Assemble Your Skirt

1 For the skirt front and back, cut one piece the width of the fabric (60 inches [152.4 cm]) by one skirt length plus 2⅝ inches (6.7 cm). This allows for a 2-inch (5.1-cm) hem and a ⅝-inch (1.6-cm) waistband seam. From the remaining fabric, cut a strip 3½ inches (8.9 cm) wide by 60 inches (152.4 cm) long for the waistband.

If you are using 45-inch (114.3-cm)-wide fabric, cut two pieces, each 32 inches (81.3 cm) wide by one skirt length plus 2⅝ inches (6.7 cm). Sew the two pieces together so your total front and back width is about 60 inches (152.4 cm). A piece much wider than 60 inches (152.4 cm) creates too much bulk at the waist. Then cut one piece for the waistband 3½ inches (8.9 cm) by the width of the fabric.

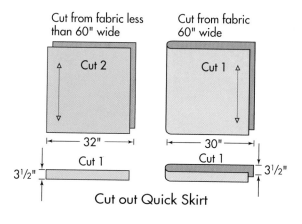

Cut out Quick Skirt

2 Make a pocket pattern by enlarging the pattern below. Then cut two pocket pieces from the matching lining fabric or self-fabric.

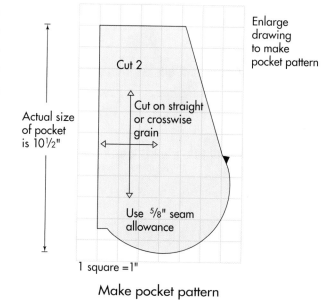

Make pocket pattern

3 Finish all of the raw edges on the skirt and the edges on the pocket pieces from the notch to the top, using one of the *Fast, Faster, Fastest* techniques from "Edge Finishes" on page 80. With a ¼-inch (0.6-cm) seam allowance, sew one pocket piece to each side of the skirt. Then press each pocket piece away from the skirt with the seam allowance pressed toward the pocket.

HERE'S WHAT **I DO**...
to Avoid Wasting Elastic

To eliminate those short pieces of elastic left over from cutting waistbands, I purchase elastic by the yard instead of buying it in packages. For the Quick Skirt, I determine my waist measurement and then add 5 inches (12.7 cm) to allow for a pocket extension, or for a pull-on waistband, I use my waist measurement minus 2 inches (5.1 cm). Then I buy multiples of those amounts. For instance, for a pull-on waistband, if my waist measures 29 inches (73.7 cm), I'd need 27 inches (68.6 cm), or ¾ yard (0.7 m), of elastic for one waistband. So twice that, or 1½ yards (1.4 m) of elastic, yields two waistbands, and so on.

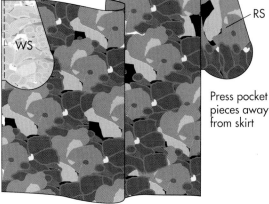

Sew pocket piece to each side of skirt

¼" seam allowance

WS

RS

Press pocket pieces away from skirt

Sew pocket pieces to skirt

6 Press the pocket and seam allowances toward the skirt front and remove the machine basting from the seam allowance. Then machine baste the pocket front to the skirt front. (Hint: The pocket is usually placed on the left side of the skirt, so the easiest way to determine which way to press it is to hold the skirt up to your body right side out.)

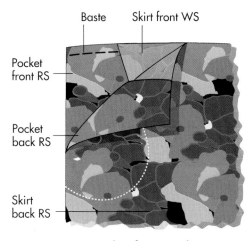

Baste

Skirt front WS

Pocket front RS

Pocket back RS

Skirt back RS

Baste pocket front to skirt

4 Pin the skirt side seam(s) and pocket pieces with right sides together, carefully matching the pressed seamlines.

5 Machine baste from the top of the pocket to 1½ inches (3.8 cm) above the lower edge of the pocket along the ⅝-inch (1.6-cm) seam allowance. Then with a ⅝-inch (1.6-cm) seam allowance, stitch from the bottom edge of the skirt to 1½ inches (3.8 cm) above the lower edge of the pocket, pivot, and stitch around the lower curve of the pocket, stopping and securing the stitches at the notch.

7 Decide whether you want your skirt to have gathers or pleats, then look at the options in "Gathering" on page 101 or in "Pleats" on page 110. For the front of my Quick Skirt, I prefer these tummy-flattering pleats.

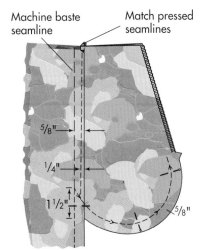

Machine baste seamline

Match pressed seamlines

⅝"

¼"

1½"

⅝"

Join pocket and skirt seam

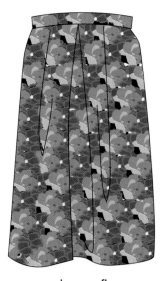

Use center pleat to flatter tummy

To insert pleats in the skirt front, mark the center front, press 2-inch (5.1-cm) pleats toward each side of the center, and press 1-inch (2.5-cm) pleats on each side. Machine baste the pleats in place. Try the skirt on, and add pleats or gathers as needed.

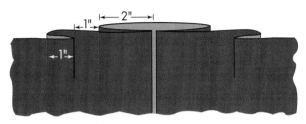

Fold pleats toward center

Finishing Fast, Faster, Fastest

Use the *Fast* method on page 121 to make a waistband with a hook and eye. To attach the hook and eye, see the *Faster* method in "Buttons" on page 159. Finally, choose a technique from "Hems" on page 167, and you are ready to go.

Sew hook and eye

Finish waistband with hook and eye

SUE'S QUICK YOKED SKIRT

Often a gathered skirt with an elastic waistband is not flattering because there is too much fabric fullness at the waist. I reduce this bulk with a yoke, which adds a nice design detail. This skirt is a breeze when you use my *Fastest* method for the one-piece elastic waistband on page 124 and

---

SUE'S SNIPPETS
WHERE MY IDEAS COME FROM

Several years ago I fell in love with a beautiful imported wool challis and wanted to make a skirt. The challis was $59 a yard, and every pattern I found called for at least 1⅞ yard (1.7 m). The challis was 58 inches (147.3 cm) wide, which was enough to go around me with plenty of ease for pleats or gathers. I decided that if I didn't use a pattern, I could get a skirt from one length of fabric—less than a yard. And the idea for the Quick Skirt was born. Because this skirt is cut straight across the bottom edge, it is the perfect choice for border prints and plaids. The best part is that with practice, you can make it in an hour—start to finish!

---

one of the methods from "Gathering" on page 101 and from "Hems" on page 167.

1 Cut two yoke pieces 9 inches (22.9 cm) long (which includes seam allowances and a self-casing for 1-inch [2.5-cm] elastic) by half your hip measurement plus 3 inches (7.6 cm) for ease. Cut two skirt pieces, 30 to 35 inches (76.2 to 88.9 cm) wide, making the length of each piece your finished skirt length minus 5 inches (12.7 cm). This allows for a 2-inch (5.1-cm) hem.

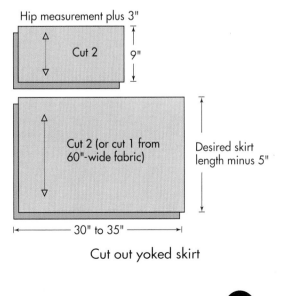

Hip measurement plus 3"

Cut 2 9"

Cut 2 (or cut 1 from 60"-wide fabric)

Desired skirt length minus 5"

30" to 35"

Cut out yoked skirt

2 With right sides together, sew one side seam in the yoke and one side seam in the skirt. Then choose a *Fast, Faster, Fastest* method from "Gathering" on page 101. Use the method you prefer to gather the top edge of the skirt to match the width of the yoke. Pin the skirt to the yoke right sides together, matching the side seam of the yoke to the skirt side seam. Adjust the gathers to distribute them evenly.

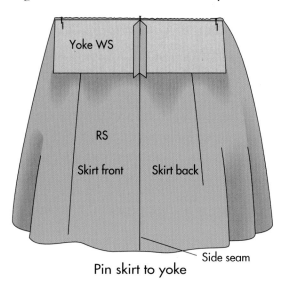

Pin skirt to yoke

3 Sew the skirt and the yoke together with a ⅝-inch (1.6-cm) seam allowance, then with right sides together, sew the second side seam closed. Sew the one-piece elastic waistband according to the directions for the *Fastest* waistband on page 124; put in the hem, and it is ready to wear!

SUE'S 10-MINUTE SKIRT

All you need to make my favorite ten-minute skirt is one length of a very lightweight, drapey fabric. You can cut this skirt out, sew it, and wear it out the door in ten minutes—or close to it. To make this skirt, you will sew the one-piece elastic waistband according to the

directions for the *Fastest* waistband on page 124, then sew a single seam down the center back, and put in a hem using a technique from "Hems" on page 167. This is not couture sewing, but it is great for spur-of-the-moment creations.

1 Decide how long you want your skirt to be. Then cut a piece of 60-inch (152.4-cm)-wide fabric the desired finished skirt length. Add 5 inches (12.7 cm) to the desired length, which allows for a 1½-inch (3.8-cm) elastic casing and a 2-inch (5.1-cm) hem.

2 Sew the *Fastest* waistband in top edge of your skirt. (See page 124.) Stitch casing in flat piece of fabric, then insert elastic. With right sides together, sew skirt seam, beginning at the waist. Be sure to catch the elastic securely in the seam, and continue sewing to the bottom edge.

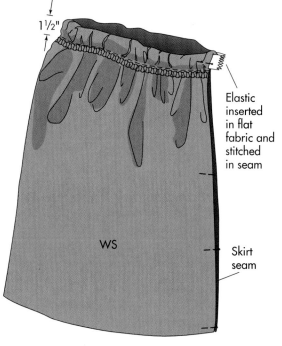

Sew center back seam of skirt

3 Press a 2-inch (3.2-cm) hem in the skirt. Straight stitch the hem in place, and you are out the door.

Stitch & Stretch Belt

Use the same fabric in your skirt to make a stretchy belt that won't cut you in half.

Many times it is impossible to find the perfect belt for an outfit, and I find that belts usually cut me in half, emphasizing my lack of height and ample width! This quick belt is made from scraps and adds a designer detail to a simple outfit.

1. Select a 2- or 3-inch (5.1- or 7.6-cm) width of Stitch & Stretch elastic in black or white. It is available by the yard or in packages at your local sewing store. Purchase 1½ yards (1.4 m) for an average belt.

2. Cut a strip of fabric 1¼ inches (3.2 cm) wider than the elastic and 45 to 60 inches (114.3 to 152.4 cm) long, and press a ½-inch (1.3-cm) hem to the wrong side along both long edges. (You can sew and turn a tube for lightweight fabrics. Begin with a strip twice the width of the elastic plus ¾ inch [1.9 cm] to seam the tube with a ¼-inch [0.6-cm] seam allowance.) The long edges of the

strip must be finished, and the finished strip should be slightly wider than the elastic. I have made several belts with ribbon as the strip.

3. Place the Stitch & Stretch elastic on the wrong side of the fabric strip, and stitch it in place, sewing along all the marked lines with a straight stitch.

4. After stitching, pull up the elastic threads to create the shirred belt. Try the belt on and adjust the shirring as needed.

5. Tie the elastic thread ends one to another with a square knot, and stitch across both ends several times with a three-step zigzag to secure them well.

6. Add a decorative two-sided clip-type belt buckle. Before you spend a lot of money on belt buckles, look for belts that are on sale. I have purchased many belts at reduced prices and have removed the buckles to use on my designer Stitch & Stretch belts!

SUE'S CAREER CHANGE BLOUSE

Of all the projects I have taught, this has been a favorite. Many people laugh when they see the idea, but then try it and love it. The idea came from a ready-to-wear tank top I once spotted that was made from four different fabrics. It is reversible inside and out and front to back— a blouse that can be worn four different ways! It is perfect for wearing under a jacket where you see only one side of the blouse at a time. To make this blouse, you cut four different fabrics from a single pattern piece, sew two blouses that each have two "fronts," then use one blouse as the reversible "lining" of the other—it is easier to do than to explain!

QUICK LIST

Four different fabrics
You will need one blouse length of each fabric. Since this is a double-thickness blouse, light-weight fabrics are best. (Silk, rayon challis, and batiste work well.) Only one side of the blouse will show under a jacket, so the fabrics do not even need to match or blend.

Fusible interfacing
You will need enough to interface the neckline of the outer blouse.

Blouse pattern
A basic dartless, collarless shell pattern with cap sleeves is ideal.

Cut and Assemble Your Blouse

1 Start by preparing one pattern piece, which you will use for cutting all four blouse pieces. On most simple shell patterns, the front and back bodice pieces are the same except for the neckline. Select the pattern piece with the higher neckline, and use it for each front/back piece. (Do not worry about whether this neckline will allow the blouse to fit over your head; we will get to that in a minute.) Cut a full front/back pattern piece from paper pattern tissue. If needed, trim the hem allowance on the sleeve to ⅝ inch (1.6 cm) from the hemline of the sleeve.

2 Cut one front/back piece from each fabric, and cut fusible interfacing for the necklines of two front/backs using the neckline-facing pattern. (Cut the outer edge of the interfacing with pinking shears to prevent its edge from showing through to the right side of the garment.) Fuse the neckline interfacing to the wrong sides of two front/backs.

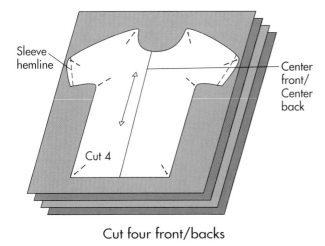

Cut four front/backs

3 To sew the outer blouse, stitch the interfaced pieces with right sides together at the shoulders, then sew the remaining front/back pieces together at the shoulder seams to make the lining.

4 With right sides together, pin the outer blouse and lining necklines, matching the shoulder seams. Sew around the neckline with a ⅝-inch (1.6-cm) seam allowance, and trim the seam allowance with pinking shears. Now try on the blouse to see whether it fits over your head. If the opening is too small, stitch the neckline again ¼ inch (0.6 cm) in from the first seamline, trim, and try it on again. Turn the blouse right side out, and press the neckline. Topstitch if desired.

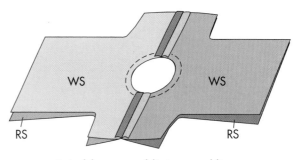

Join blouse and lining necklines

5 Keep the blouse right side out, and with right sides together, pin the outer blouse-sleeve hems to the lining-sleeve hems at the shoulder seams, turning the hems inside. Pull the hem out one side of the sleeve with right sides together, then sew the sleeve hems together with a ⅝-inch (1.6-cm) seam allowance. Trim them with pinking shears.

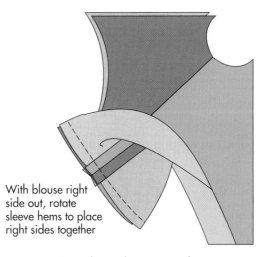

With blouse right side out, rotate sleeve hems to place right sides together

Sew sleeve hems together

Finishing Fast, Faster, Fastest

1 Pin the outer blouse front and back side seams with right sides together, matching the underarm seams, and sew the side seams end to end with a ⅝-inch (1.6-cm) seam allowance. Then trim the seam allowances, press them, and turn the blouse right side out.

Bring ends of front/back side seams together

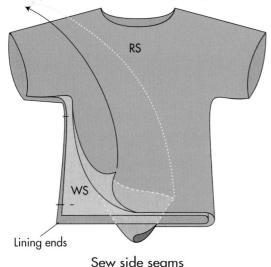

RS

WS

Lining ends

Sew side seams

2 Do not attach the outer blouse and the lining along the bottom edge. Instead, if the blouse will always be worn tucked in, just serge the raw edges separately, or use some other edge finish to prevent fraying. If you plan to wear the blouse untucked, select a *Fast, Faster, Fastest* technique from "Hems" on page 167, and hem the outer blouse and the lining separately. Then, whichever layer you are wearing on the outside, tuck in the inside layer so the hem does not get caught peeking out from under the outside blouse.

I think you will love this Career Change Blouse. After you've made your first blouse, you'll be ready to add some variety to your second blouse by cutting two of the fronts with a V-neck and two with the neckline you used on your first blouse.

SUE'S TRICKS FOR QUICK CLASSIC BLOUSES

Classic blouses with set-in sleeves, collars, and cuffs are staples in any wardrobe. I often make a matching skirt and blouse to wear for the look of a dress because I find two pieces more comfortable than one and because they can be worn separately with other garments. Here are some tips for sewing professional-quality blouses quickly.

Cut Down on Cutting Because blouse patterns with many pieces take longer to cut out and sew, look for patterns with just a few pieces.

Create Dartless Darts You can eliminate the dart in a blouse without completely losing the shaping the dart provides at the bustline. (This trick is not really "legal," because it throws the grainline off, but on many fabrics this is not noticeable.) Add ½ to ¾ inch (1.3 to 1.9 cm) to the length of the blouse front, starting at the side seams and tapering to nothing at the center front. Then when sewing the side seam, ease this excess length into the side seam in the bust area.

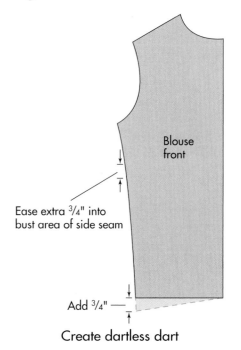

Blouse front

Ease extra ¾" into bust area of side seam

Add ¾"

Create dartless dart

Make Collars with Body For extra crispness to your collars, put interfacing in both the upper and lower collar pieces. (You can use the same trick to add extra crispness to cuffs, too). To hide the seam at the edges, trim away $1/16$ inch (0.2 cm) all the way around the undercollar (or undersides of the cuffs) so the seam will pull slightly toward the underside and not be visible on the right side.

Get Out the Gap Sometimes we don't realize there's a little too much fabric in the neckline until the garment is finished and it's too late to change it. There is a quick way to eliminate the gap and keep a scoop neck or V-neck hugging your body in home-sewn as well as ready-to-wear garments: After sewing the facing in the neckline, grade the seam allowance with pinking shears. Lay a piece of $1/4$-inch (0.6-cm)-wide clear elastic on the seamline, and stitch it in place using a long straight stitch or zigzag stitch, pulling slightly on the elastic as you sew. Start with a piece at least as long as the total neckline, then clip off the excess.

Let's Face It Use a small zigzag stitch to understitch the facing to its seam allowance. The zigzag makes the seam allowance lie flatter than a straight stitch and is more forgiving if your understitching is not exactly straight.

Mark Away Buttonhole Gap Ideally, to prevent a gap in the blouse front at the bustline, one buttonhole should be positioned at the fullest part of the bust. However, too often the markings on a pattern result in buttonholes above and below the ideal position. Before sewing the buttonholes, try on the blouse and mark one buttonhole at the fullest part of the bust, then space the remaining buttonholes evenly above and below the mark.

HERE'S WHAT I DO...
to Add Design Details to Collars

A scalloped edge is the perfect finish for collars and cuffs. Here are two easy ways to add this design detail.

Cut out the facing piece from the pattern, and place it along the garment edge to be scalloped, right sides together. Mark the scallops along the stitching line. (There are scallop rulers available, but a large coin or other circular item will suffice.) Straight stitch along the marked scallops with a short stitch length, about 1.5.

Trim the seam allowance of the scalloped edge close to the stitching with pinking shears. Clip the points almost to the stitching. Finally, turn the facing to the right side, and press well.

A quicker way to make a scalloped edge is to use a built-in sewing machine stitch. Many sewing machines feature a straight-stitch scallop that will eliminate the marking step.

Start this scalloped edge the same way as described above. Place a facing along the garment edge to be scalloped, right sides together.

Select a straight-stitch scallop or running stitch on your sewing machine (experiment on scraps to find the best width setting for the stitch you chose), and use this stitch to sew along the outer edge of the collar. Trim the scallops close to the stitching with pinking shears, and clip the points. Turn the facing to the right side, and press well.

Faux-Woven Scarf

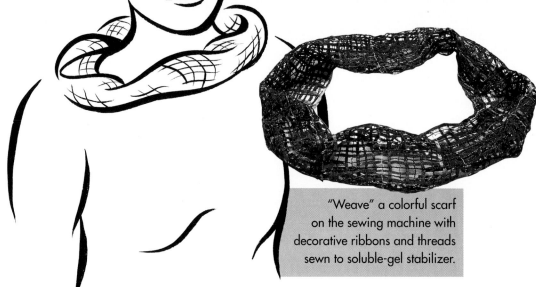

"Weave" a colorful scarf on the sewing machine with decorative ribbons and threads sewn to soluble-gel stabilizer.

One of the most incredible accessory projects I have seen is the faux-woven scarf that Joyce Drexler demonstrated on my "America Sews" television program. The concept of faux weaving ribbons, yarns, braids, threads, and trims that have been sewn onto a stabilizer is based on techniques developed by several creative people, including Brenda Duncan, Yvonne Perez-Collins, and Sharee Dawn Roberts.

The technique is easy! The ribbons and threads are stitched to a disintegrating-type stabilizer (Heat-Away) or two layers of heavy dissolving-type stabilizer (Super Solvy). I prefer Heat-Away, but you must use Super Solvy when the trims will not take the heat of an iron.

1. Cut a piece of stabilizer the desired size of the finished scarf. The circular scarf shown in the photo above is 8 by 45 inches (20.3 by 114.3 cm). You can make your scarf longer or shorter around than mine. But if you make it shorter, be sure it will still fit easily over your head. If you use Heat-Away, cut it with pinking shears to hinder fraying.

2. Thread your machine with Sulky invisible polyester thread on the top and in the bobbin for the best results. For the circular scarf, overlap the short edges of the stabilizer about ¼ inch (0.6 cm), and stitch the stabilizer into a circle to create a tube. (If you prefer a straight scarf, do not sew the stabilizer into a circle.)

3. You will need at least 30 to 50 yards (27.4 to 45.7 m) of a soft ribbon or braid or flat yarn as the base, plus a variety of threads and trims for the scarf. Starting at the overlapped seam, place a ribbon ¼ inch (0.6 cm) from the pinked edge, and stitch it all the way around the circle with a straight stitch. Use the free arm and a braiding foot for easy guiding.

4. When you have sewn the first row of ribbon all the way around the tube of stabilizer, angle the ribbon 90 degrees, and sew it about ¾ inch (1.9 cm) along the seam that joins the ends of the stabilizer. Then angle the ribbon 90 degrees again to sew a second row of ribbon parallel to the first row you stitched.

Continue around the stabilizer tube in this manner, adding rows until the entire stabilizer is covered with rows of ribbon. Don't worry if your stitching is not perfectly straight; it will not be noticeable on the finished scarf. Also, don't worry if one piece of ribbon is not long enough to go all the way around a row or multiple rows. You can use several pieces of ribbon by overlapping the new piece and continuing to sew.

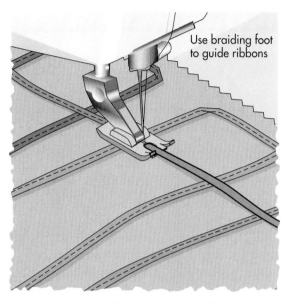

Use braiding foot to guide ribbons

Stitch layer of ribbon across first rows

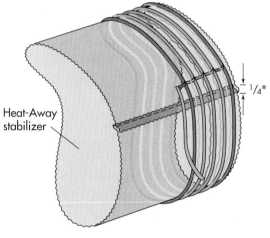

Heat-Away stabilizer

¼"

Stitch ribbons to Heat-Away stabilizer

5. Turn the stabilizer sideways, and continue to stitch the same ribbon in the same manner but across the first rows to create a waffle or faux-woven effect.

6. Once the stabilizer has been covered with ribbon, add rows of decorative thread stitching or couched yarns and trims between the ribbon rows. I like to use a zigzag or decorative stitch to couch (stitch onto the surface) some surface threads to the stabilizer between the rows of ribbon for texture. Always use a stitch wider than the thread or trim to couch it in place.

7. Remove the stabilizer. To disintegrate the Heat-Away, use a dry iron, and hold it in place until the Heat-Away turns a scorched color. Then brush the stabilizer away. To make cleanup easier, place the scarf in a plastic bag, and rub carefully to remove the disintegrated stabilizer. Do not use steam or let water come in contact with the disintegrating stabilizer, because it will activate the chemical and damage the fabric. To remove Super Solvy, place the scarf in water to dissolve it away.

SUE'S COLLARS THAT COME AND GO

Any blouse can lead a double life—you may want a professional look during office hours and then a more feminine, dressy look after hours. You can change the look of a classic blouse by adding a detachable collar, which can be removed when the blouse is dry-cleaned or laundered.

Making a detachable collar gives you a great way to experiment with a variety of creative sewing techniques. You can use fine lace, add heirloom hemstitching or machine embroidery to batiste or linen, or sew a satin-stitched scalloped edge. The possibilities are endless.

QUICK LIST

Fabric to complement your blouse
You will need enough to cut an upper and a lower collar.

Decorative rayon thread
Use thread that matches your fabric for satin stitching.

Four or five clear, flat buttons
Use buttons the same size as those on the blouse, usually ½ to ⅝ inch (1.3 to 1.6 cm) in diameter.

Cut and Embellish Your Collar

1 Cut an upper and a lower collar, adding ½ inch (1.3 cm) to the neck edge, which will allow it to tuck into the blouse collar and to button on.

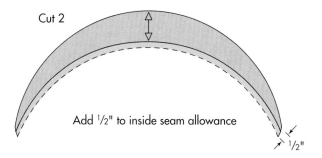

Cut 2

Add ½" to inside seam allowance

½"

Extend seam allowance for detachable collar

2 With wrong sides together, serge or overcast the upper and lower collars together along the neck edge. Machine baste the outer edges of the upper and lower collars along the ⅝-inch (1.6-cm) seamline.

3 Place a stabilizer under the edge of the collar. Then with decorative rayon thread in both the needle and the bobbin, sew a decorative satin scallop stitch or a satin zigzag stitch along the basted seamline.

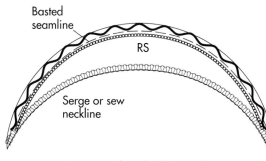

Basted seamline

RS

Serge or sew neckline

Baste and embellish collar

4 Place a fray-stopping liquid along the outer edge of the satin stitching. Allow it to dry, then carefully trim away the excess seam allowance on the outer edge of the collar.

HERE'S WHAT **I DO**...
to Embellish Light Fabrics

As a rule, I use white or pastel thread colors to embellish white or sheer fabrics. One of my favorite quick ways to embellish sheers is to stitch "shadow tucks" with a twin needle. When embellishing sheers, I use a water-soluble stabilizer so no pieces of the stabilizer are left to show through the sheer fabric.

Finishing
Fast, Faster, Fastest

1 To create an additional lacy effect on your detachable collar, add a row of hemstitching, as explained in "Here's What I Do to Sew Heirloom Hemstitching" on page 36.

2 Try on the blouse with the collar to mark where it will be buttoned to the facing. (You might want three buttonholes—the one on the blouse and the two on the ends of the collar—to slip over the top button of the blouse. Add a thread shank to the top button to make it easier.)

Stitch the buttons to the neckline facing as shown below. Choose a *Fast, Faster, Fastest* method from "Buttons" on page 158.

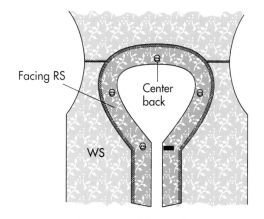

Facing RS

Center back

WS

Sew buttons to blouse facing

3 To determine the buttonhole placement on the detachable collar, try on the blouse, position the collar, and mark the buttonhole placement on the detachable collar ⅜ inch (1 cm) from the inside edge.

4 Stitch the buttonholes where they are marked. Button the collar onto the blouse, and enjoy.

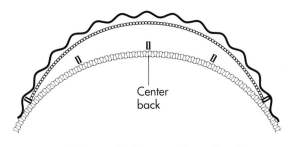

Stitch buttonholes on edge of collar

HERE'S WHAT **I DO**...
to Sew Heirloom Hemstitching

Hemstitching is my favorite heirloom technique. It is magic to watch the wing needle create a lace effect in the fabric by punching holes and sewing them open. Most sewing machines have some stitches for hemstitching. Select a stitch that goes back into the same hole several times. This is usually called a stretch stitch or tri-motion stitch. Even the most basic machines have a stretch stitch called a rickrack stitch. The computerized machines will feature a variety of stitches designed especially for hemstitching.

The key is to use a wing needle and a fine (2-ply) thread. (Heavy thread will fill the holes, but experiment! You can stitch beautiful hemstitches with rayon machine embroidery threads.) Thread the top and bobbin with the same color and type of thread. Hemstitching is usually sewn with the thread matching the fabric color for a rich tone-on-tone embellishment. Use a standard presser foot or a transparent foot for better visibility. A stabilizer is optional as some fabrics will hemstitch better with stabilizer, some without. Always experiment on scraps first, adjusting width and length to the most pleasing stitch before hemstitching on your garment.

1 Use a water-soluble marking pen to mark a line to hemstitch on.

2 Select a hemstitch, and sew with a wing needle along the marked line.

Holes made by wing needle enhance heirloom look

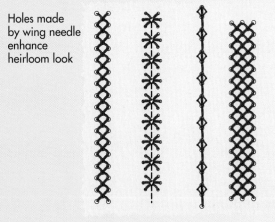

Use wing needle with heirloom stitches on sewing machine

SUE'S QUICK HALF-SLIP

I have found it takes less time to sew a slip than to shop for one. Besides, by making my own, I get a slip that is exactly the size I need and the color I want. To make the Quick Half-Slip, you cut a rectangle of fabric, sew a piece of flat lace to the bottom of the rectangle, sew elastic to the top, stitch up the back seam, and that's it—this project could not be quicker!

QUICK LIST

108-inch (2.7-m)-wide nylon tricot
You will need one length. The traditional fabric for slips is nylon tricot, but I often use silk shantung or china silk or, for an heirloom look, a fine cotton batiste. You need a length of fabric that is your hip measurement plus 4 to 10 inches (10.2 to 25.4 cm).

½-inch (1.3-cm)-wide lingerie elastic
Use your waist measurement minus 2 inches (5.1 cm). You can substitute ¾-inch (1.9-cm)-wide stretch lace for the lingerie elastic.

Flat edging lace, any width
You will need a length to match the bottom edge of the slip.

on the
FAST
TRACK...

to a Quick Lingerie Hem

The shell hem is a quick and inexpensive alternative to a lace hem on lingerie made from tricot or lightweight woven fabrics. To make the shell hem, eliminate the lace altogether, and cut the slip ½ inch (1.3 cm) longer than the desired finished length. Turn and press the ½-inch (1.3-cm) hem allowance to the wrong side, then stitch along the folded edge with a blindhem stitch, as shown, letting the zigzag stitch jump off the edge of the fabric to create the shell effect. To increase the scallop effect, increase the needle-thread tension.

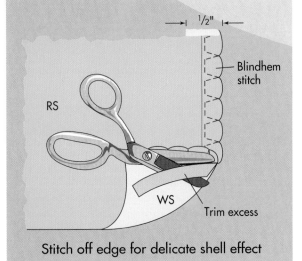

Stitch off edge for delicate shell effect

Cut and Assemble Your Half-Slip

1 The beauty of this project is that you don't need a pattern for it. Instead, you will start by cutting a rectangle of fabric. To determine the size of the rectangle, use the measurement of your hips at the fullest point, then add 4 to 6 inches (10.2 to 15.2 cm) to the hip measure-ment for ease if you are using tricot or other stretch fabrics. If you plan to make your half-slip from woven fabrics such as China silk or cotton batiste, use the measurement of your hips at the fullest point and add 8 to 10 inches (20.3 to 25.4 cm) for ease. Cut the rectangle at this width by the desired finished length of the slip (minus the width of the lace you selected for the hem).

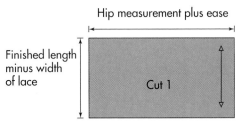

Cut slip according to body measurements

2 Place the flat lace along the bottom edge of the slip, lapping the lace over the right side of the fabric at least ½ inch (1.3 cm). Sew the lace to the fabric, stitching along the top edge of the lace with a narrow zigzag stitch. If you are using a woven fabric (but not a stretch fabric), you can add an heirloom stitch using a wing needle and a hemstitch for an additional decorative effect. (See "Here's What I Do to Sew Heirloom Hemstitching" on page 36).

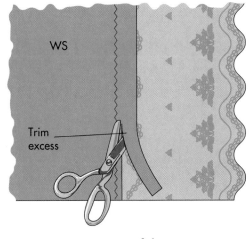

Trim excess fabric

3 To stitch the elastic to the top of the slip so the waistline will be evenly gathered, divide the slip and the elastic into quarters. Pin the elastic to the slip at the quarter points, with the wrong side of the elastic to the right side of the slip, with about ½ inch (1.3 cm) of the slip extending beyond the upper edge of the elastic.

4 Sew the elastic to the top of the slip with a serpentine stitch, a regular zigzag stitch, or a three-step zigzag stitch, stretching the elastic as you sew. Since too short a stitch length will actually sew the stretch out of the elastic, I increase the stitch length considerably when sewing elastic on the machine or serger. A Schmetz stretch-type sewing machine needle is best to use for sewing elastic to prevent skipped stitches.

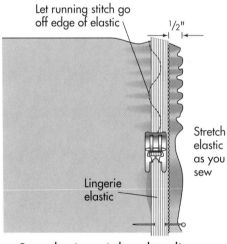

Let running stitch go off edge of elastic

½"

Stretch elastic as you sew

Lingerie elastic

Sew elastic waistband to slip

5 Trim the excess fabric close to the stitching where the lace is sewn at the hem and where the elastic is sewn to the waistline. When trimming the excess after sewing lace or elastic to a fabric, I use blunt-tipped scissors, such as kindergarten or pocket scissors. This helps prevent poking holes in the lace or accidentally snipping the fabric.

Finishing Fast, Faster, Fastest

To finish the slip, use a sewing machine overcast stitch or a serger four-thread overlock stitch to sew the center back seam. Sew with right sides together, matching the edges of the elastic at the waist and the flat lace at the hem.

HERE'S WHAT **I DO**...
to Embellish with Rolled-Edge Tucks

Pintucks are a great decorative design detail to add to a garment. But sewing pintucks can be time-consuming. You can sew serger tucks twice as fast as sewing machine tucks using the rolled-edge stitch.

1 Set the serger for a rolled-edge stitch. Consult your instruction book. Only the upper looper thread will be seen on the tuck, so thread the upper looper with decorative rayon machine embroidery thread. Thread the needle and lower looper with regular sewing thread. Set a satin stitch length so the stitches are very close together. Experiment on scraps before tucking on the garment.

2 Mark the tuck line on the right side of the garment. (Be sure to use a marker that you've tested and know will come out of the fabric.) Fold the fabric with wrong sides together along the marked tuck line.

3 To get a very straight tuck, use a serger blindhem or multipurpose foot to guide the fold as you sew. Serge the rolled edge along the fold.

SUE'S QUICK CAMISOLE

A camisole to match your half-slip can be finished in minutes. The materials and construction are similar to the Quick Half-Slip. To make the camisole, you will begin with a rectangle of fabric, add lace to the top and bottom, close up the rectangle with a side seam, and add straps. It is as quick and easy as that!

QUICK LIST

Lightweight silk or nylon tricot
You will need enough fabric for your bust measurement plus 4 to 10 inches (10.2 to 25.4 cm) for ease by one camisole length.

Wide flat edging lace
Measure the bottom edge of the camisole to determine how much you need.

Narrow flat edging lace
Use the length measurement on the top of the camisole (which is the same as its bottom measurement). Stretch lace works well on the top edge of the camisole.

Embellishments (optional)
Use any laces or decorative threads as desired for embellishment.

SUE'S SNIPPETS
GIFTS THAT KEEP ON GIVING

The Quick Half-Slip and camisole make a beautiful lingerie set for a bridal-shower gift or other special occasion. I love to make gifts for special people because I think about them as I sew and because these gifts carry the love that went into them. I keep all my scraps, and it's so much fun to come across a piece of fabric that was part of a gift for someone special!

Cut and Assemble Your Camisole

1 Measure your bust at the widest part and add 4 to 6 inches (10.2 to 15.2 cm) for ease in a stretch fabric or 8 to 10 inches (20.3 to 25.4 cm) in a woven. Determine the finished length of the camisole, and subtract the widths of the edging lace. Cut a rectangle of fabric (with the crosswise grain going around your body) that equals your bust measurement plus ease by the desired length.

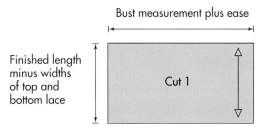

Cut camisole according to body measurements

2 Now is the time, before assembling the camisole, to add any desired embellishments. (See "Finishing Techniques" on page 144 for ideas and techniques.) I like to add a combination of rolled-edge tucks (see "Here's What I Do to Embellish with Rolled-Edge Tucks" on page 39), hemstitching, and rows of lace to the center front of the camisole. Trim excess.

3 Sew the flat lace to the bottom edge of the rectangle and the narrow lace to its top edge, as explained in Step 2 under "Cut and Assemble Your Half-Slip" on page 38. Then sew the side seam of the camisole, as explained in Step 5 on page 39.

Finishing Fast, Faster, Fastest

1 To determine the placement and length of the straps, try on the camisole, and mark the top front and back where the straps will be attached.

2 For self-fabric straps, cut two strips the length of the straps by twice their desired finished width, then add 1 inch (2.5 cm) to the width for the seam allowances. Fold each strip lengthwise with right sides together, and sew each strip into a tube with a ½-inch (1.3-cm) seam allowance. Trim the seam allowances to reduce the amount of bulk inside the finished strap, then turn each tube right side out using a Fasturn tube turner. (See "Sources" on page 203.)

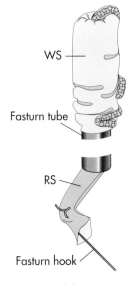

Make self-fabric strap

3 Pin the straps in place on the wrong side of the camisole, and topstitch them in place.

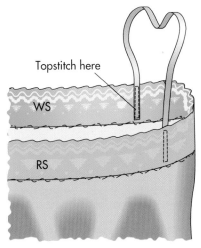

Topstitch strap in place

on the
FAST TRACK...

to Quick Lingerie Straps

You can make spaghetti straps on your serger in a jiffy. Start by chaining off a length of thread 1 inch (2.5 cm) or so longer than your strap length. Cut a strip of fabric the length of the strap by two times its desired finished width plus 1 inch (2.5 cm). Fold the strip lengthwise with right sides together, positioning the serger chain inside the folded strip. Serge the length of the strip, taking care not to catch the chain in the stitches. To turn the strap right side out, gently pull the chain through the strap.

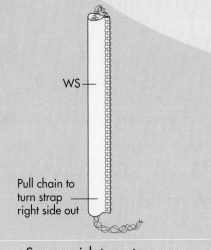

Serge quick-turn strap

Vienna Blouse Placket

Turn one blouse into a closetful of blouses by making detachable embroidered front plackets.

I was in Vienna, Austria, for a world-wide meeting of Husqvarna Viking Sewing Machine leaders and wanted to find an Austrian embroidered blouse to inspire the viewers of one of my "America Sews" television shows. Herb met me for a few days of sight-seeing and quickly tired of shopping for the "perfect" blouse. On our last day I found it! It was very expensive, but I bought it anyway. This classic tailored blouse features a front placket insert that has embroidery on both sides so it can be changed for different color schemes, seasons, and occasions. What a great idea! We planned an "America Sews" program

around the concept, but unfortunately, the blouse was sent to the cleaners and given to the wrong hotel guest, so we did not have it for the taping day. The amazing thing was that the hotel guest had flown to China with the blouse. His secretary faxed him the urgent message to please send the blouse back "because the owner said it was going to be on television and she needed it." This is why it is now affectionately known as the "around the world" blouse by our Husqvarna Viking education staff!

The blouse shown in the sketch above can be made from any front-placket blouse pattern.

1. Stitch several long, narrow embroidery designs onto the placket fabric. It is easiest to stitch the embroidery before the placket has been cut out because the fabric will fill the embroidery hoop. If you have a narrow placket to embroider, hoop one of the sticky stabilizers and stick the placket onto it. Or you can straight stitch the placket piece to a piece of tear-away stabilizer that is large enough to be hooped.

2. Measure the finished width of the blouse placket and the distance between the buttons that the detachable placket will button on to. Cut the placket pieces ½ inch (1.3 cm) wider and at least 1½ inches (3.8 cm) longer than these measurements to allow for seam allowances and an extension at the top and bottom.

3. Pin two placket pieces right sides together with the embroidery designs lined up. Mark a line to guide your stitching ¼ inch (0.6 cm) from each edge with a point at each end. Stitch all the way around the placket on this line, leaving an opening for turning along one angled edge of the point at the bottom edge. Trim the seam allowance with pinking shears.

4. Turn the placket right side out, and press. Topstitch the placket if desired.

5. Place the placket on the blouse, and mark the buttonhole placement on the placket to line up with and fit the blouse buttons. Stitch the buttonholes. Use a balanced tension setting for reversible buttonholes.

6. Hold the detachable placket in place with two bias loops (similar to belt loops) sewn to the blouse placket. To do this, cut self-fabric bias strips the width of the detachable placket plus 2 inches (5.1 cm). Prepare the loops using the *Fast* method for "Belt Loops" on page 151.

Button the detachable placket to the blouse, and mark the placement of the loops on the blouse placket just above and below the embroidered design on the detachable placket. Pin the strips to the blouse as you would belt loops, allowing enough length in the loops for the detachable placket to slip through easily. Trim the excess from the ends of the loops, and blindstitch in place.

7. You may want to sew decorative buttons for the top and bottom of the placket and plain buttons down the rest of the blouse. The beauty of this blouse is that it can be worn over and over again because you can make many reversible plackets for the same blouse. I like to make several detachable plackets for special occasions such as Christmas, Valentine's Day, birthdays, and more.

Stitch plackets together

SUE'S FAVORITE FAST COVER-UP GARMENTS

Coats, jackets, and other cover-up garments are basic to every wardrobe and don't have to be time-consuming to make. In this chapter I have included my favorite fast vests, capes, and reversible garments, which you can use to round out any outfit. Cover-up garments are a good investment to make with your sewing time.

SUE'S INVESTMENT DRESSING

I love making vests. They are high-yield wardrobe investments that update any garment and flatter every figure type and age group. Most vests require less than 1 yard (0.9 m) of fabric, so you can splurge on a beautiful tapestry, boiled wool, or even suede. Making a vest is a good way to limit the size of a project as you try new embellishment and fabric-manipulation techniques.

Here is my favorite way to make a simple lined vest, which can be finished in an hour, will look professionally made, and will give years of pleasure. The trick is in the way the lining is sewn.

QUICK LIST

Fabric for outer-vest front
Use one length, about ¾ yard (0.7 m).

Lining fabric
Use two lengths, about 1½ yards (1.4 m) each, enough to cut two backs (for the outer back and lining) and two lining front pieces.

Fusible weft-insertion interfacing
You will need enough to underline the outer-vest fronts and back.

Vest pattern
If you are going to embellish the vest or use a specialty fabric, such as a tapestry, start with a simple pattern without darts or details.

Cut and Assemble Your Vest

1 To keep the lining from peeking out along the edges of the vest, I cut out the lining, then I trim ⅛ inch (0.3 cm) off all the outside edges of each lining piece before beginning to construct the vest. Since the lining is now slightly smaller than the outer vest, it pulls the outer fabric slightly to the inside, hiding the seamlines along the edges of the vest.

2 Underline the vest fronts and back pieces with the fusible weft-insertion interfacing. (This prevents the "droop" often seen in ready-to-wear vests.) If called for in the pattern, sew the vest and lining center back seams. Sew the shoulder seams of the outer vest, then sew the lining shoulder seams.

3 Lay the vest on a large, flat surface, and pin the lining to the vest with right sides together at the armholes and around the vest front and back neckline. Sew the armholes and the vest front, starting and ending 2 inches (5.1 cm) from each side seam. Trim the seam allowances with pinking shears, then turn the vest right side out, and press.

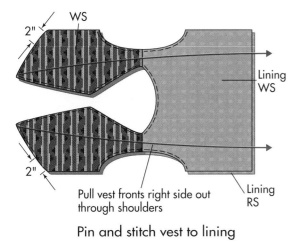

Pull vest fronts right side out through shoulders

Pin and stitch vest to lining

4 Pin the vest front to the vest back at the side seams and the lining front to the lining back

at the side seams with right sides together, matching the armhole seams. Sew one side seam end to end, beginning at the bottom of the vest and continuing to the bottom of the lining. Sew the other side seam the same way but leave 4 inches (10.2 cm) unsewn in the middle of the lining seam, creating a hole in the lining side seam.

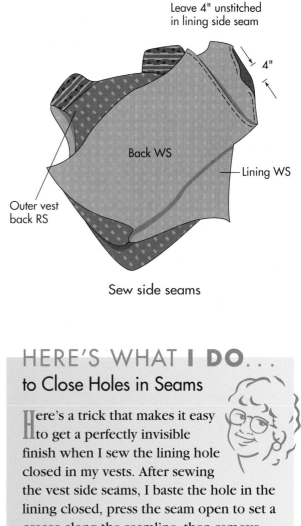

Sew side seams

HERE'S WHAT I DO...
to Close Holes in Seams

Here's a trick that makes it easy to get a perfectly invisible finish when I sew the lining hole closed in my vests. After sewing the vest side seams, I baste the hole in the lining closed, press the seam open to set a crease along the seamline, then remove the basting to reveal the hole. Later, when I'm ready to whipstitch the hole closed again, the seamline is clearly marked since it was "trained" in place, and it's easy to stitch closed invisibly.

on the
FAST TRACK...

to a Quick Unlined Vest

Here's my super shortcut to a quick unlined vest—cut, sew, serge, and you're done. The secret lies in turning a two-piece vest pattern into a one-piece pattern by eliminating the side seams, as shown. A piece of blanket wool or tapestry is a perfect fabric choice for this type of unlined vest.

With a decorative rayon or metallic thread in the loopers, serge the raw edges of the vest with a wide three-thread stitch shortened to create a serged binding (a finish often found in high-end designer ready-to-wear). To finish the vest, sew the shoulder seams with right sides together.

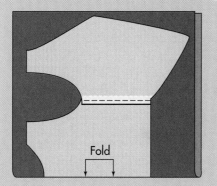

Fold

Eliminate side seams for unlined vest

Finishing Fast, Faster, Fastest

1 To finish the bottom edge, keep the vest right side out. Pull the bottom edges of the vest and lining through the hole in the lining side seam. Pin the bottom edges of the vest and the lining with right sides together, matching the side seams, then sew the bottom edges, including the 2-inch (5.1-cm) openings.

2 Pull the vest back through the side-seam hole, and press the lower edge of the vest. Then hand sew the lining hole closed with a blind stitch, or use a narrow zigzag stitch to sew the hole closed on the sewing machine.

3 Finally, mark and sew buttonholes and buttons on the vest.

HERE'S WHAT I DO...
to Make a Vest More Fitted

When I want a fitted vest, I add a piece of elastic to the vest back. Before closing the hole in the lining side seam, I mark the waistline at the vest center back and stitch a casing through the vest and lining about 8 inches (20.3 cm) long by $5/8$ inch (1.6 cm) wide. Next, I reach in through the hole and with a safety pin or bodkin, I slip a 6-inch (15.2-cm) piece of $1/2$-inch (1.3-cm)-wide elastic into the casing. Then from the right side of the vest, I stitch through all layers, catching the ends of the elastic.

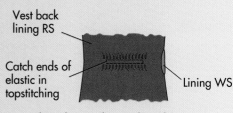

Vest back lining RS

Catch ends of elastic in topstitching

Lining WS

Slip elastic through side-seam hole and into stitched casing

SUE'S QUICK COVER-UP CAPE

Capes are the perfect cover-up for any season. They are fun to wear and so quick and easy to make that you can have several capes in different colors and lengths. Make a short one from wool knit or waterproof fabric for quick trips to the grocery store, and make a long one from wool, mohair, or even velvet for evening wear. A beautiful new cape is a favorite project for the mother-to-be, who will outgrow every coat she owns!

QUICK LIST

60-inch (152.4-cm)-wide fabric

Your fabric should have some drape to it and be appropriate to the season. You will need one piece twice the length of the finished cape. If you are making a gift, it is safe to start with 3 yards (2.7 m) of fabric, which will make a standard calf-length cape.

¼ yard (0.2 m) extra fabric

You can use this extra fabric to make a belt or scarf to match your cape.

Binding for edges (optional)

If your cape fabric is loosely woven like the one shown in the photo at right, consider using a tightly woven fabric for the binding. Look through the trim section of your local fabric store to find a binding in a color that matches or coordinates with your cape fabric.

Cut and Assemble Your Cape

1 Fold the length of fabric in half crosswise, and mark the foldline. (This will be the shoulder line.)

2 Mark and cut a center front line through one thickness of fabric from the bottom front edge to the marked shoulder line and 4 inches (10.2 cm) past the line, down the back. To create the neck opening, cut a slight curve in the 4 inches (10.2 cm) beyond the shoulder line. Staystitch the curve to prevent the opening from stretching.

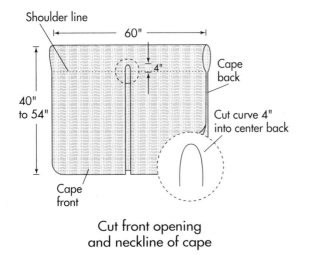

Cut front opening
and neckline of cape

Finishing Fast, Faster, Fastest

1 Try on the cape to see if you want to round the corners on the hem at the center fronts and at the side seams. Finish all the edges with your choice of the *Fast, Faster, Fastest* techniques in "Binding" on page 146 or in "Edge Finishes" on page 80. My favorite finish is a three-thread serged edge using a decorative thread. On loosely woven fabrics, you may want to create fringe along the bottom of the cape edge by pulling out the crosswise-grain threads.

2 After you have finished the edges, try on the cape, and match up the bottom edges so the length is the same in the front and back. To keep the cape from slipping forward or back while you are wearing it, join the cape front and back at the underarm. To do this, pin the side edges with wrong sides together 8 to 10 inches (20.3 to 25.4 cm) below the shoulder line, then stitch the front and back together in a large triangle, using the measurements suggested in the illustration below to create sleeves.

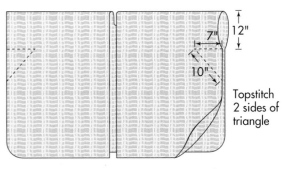

Create "sleeves" with triangles

3 Dress up your cape with the "Stitch & Stretch Belt" described on page 27 or the "Faux-Woven Scarf" described on page 30. You can also accessorize with the quick scarf described in "On the Fast Track to a Warm Scarf" on the opposite page.

on the FAST TRACK...

to a Warm Scarf

For a quick, warm scarf, cut ¼ to ⅜ yard (0.2 to 0.3 m) of polar-fleece-type fabric with a rotary cutter. (Try the wave or zigzag rotary blade for a fun look.) Cut fringe 3 to 4 inches (7.6 to 10.2 cm) long at each end with the rotary cutter. Finally, add a monogram or embroidery detail. This also makes a great gift!

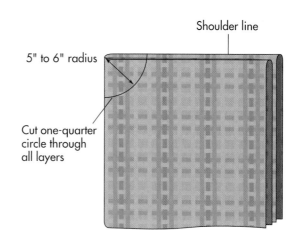

Cut neck opening for poncho

SUE'S RIBBED COWL-NECK PONCHO

For a warm winter wrap with a sporty look, you can create a poncho instead of a cape. Just cut a neck hole, add a ribbed cowl neck for extra warmth, finish the edges, and you are done.

QUICK LIST

60-inch (152.4-cm)-wide fabric
Begin with a single piece two times the length of the finished poncho.

Light- to medium-weight ribbing
You will need a piece 18 inches (45.7 cm) long by 28 to 30 inches (71.1 to 76.2 cm) wide.

1 After folding and marking the shoulder line, as explained in Step 1 under "Cut and Assemble Your Cape" on the opposite page, fold the fabric in half again along the center front and back, and cut a quarter-circle hole with a 5- to 6-inch (12.7- to 15.2-cm) radius.

2 This collar will be sewn on in a single thickness, so you'll need to finish one crosswise edge of the ribbing by serging or zigzag stitching. Then sew the ribbing lengthwise into a tube. Divide and mark the unfinished crosswise edge of the ribbing and the neck opening into quarters, then pin them, right sides together, matching the markings. Sew or serge the ribbing to the neck opening, stretching the ribbing as you stitch.

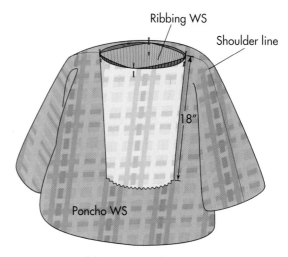

Pin ribbing to neck opening

3 Finish the edges around the poncho, using one of the techniques suggested in Step 1 under "Finishing Fast, Faster, Fastest" on the opposite page.

51

SUE'S BLANKET TO GO

One way to speed up a sewing project is to start with fabric that has part of the work done for you. Sewing a coat from a fringed cotton-knit afghan is a good example. To make this coat, you eliminate all the facings from a simple coat pattern, and place the pattern pieces on the blanket with all the hemlines falling along the fringe, which eliminates any hemming. Then all you do is sew the sleeves and collar, and you will have a great-looking coat.

QUICK LIST

Blanket
A blanket 45 to 64 inches (114.3 to 162.6 cm) wide by 54 to 64 inches (137.2 to 162.6 cm) long will make one adult coat. (Be sure the width of the blanket will wrap around you.) A fringed cotton-knit afghan is used most often, but any blanket suitable to the climate and season will do.

Coat or jacket pattern
You can use a pattern designed for making coats from blankets (see "Sources" on page 203), but any simple coat or jacket pattern with a shawl collar will work. Look for patterns with four pieces: front, back, sleeve, and collar.

Cut and Assemble Your Coat

1 Before cutting out your coat, you may want to eliminate the side seams by overlapping the front and back side seams on the seamlines. At the same time, make sure that the width of the coat pattern matches the width of the blanket. For smaller sizes, you can make the armhole fit the sleeve without losing fullness in the coat at the hip by creating a dart in place of the underarm seam. To do this, line up the front edge of the pattern along a fringed edge of the blanket, then draw a dart, as shown in the illustration below.

Lay out your pattern pieces so the hemline of the front, back, sleeves, and outer edge of the collar lie along the fringe. If needed, shorten the coat slightly to make room for the sleeves and collar along the fringe of the blanket. Also, before cutting, check to see how the design on the blanket will fall on your body, and adjust the pattern placement so the design is flattering on you.

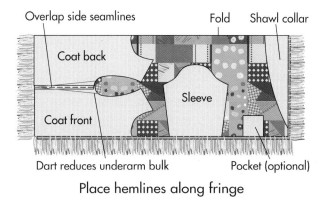

Place hemlines along fringe

2 Before sewing the coat, test your stitches on blanket scraps, experimenting with needle size and stitch length to prevent wavy distorted seams in the loosely woven blanket fabric. On the sewing machine use a size 90/14 needle, select a slightly longer stitch length than normal, and adjust the presser foot pressure to prevent the loose weave of the blanket from distorting. Sew ⅝-inch (1.6-cm) seams, then finish the raw edges with a zigzag or overcast stitch close to

the seam. Trim the excess from the seam allowance, or sew the edge in one step using a seam/overcast stitch. (On the serger, use a wide four- or five-thread stitch and a long stitch length. Adjust the differential feed toward 2 to prevent waving and distortion in the fabric.)

3 Sew the shoulder seams first. To prevent the seam from stretching when the coat is worn, stitch or serge over a piece of ribbon or twill tape as you sew the shoulder seam.

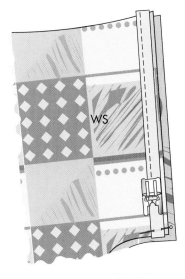

Sew stay tape into shoulder seam

4 Next, pin the right side of the collar to the wrong side of the neck edge, matching the center backs. (I have done this wrong so many times I suggest you pin it first to be sure the seam will be under the collar!)

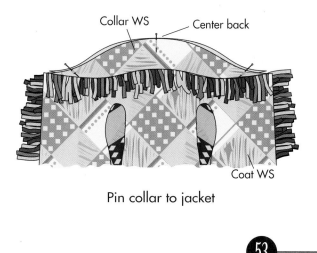

Pin collar to jacket

53

5 You have two choices for adding the sleeves, depending on how you cut out the coat. If you left the side seams in the pattern, sew or serge the sleeves to the jacket in the flat, then finish the side seams and the underarm sleeve seams together. If you eliminated the side seams, sew the underarm sleeve seams, then set the sleeves into the coat.

Finishing Fast, Faster, Fastest

1 Pockets are optional, but here is a quick patch pocket if you want one. Cut the pocket with the fringe along the top edge of the pocket. Cut a lining for the pocket from a piece of fusible tricot interfacing cut slightly narrower and shorter than the pocket minus the fringe.

2 Pin the interfacing to the pocket, right sides together (yes, with the adhesive on the outside). Stitch the interfacing to the pocket along the sides and bottom, leaving the fringed edge unstitched.

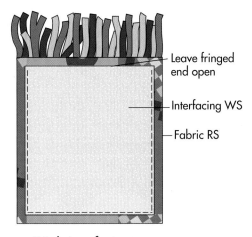

— Leave fringed end open

— Interfacing WS

— Fabric RS

Stitch interfacing to three sides of pocket

3 Trim the seam allowance around the interfacing with pinking shears to reduce the bulk of the blanket fabric. Turn the pocket right side out through the fringed edge, and press to fuse the interfacing to the inside of the pocket. Pin the pocket to the coat front, and topstitch it in place. Add another pocket if you have enough blanket scraps for a second one.

Once you've tried this blanket coat, you can try some variations, such as using a Battenberg tablecloth for a summer coat without the collar, or a fringed rayon shawl to make a swimsuit cover-up. The possibilities are endless. Save the scraps from your blanket coats, and use them later to make great totes and purses to match your cover-ups and coats.

SUE'S SNIPPETS
A NEW COAT "ON THE FLY"

I first saw a blanket coat at the Dallas, Texas, airport on my way to catch a plane to Minneapolis. The price tag on the coat was $175, but as I boarded the plane, I thought "I can make that!" That night, in the hotel gift shop, I found a wonderful blanket for $38 and liked it even better than the coat I'd seen in Dallas, so I bought the blanket. All I needed to make a coat from the blanket was a quick trip to a fabric shop the next day to buy a basic jacket pattern with a shawl collar. Then back in my hotel room, it took me only about 40 minutes total cutting and sewing time, and I was wearing my new blanket coat on the flight home that night!

FROM SWEATSHIRT TO JACKET

Because I start with a completed garment, converting a ready-to-wear pullover sweatshirt to a jacket is one of my favorite ways to create a one-of-a-kind garment in no time at all. The finished jacket is comfortable, washable, and beautiful, and most people have to be told that it started out as a sweatshirt. Let's start by converting a basic sweatshirt to a plain jacket, using the ribbing from the bottom band of the sweatshirt to make the facing of the jacket. Then I will show you some ideas for creating your own "conversion version" with a woven-fabric "ribbing," front band, and cuffs, like the jacket shown in the photo at right. (To make this jacket, see the instructions for the Trim-to-Match Conversion Sweatshirt on page 61.)

QUICK LIST

Oversize sweatshirt
Buy the best-quality sweatshirt your budget will allow. I prefer sweatshirts with set-in sleeves.

¼ yard (0.2 m) fusible tricot interfacing
The interfacing will be used to stabilize the front facing of the conversion jacket.

Cut and Assemble Your Jacket

In this basic conversion, you are going to remove the bottom-band ribbing and use it as the center front facing. This accomplishes two things at once. It eliminates the unflattering pull from the ribbing that accentuates the tummy area in a cardigan sweatshirt, and it provides a perfectly dyed-to-match front facing.

1 Cut off the bottom ribbing, cutting through the sweatshirt next to the seamline, then cut the seam allowance off the ribbing.

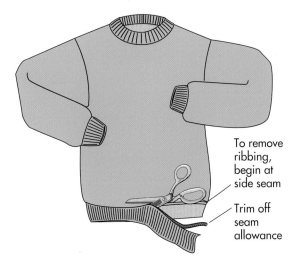

To remove ribbing, begin at side seam

Trim off seam allowance

Remove ribbing and trim off seam allowance

2 Cut the circle of ribbing into a long strip. (If there is a seam where the ribbing was originally sewn into a circle, begin cutting the ribbing at the seam.) Pin the ribbing to your ironing board, and steam it to straighten and block it flat.

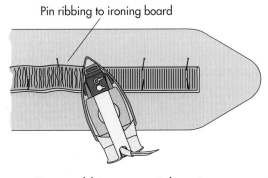

Pin ribbing to ironing board

Steam ribbing to straighten it

3 Mark the center front of the sweatshirt by folding the front in half and pressing a crease from the neck to the bottom edge. If the sweatshirt is made of very stretchy knit, first stabilize the center front from the neckline to the bottom by fusing a 2-inch (5.1-cm) strip of interfacing to the wrong side of the sweatshirt. Cut the sweatshirt open along the center front foldline.

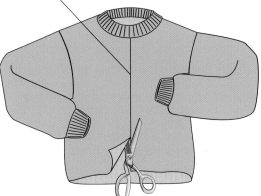

Press crease in center front

Mark and cut sweatshirt front

4 Try on the sweatshirt, and mark the desired hemline of the jacket plus 1½ inches (3.8 cm) for the hem allowance. I prefer to make a conversion-sweatshirt hem fall just below the waistline because it flatters most figures, disguises a tummy, and eliminates the baggy appearance of an oversize sweatshirt.

If there is any excess below the marked hem allowance, trim it off. Turn and press the hem toward the wrong side.

5 Now it's time to determine whether you have enough ribbing for the front facing. You will need two pieces the length of the jacket center front from the top of the neck ribbing to the hemline plus ½ inch (1.3 cm).

If the ribbing is long enough to provide two pieces for the front facing, cut the pieces now and continue with the next step. If the ribbing is not long enough to make two pieces, cut it in half lengthwise to create two long, narrow strips. Press lightweight fusible interfacing to the wrong side along the length of the ribbing strip to stabilize it.

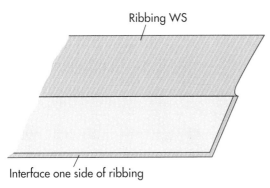

Ribbing WS

Interface one side of ribbing

Interface ribbing for front facing

6 Next, fold the ribbing in half lengthwise with right sides together, and sew or serge across the ends with a ¼-inch (0.6-cm) seam allowance. Turn each strip right side out and press, then double-check that the sewn strips are exactly the same length.

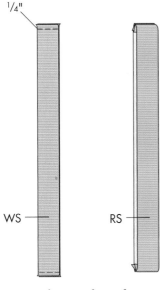

¼"

WS   RS

Prepare front facing

Finishing Fast, Faster, Fastest

1 Pin the facing pieces to the center front edges of the jacket with right sides together,

matching the top of each ribbing strip to the neckline edge and the bottom of each strip with the marked hemline. Fold the hem allowance to the right side over the facing, and pin it in place.

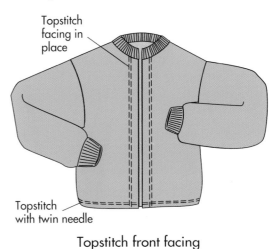

Topstitch facing in place

Topstitch with twin needle

Topstitch front facing

2 Stitch the ribbing strips to the jacket front (do *not* stretch the ribbing as you stitch), then press them to the wrong side of the jacket, and topstitch them in place.

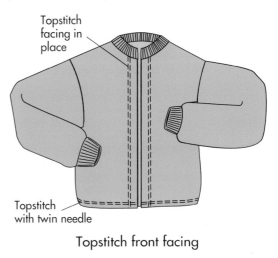

Topstitch facing in place

Topstitch with twin needle

Topstitch front facing

Once you have made a jacket from this basic sweatshirt conversion, consider the endless creative options, such as some of the variations on pages 59–66. Also, a conversion sweatshirt is a good project for trying out different embellishment techniques.

Embroidery Pin

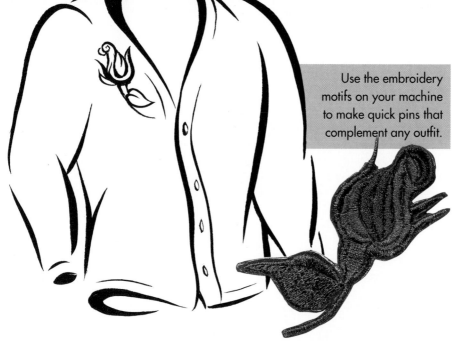

Use the embroidery motifs on your machine to make quick pins that complement any outfit.

If you have a machine that will embroider large motifs, here's a way to make an accessory for any occasion. My rose pin was created by Snez Babic from Husqvarna Canada. But the original idea came from snowbird Sue Heck, who gave me an embroidered pumpkin pin she had made. Sue's pins have inspired a variety of variations from country to fashion. With embroidery motifs available on today's machines, a pin can be created for every occasion and every garment. Pins especially add pizzazz to sweat-shirt jackets. In addition to embroidery motifs, fabric prints and appliqué motifs are other sources for these creative accessories and fun gifts.

1. From the designs available on your sewing machine, select a rosebud or other flower motif, and embroider it on a double layer of organza. (If you don't have built-in embroidery designs on your machine, you can free-motion embroider a motif on a double layer of organza, then continue with the rest of the steps described here.)

2. After stitching the motif, cut it out, being careful not to cut the stitches.

3. Roll or press a craft clay such as Fimo until it is about ¼ inch (0.6 cm) thick. Mold or cut the rolled-out craft clay in the general shape of the rosebud.

4. Press the embroidered rose into the clay. Cut around the embroidered rose with a sharp craft knife, leaving a narrow border of clay. Bake it in the oven as directed on the clay package. Paint a thin coat of a sealant/glaze such as Sculpey Glaze over the embroidery pin. Glue a pin back to the back side.

SHIRRED SLEEVES

Sloppy extralong sleeves are dead giveaways that you are wearing a sweatshirt. To eliminate droopy sleeves, try adding a length of elastic inside the top of the sleeve. The shirring created by the elastic shortens the sleeve and creates the designer push-up sleeve found in upscale exercise jackets and other casual ready-to-wear.

1 Turn the sweatshirt sleeve wrong side out, lay it flat as you would to iron a shirtsleeve, and press a fold in the top of the sleeve from shoulder to cuff.

2 Pin the ends of the elastic from a few inches above the elbow to the cuff. Use a zigzag or three-step zigzag stitch to sew the elastic to the wrong side of the sleeve along the crease, stretching the elastic to fit as you sew.

MY MOTHER'S SPECIAL REQUEST

If you use a double thickness of ribbing for your facing, you can let the ribbing serve as a front band instead of a facing, adding buttonholes and buttons instead of topstitching it down. This is the way my mother wanted me to make her jacket. She saw the conversion-sweatshirt project on my "America Sews" television program from her home in Arizona. Then the next time I visited her home, she had several pullover sweatshirts lined up for me to convert!

Front band that my mother prefers

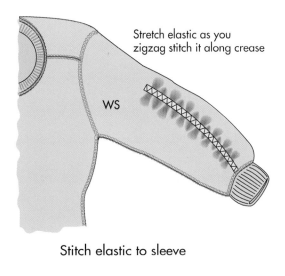

Stretch elastic as you zigzag stitch it along crease

WS

Stitch elastic to sleeve

59

EPAULETS THAT COME AND GO

I saw this idea for detachable epaulets in a very upscale women's shop in California. Begin with a converted-sweatshirt jacket in a basic color, then make a variety of epaulets—plain and fancy and held in place with hook-and-loop tape—that can be changed to match any outfit. To make a pair of epaulets, you cut fabric strips, serge rolled hems on the edges, and sew the strips to the hook side of hook-and-loop tape.

QUICK LIST

Six different fabrics
Use ¼ yard (0.2 m) each of color-coordinated light- to medium-weight fabrics.

Hook-and-loop tape
You will need 8 inches (20.3 cm).

1 From each fabric, cut a rectangle 9 inches (22.9 cm) by 11 inches (27.9 cm). (Save time by cutting all six fabrics at once with a rotary cutter.) Finish both of the 9-inch (22.9-cm) raw edges of each rectangle with a serger rolled-edge finish.

2 Cut the rectangles lengthwise into 1-by-11-inch (2.5-by-27.9-cm) strips, and finish the 11-inch (27.9-cm) raw edges with a serger rolled-edge stitch.

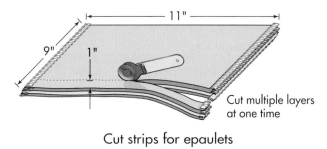

Cut strips for epaulets

3 For each epaulet, layer the strips in a pleasing arrangement. Center a 4-inch (10.2-cm) strip of the hook-and-loop tape hook side down under the strips, and stitch down the center to hold it in place. Sew the loop side of the epaulet to the shoulder of your conversion sweatshirt.

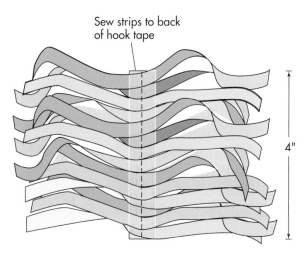

Sew strips to back of hook tape

4"

Sew strips to hook-and-loop tape

HERE'S WHAT **I DO**...
to Make Fringed Epaulets

The epaulets I saw in an upscale California designer shop had serger rolled-edge chains hanging off the corners of a number of the strips. To create this effect, I begin with a chain several inches long, serge the rolled edge, then chain off for several inches. If I want the chains to curl, I thread the lower looper and the needle with nylon monofilament thread.

Here are two epaulet variations. You can make lettuce-edged strips from knit fabric by cutting the strips with the greater stretch of the knit running lengthwise. Stretch slightly as you stitch a rolled edge. Or you can use ribbon or other trims in place of some of the fabric strips in the epaulet, and sew the ends to a point.

TRIM-TO-MATCH CONVERSION SWEATSHIRT

To add a fashion coordinate to your wardrobe, make a conversion-sweatshirt jacket (see photo on page 55) with the materials from the Quick List on page 55. Use leftover fabric from "Sue's No-Pattern Quick Skirts" on page 22 to make the front band and to create ribbing for the cuffs and bottom band for the conversion sweatshirt.

QUICK LIST

60-inch (152.4-cm)-wide fabric
You will need ⅞ yard (0.8 m) for the bottom band, cuffs, and front band. Use the same light- to medium-weight, drapey fabric you used in your Quick Skirt. (See "Sue's No-Pattern Quick Skirts" on page 22.)

Cut and Assemble Your Jacket

1 To prepare the sweatshirt, cut off the bottom band and cuff ribbing, cutting through the sweatshirt next to the seamline. Set aside the ribbing to save for another project. Try on the sweatshirt to determine the length you would like the finished jacket to be, then cut the sweatshirt 2¾ inches (7 cm) shorter than the desired length. Likewise, cut each sleeve 2¾ inches (7 cm) shorter than its desired finished length.

2 Fold the sweatshirt in half lengthwise, and press a crease up the center front. Cut the sweatshirt open along the line created by the pressed crease.

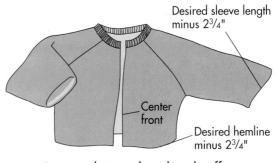

Remove bottom band and cuffs

3 To prepare the shirred bottom band and cuffs, cut two strips crosswise on the fabric 7 inches (17.8 cm) wide by 60 inches (152.4 cm) long. Sew the ends together to make a strip approximately 120 inches (304.8 cm) long. (The gathers that create the shirring will reduce the length of the strip by about half.)

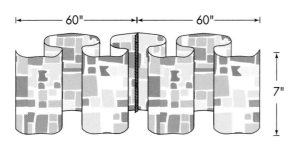

Make one long strip for shirring

4 Wind several bobbins with elastic thread. If you cannot wind the bobbins on the machine without stretching the elastic thread, wind them by hand.

5 Place the bobbin in the machine as you normally do, thread the needle with polyester thread, and set the machine for a straight stitch at a long stitch length of about 4 (6 to 6.5 spi). Sew rows of stitching down the length of the strip about ½ inch (1.3 cm) apart. (A quilting guide or edge guide is handy to keep the rows straight.) The fabric will shirr, or pucker, as you sew. Be sure to check how much elastic thread is left on the bobbin at the end of each row to avoid running out in the middle of a row.

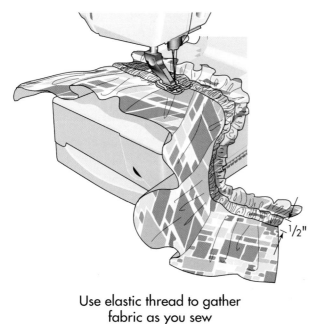

Use elastic thread to gather fabric as you sew

6 To set the elastic thread so it returns to its original shape after all the rows have been stitched, lay the shirred strip on the ironing board. Hold the iron close but not touching the strip, and steam the strip with bursts of steam. Let the shirring dry.

7 Adding the shirred strip to the conversion sweatshirt is the same as using ribbing for the bottom band and cuffs.

To determine the length you will need for the bottom band, pull the shirred strip around your body (without stretching it) where the bottom band will be worn when it is sewn to the jacket. Cut the shirring for the bottom band 2 inches (5.1 cm) shorter than the distance around your body.

8 Fold the shirred band in half lengthwise, divide the band and the jacket hem in quarters, and pin them right sides together. With a ½-inch (1.3-cm) seam allowance, sew or serge the band to the jacket, stretching the band as needed.

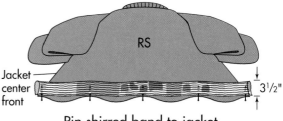

Pin shirred band to jacket

9 To prepare the shirring to make the cuffs, cut two pieces of the shirred strip 7½ inches (19.1 cm) long. Fold the strips in half, matching the short ends, and sew each strip into a circle with right sides together.

Fold each cuff in half with wrong sides together. Divide the sleeves and cuffs into quarters, pin them with right sides together, and sew or serge, stretching the cuffs as needed.

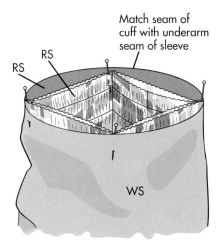

Match seam of
cuff with underarm
seam of sleeve

RS

RS

WS

Pin and sew shirred cuff to sleeve

Finishing Fast, Faster, Fastest

1 To prepare the front bands of the jacket from the same fabric you used for the bottom band and cuffs, cut two strips 3½ inches (8.9 cm) wide by the length of the jacket front from the top of the neckline ribbing to the bottom of the shirred bottom band plus 2 inches (5.1 cm) to turn under at the top and bottom. Fuse tricot interfacing to the wrong side of each strip.

2 Pin the bands to the center front edges of the jacket with right sides together, and sew or serge in place. Then press the bands away from the sweatshirt with the seam allowances toward the bands.

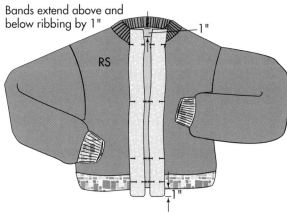

Bands extend above and
below ribbing by 1"

1"

RS

1"

Pin and stitch front bands to jacket

3 Press under the remaining lengthwise edge of each band ¼ inch (0.6 cm), and edgestitch. Turn under the excess fabric at the top and bottom of the band.

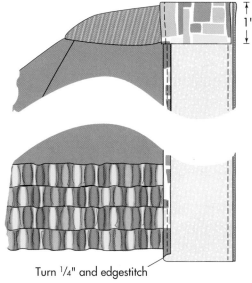

1"

Turn ¼" and edgestitch

Finish raw edge of band

4 Turn half of the band under to the wrong side of the jacket, matching the edgestitched fold to the seamline, and whipstitch the fold in place. A faster way to stitch the band is to pin from the right side and stitch in the ditch by machine.

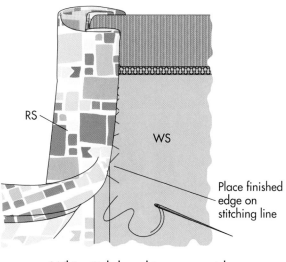

RS

WS

Place finished
edge on
stitching line

Whipstitch band to wrong side

TRACY'S PINTUCKED CONVERSION JACKET

One of the teaching guests on my "America Sews" television program, Tracy Helmer, brought this great quick and easy sweatshirt conversion idea to one of our programs. So many viewers have written to ask for the directions, I thought it would be a good project to include among my favorite cover-up garments. With slightly tapered sleeves and the shaping provided by the pintucks at the neck and waistline, Tracy's conversion jacket definitely eliminates the sloppy sweatshirt look. To make this jacket, you will remove all the ribbing, mark and stitch the pintucking, cut a V-neck, and add a front band.

QUICK LIST

Oversize sweatshirt

Buy the best-quality sweatshirt your budget will allow.

Three buttons

Choose buttons that match or contrast with the sweatshirt. The buttons should be ½ to ⅝ inch (1.3 to 1.6 cm) in diameter.

Cut and Mark Your Jacket

1 Cut the bottom ribbing and cuffs off the sweatshirt. Determine the finished length of the jacket, add 1 inch (2.5 cm) to the desired hemline, and trim off the excess.

2 Cut the sweatshirt open along the center front. Try on the sweatshirt, and mark your waistline at the center front and back and at your bust point.

Cut sweatshirt along center front

3 Lay the sweatshirt front flat, and mark a line along the waistline, which will be the bottom of the pintucks. On each side of the jacket front, draw a line for a tuck from 1 inch (2.5 cm) below the bust point to the waistline. Draw four or five lines 1 inch (2.5 cm) apart on either side of the center line, with each line starting about 1 inch (2.5 cm) lower than the previous one and extending to the waistline.

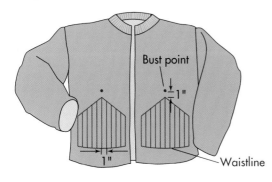

Mark front for pintucking

4 Mark the center back with a line from just below the shoulder blades to the waistline, then mark one or two pairs of lines the same way you marked the jacket front.

5 Use a twin needle to stitch the front tucks. Try on the jacket after sewing each pair of back tucks to make sure the jacket doesn't get too tight.

6 For the V-neck, mark three buttonholes, one at the waist, one even with the top of the longest tuck, and one spaced evenly between these two. Mark and cut the V-neckline, as shown, then cut off the neckline ribbing.

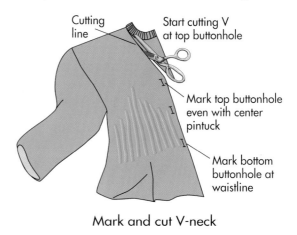

Mark and cut V-neck

7 Staystitch the neckline a scant ¼ inch (0.6 cm) from the edge. Mark and stitch tucks 2 to 3 inches (5.1 to 7.6 cm) long at the center back neckline.

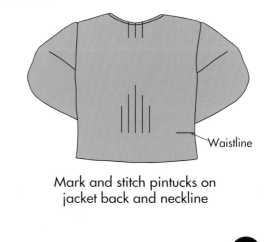

Mark and stitch pintucks on jacket back and neckline

Finishing Fast, Faster, Fastest

1 To hem the jacket, serge or finish the lower edge with a zigzag stitch, then turn up a 1-inch (2.5-cm) hem. Topstitch the hem from the right side with a 2.0- or 3.0-mm twin needle.

2 To taper the sleeves, try on the jacket, and mark the desired hemlines. Then mark and stitch a tapering line in the underarm seam of each sleeve from the elbow to the hemline. Add 1 inch (2.5 cm) to the desired hemline, trim the excess, then stitch the sleeve hem the same way you did the jacket hem.

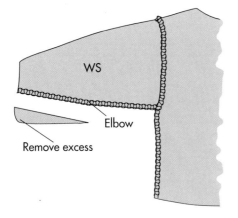

WS

Elbow

Remove excess

Taper sleeve from elbow to wrist

3 To prepare the neckline/front band, pin the bottom ribbing band to the ironing board, and steam it flat and straight. Cut the ribbing lengthwise to make two long strips. Sew or serge the short ends of the strips together to create one long strip.

4 Fold the ribbing right sides together to create the front band. Measure your jacket to determine the exact length needed to face the jacket center front and neckline, and add ½ inch (1.3 cm). (This measurement will be the length of the ribbing band.) Trim the ribbing band to the correct length, centering the seam at the back neckline. Sew or serge the ends

with a ¼-inch (0.6-cm) seam, then turn the band right side out.

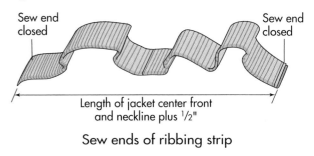

Sew end closed

Sew end closed

Length of jacket center front and neckline plus ½"

Sew ends of ribbing strip

5 Stitch the ribbing band to the jacket edge, with the right side of the band to the *wrong* side of the jacket, matching the hemline of the jacket with the band ends.

¼"

Pin and stitch band to jacket

6 Turn and press the band to the right side of the jacket, then topstitch the band in place. Finally, mark and sew the buttonholes and buttons to the band.

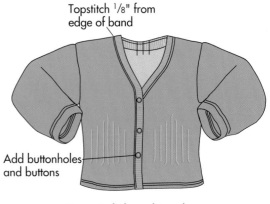

Topstitch ⅛" from edge of band

Add buttonholes and buttons

Topstitch band in place

REVERSIBLE GARMENTS

I love sewing garments that can be worn more than one way. It maximizes sewing time and cuts down on the bulk in my luggage when I am traveling! The best part about reversible garments is that they are great to wear. What fun to flash to the wrong side!

All it takes to make a great reversible garment is a simple pattern and two good-quality fabrics for the two "right sides" of the garment. Once you've made a reversible garment, you can add a few sewing hours to create a mix-and-match wardrobe you will enjoy for years.

Beginning on page 74, I'll give you some tips for making garments from reversible fabrics. Many fabrics are not meant to be reversible. But if you like both sides and cannot decide which side to use, why not treat the fabric like a reversible? I have found many knits that look great on both sides. Reversible wovens are usually two fabrics bonded together to create the reversible look.

Here are some of my favorite ideas and techniques for making reversible garments.

Make Two

As long as you are using two lightweight fabrics, you can make two identical garments and sew them wrong sides together to create a reversible garment. A reversible garment travels well because it resists wrinkles. Make two-in-one garments to double the size of your wardrobe. Follow these easy steps whether you are making a pair of slacks, a vest, a top, or a jacket.

1 Use the basic pattern pieces for the garment front, back, and sleeves. Look for simple patterns in loose-fitting styles. Your reversible garment does not need facing pieces, so you can eliminate these from the pattern. Trim each hem allowance to the hemline plus a ⅝-inch (1.6-cm) seam allowance.

2 Cut out the entire garment from two different fabrics. I believe that accurate cutting, marking, and sewing with accurate seam allowances are important for a professional look for every garment but absolutely crucial for reversibles so they end up the same size and lie and hang well on the body.

3 Sew all of the basic seams on each garment so you have two identical garments. Then add specific finishing techniques, such as buttonholes and hems, according to the garment type.

4 For slacks or a simple skirt style, put the two garments right sides together, and sew around the top edge.

5 Turn the two layers right side out, and insert waistband elastic sewn into a circle into the slacks or skirt at the waist. Straight stitch below the elastic to create a casing. Sew another row of stitching through the elastic,

stretching it as you sew. You can also stitch multiple casings for multiple pieces of narrow elastic if you prefer.

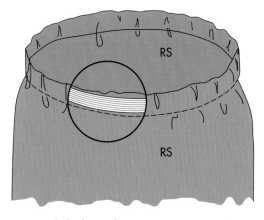

Stitch below elastic to create casing

6 I have found that for the hem edges on fuller styles it is better to hem the legs or skirt of each side separately and let them hang freely. If they are stitched together, too often they pull and destroy the hang of the garment.

JACKET

A reversible jacket can be difficult to make because it is hard to get the two layers to hang exactly the same. Piping around the edges is the key to a successful reversible jacket since it keeps one side from peeking out from behind the other. Start with a simple jacket pattern—collarless is best and with as few seams as possible.

1 Cut the fronts, backs, and sleeves from the two fashion fabrics. Construct both jackets leaving about 4 inches (10.2 cm) open along one side seam for finishing later.

2 Make piping from self- or contrasting fabric strips cut on the bias or crosswise grain and piping cable cord. Cut each strip wide enough to cover the cord plus 1¼ inch (3.2 cm) for seam allowances.

3 Wrap the fabric strip lengthwise around the cable cord wrong sides together. With a piping foot on your machine, lay the cable cord into the groove on the underside of the foot. Then straight stitch through both layers of fabric close to the cable cord without stitching into it.

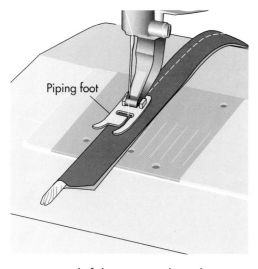

Stitch fabric around cord

4 Sew the piping to the right side of the outer edges of one of the jackets. Place the jackets right sides together, and sew all the way around the outer edges—front, neck, and bottom. Turn the jacket right side out through one of the sleeves. Pin the sleeves as they need to be sewn along the hemlines.

Pin sleeve hems

5 Pull the sleeves out the side-seam opening, and repin them so they can be sewn end to end. Stitch around the sleeve hems. Pull the sleeves back out, and slip stitch the opening.

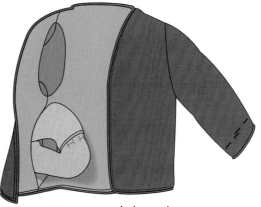

Sew around sleeve hems

QUILTED-FABRIC JACKET

Reversible quilted fabrics make versatile and fun jackets. Buy the fabric prequilted, or quilt your own by placing a piece of preshrunk garment-weight cotton batting between two layers of fabric and quilting on your sewing machine.

When you quilt your own fabric, layer the quilting and batting, and quilt as desired. The possibilities are endless with decorative threads and quick machine techniques. Spot quilt with a single decorative stitch, or use a print for one side of the jacket and a solid for the other and then free-motion quilt following the design in the print. For a channel-quilted jacket, it is great to select a striped fabric on one side and quilt along the stripes. The sleeves can be quilted with free motion or with side motion, sewing on the free arm of your sewing machine.

1 Select a simple pattern, and cut out the front, back, and sleeve pieces. Before cutting the garment pieces, eliminate the side seams if possible by overlapping the front and back pattern pieces at the side seams.

2 At the shoulder and sleeve seams, sew reversible flat-felled seams as follows: Straight stitch each seam with a ⅝-inch (1.6-cm) seam allowance. Trim one side of the seam allowance to ⅛ inch (0.3 cm). On the other side of the seam allowance, trim away the underlayer of fabric and the batting. Press under half of the seam allowance that is left, and press it over the seam. Topstitch the seam allowance in place with a transparent appliqué foot.

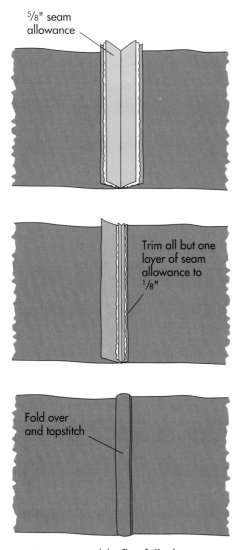

⅝" seam allowance

Trim all but one layer of seam allowance to ⅛"

Fold over and topstitch

Sew reversible flat-felled seam

3 Finish the outside edges of the jacket and sleeve seam allowances with binding.

on the FAST TRACK...

to Serger Quilting

Many five-thread sergers offer a chain stitch and/or a cover stitch that can be sewn anywhere on the fabric. The serger is perfect for speed quilting because you can sew at twice the speed of your sewing machine and never have to stop to wind a bobbin.

1 Layer the outer fabric, batting/filler, and lining, and baste them with adhesive spray or the basting stitch on your machine.

2 Mark quilting lines with a water-soluble marking pen.

3 Stitch over the marked lines with a serger chain stitch or cover stitch.

4 Cut the pattern pieces from the quilted fabric, and construct the garment.

PRINTED-PANEL VEST

For holiday or special-interest vests, you can save time by using a vest panel with the vest pattern pieces and complete instructions preprinted on the fabric. These panels make a fun project, but sometimes it is hard to justify investing in a holiday vest when you can wear it only a few days each year. That is why I line the vest with a different vest panel for another occasion.

If you decide to line the vest with another printed panel or with a fabric that you can wear year-round, purchase a vest panel, bring it home, and cut it out. Take it back to the store, and select a second vest panel printed with a similar style. Then complete the vest, as explained in "Sue's InVESTment Dressing" on page 46. My favorite is a sewing-theme vest on one side and a music-theme print on the other.

Vest Clip

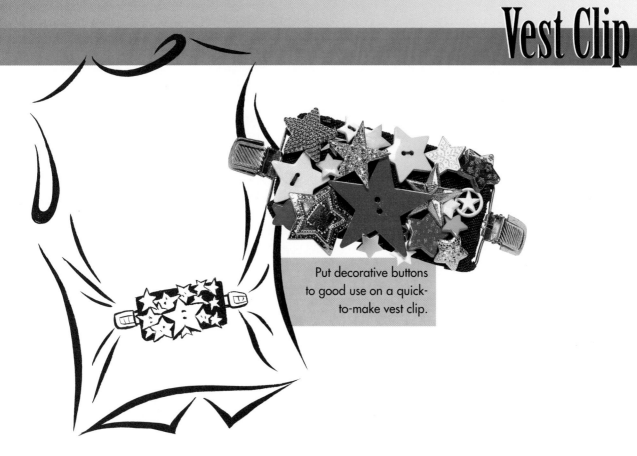

Put decorative buttons to good use on a quick-to-make vest clip.

Make vest clips that are both functional and fashionable. When Tracy Helmer demonstrated crazy-patch vests on my "America Sews" public television series, she brought me a vest clip made from antique white buttons. A vest clip adds a walk-away decorative detail to the back of the vest and helps to shape a vest that is too large (not my problem!) by tucking the back. Place a vest clip at the back waist of a one-piece unfitted dress, sweater, or conversion sweatshirt to make the back more flattering and fitted. Make two, and use them as epaulets at the shoulders of sweaters and sweatshirts to shorten sleeves with a decorative detail.

1. Begin with a piece of elastic 2 inches (5.1 cm) wide by 5 inches (12.7 cm) long, a set of suspender clips, and a collection of coordinating buttons.

2. Place the elastic ends into the loops on the suspender clips, and stitch them in place.

3. Stitch the buttons to the elastic in a pleasing arrangement.

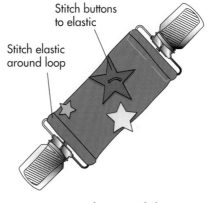

Stitch buttons to elastic

Stitch elastic around loop

Cover elastic with buttons

FOLD-AND-PRESS STRIP-QUILTED VEST

Fleece and felted fabrics are a wonderful base for reversible quilted garments. I love my strip-quilted vest. It was really a fun experiment and very economical because all the strip quilting was done with scraps from other garments.

1 Cut a simple pattern from fleece-type fabric. I eliminated the side seams by overlapping the pattern pieces at the seamlines.

2 Cut 2-inch (5.1-cm)-wide strips from fabric scraps, and seam them together end to end. If you are worried about colors coordinating, try using one color as the blender. Do not worry if the colors do not match; simply use all reds, all blues, or any color you choose. The results are amazing.

3 Fill several bobbins with a color of thread that matches the fleece. Begin with the garment back piece, and draw several vertical lines with a water-soluble marking pen to help you sew in a straight line.

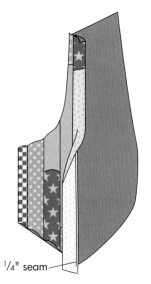

¼" seam

Stitch fabric strips to fleece foundation

HERE'S WHAT **I DO**...
to Make Reversible Buttons

Nina Kay Donovan, Husqvarna Viking educator, makes this suggestion for reversible button-holes and buttons. Sew button-holes on both the left and right front pieces of the garment. Select buttons for each side of the garment. Hand sew the buttons together back-to-back (I use elastic thread) to look like a cuff link, or sew each button to a backer button in the same manner. This is also a great way to make buttons that can be removed easily for laundering or dry cleaning. Button the reversible buttons through the buttonholes.

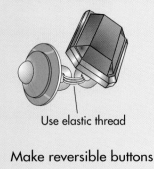

Use elastic thread

Make reversible buttons

On the back of the vest, place two strips right sides together lengthwise at the center. Sew along one edge with a ¼-inch (0.6-cm) seam allowance, stitching through the fleece and literally quilting through all layers. Finger press the top strip to the left side at the bottom edge. Lay the next strip over the strip on the right, and stitch through all layers. Fold the top strip to the right side and finger press. Use this fold-and-press method to cover the entire back. Begin the vest front at the side seam.

4 Cut off the excess strips at the bottom edge of the garment. The stitching channel quilts the reverse side of the vest as you go.

5 Construct the vest using mock flatlock seams (made by serging seams *wrong* sides together and topstitching with a matching thread) or using the reversible flat-felled seam technique, as explained in Step 2 for the "Quilted Fabric Jacket" on page 70. Bind the raw edges to complete the garment.

SWEATSHIRT JACKET

This warm bomber-style jacket is quick to complete because it is made from two ready-to-wear sweatshirts. For a personal touch, embellish each sweatshirt with appliqué or embroidery designs before making the reversible jacket.

To make this jacket, you will need two ready-to-wear sweatshirts. Be sure the sweatshirts are the same style and size. Of course, to be sure they are identical, you can start by making your own. You will also need one reversible separating zipper. It should be the same length as the center front or longer and a color that matches or complements the two sweatshirts.

1 Cut both sweatshirts down the center front, and embellish, appliqué, or embroider the sweatshirts as desired.

2 The zipper is put in the same way that piping is inserted into a seam. Separate the zipper into two pieces. Pin one side of the zipper tape along one side of the center front of one of the sweatshirts with right sides together. The bottom of the zipper will be at the bottom of the hip ribbing. If your zipper is longer than the sweatshirt, simply snip it at the top, and fold the end under.

3 Use a straight stitch set at a basting length and a standard presser foot. Machine baste the zipper in place, guiding the edge of the presser foot along the teeth of the zipper. I like to sew with the zipper down against the feed teeth and the sweatshirt on the top. This prevents the sweatshirt from feeding ahead of the zipper. Reduce the presser foot pressure as needed to prevent the layers from shifting. Repeat this for the other side of the zipper.

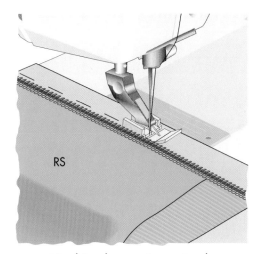

Machine baste zipper in place

SUE'S SNIPPETS
WHEN I TRY SOMETHING NEW

Here is a rule that I like to suggest when you are making any project using a new technique. If partway through the project you are concerned that you do not like the way it looks, finish it anyway for two reasons. First, you need to practice the new technique, and second, it may look totally different when it's finished. If you still really do not like it, call it a learning experience, and give it to the first person who admires it! You will have made a friend for life, and now you have the perfect excuse to buy more fabric and start over!

4 Place the second sweatshirt right sides together with the first sweatshirt. Adjust the needle position to stitch slightly closer to the zipper teeth than the first basting line. Pin along the center front zipper seam. Stitch the zipper between the two sweatshirt layers along the zipper on both center fronts.

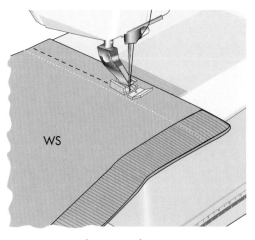

Stitch zipper between two
sweatshirt layers

5 With wrong sides out, tuck the hip ribbing into the right side of the sweatshirts, and bring the ribbing seams of both sweatshirts together. Sew these seams together along the edge with a zigzag stitch set at a length of 4 and at a width of 4 to allow for stretch along the edge. Stitch up as close as possible to the zipper at each end.

Sew ribbing seams with
wide zigzag

6 With the sleeves wrong side out, tuck the ribbing cuffs into each other end to end, bringing the ribbing seam allowances together in the round. Stitch the seam allowance together.

7 Turn the sweatshirt jacket right side out through the neckline. Stitch in the ditch through both layers of neck ribbing around the neckline.

REVERSIBLE FABRICS

Reversible fabrics are easy to sew and easy to wear. But such fabrics can be hard to find, so I add them to my collection whether I have an immediate project in mind or not. Many fabrics that are not actually designed to be reversible can be if they are interesting on both sides. I have found many knits that look great on both sides. Reversible wovens are usually two fabrics bonded together to create the reversible look. To sew with these fabrics, begin by simply cutting the basic pattern pieces and eliminating facings and other extra pieces. Here are some tips for working with reversible fabrics.

Serge Reversible Seams My favorite way to sew reversible fabrics is with my serger, which makes quick work of these garments. To sew seams with a flatlock stitch, thread your serger for a wide three-thread stitch. A three-thread flatlock will be stronger for seams than a two-thread flatlock. Reduce needle tension to 0–1, leave the upper looper about normal, and increase the lower looper slightly. Experiment on scraps, and fine-tune the tensions as needed, according to your instruction book and the type of thread you are using. The ladder stitch (needle thread) will show on the side of the two pieces you place together, and the flatlock part of the stitch (upper looper thread) will show on the side of the fabric that is to the outside. Thread with colors and thread type accordingly. Serge the seams letting the stitch loops fall very slightly off the raw edge of the fabrics. Once the seam is sewn, open the garment, and pull the fabric on either side of the seam flat, and press it.

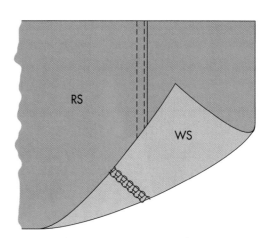

Topstitch serger seam with double needle

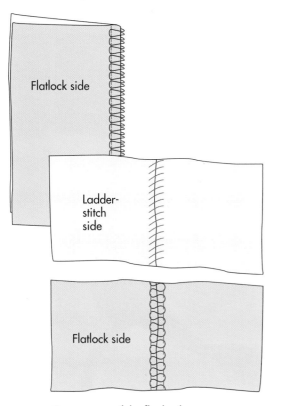

Sew reversible flatlock seam

Sew Strong Mock Flat-Felled Seams While a flatlock seam provides an interesting decorative effect and eliminates bulky seam allowances, I prefer mock flat-felled seams on reversible garments because they are stronger. Thread your serger for a three-thread stitch (or four-thread stitch, which prevents fraying better). Serge the seams, and press them to one side.

Topstitch the serged seam along the edge through all layers. I often use a twin needle for this step because the seam will lay flatter and be stronger. I recommend using the appliqué or satin stitch foot on your sewing machine because it has a tunnel on the underside to feed over the seam.

Serge a Quick Edge Finish On reversible fabrics, you can finish neckline, hem, and armhole or sleeve edges with a three-thread serger stitch and specialty thread for decorative detail, or you can use a closely matched thread color or transparent polyester thread for an invisible finish. On curved necklines and knit sleeves, use the *Fastest* facing alternative of sewing clear elastic to the edges before turning them under, as explained on page 98.

as explained on page 98.

SUE'S SNIPPETS
TEACHING THE BASICS

Too often when sewing with beginners, we take too much for granted. One of my favorite classes to teach is "Quick Gifts to Make," and I always show the scarf made from ¼ yard (0.2 m) of 60-inch (152.4-cm) wool fabric. The long edges are finished with a narrow rolled hem or serged rolled edge, and the short ends are fringed. After one demonstration-style class, one student came up very excited to share that she was planning to make wool mufflers for her family for Christmas but wanted to know where she could buy the matching fringe. I had neglected to teach that you cut off the selvage and pull the threads to create the fringe.

Fast Faster Fastest

CONSTRUCTION TECHNIQUES

There's never enough time to sew, no matter how much time we have. That is why I'm always looking for faster ways to do things. In this chapter I show you my favorite *Fast, Faster, Fastest* methods for the most frequently used basic construction techniques, such as staystitching, basting, and easing. Select the method that suits the purpose of your garment as well as the type of fabric you'll be using. I hope this chapter will inspire you to be on the lookout for your own fast, faster, and fastest ways to do your everyday sewing.

STAYSTITCHING

The main purpose of staystitching, a row of stitches sewn in the seam allowance, is to stabilize the edge of the fabric. This row of stitching prevents bias-cut edges, such as the curves in a neckline, from stretching. This limits distortion of garment pieces that will be handled a great deal during construction or embellishment. Staystitching is also useful for preventing seam allowances of loosely woven fabrics from raveling.

You can eliminate staystitching from many, if not most, garments. Yet on certain garment styles and fabric types, staystitching is necessary for a professionally sewn result.

Fast **Staystitching by Machine** With a straight stitch at a normal stitch length of 2.5 to 3, sew just outside the seamline in the direction of the straight grain of the fabric. There is no need to remove this type of staystitching later.

Faster **Staystitch and Edge Finish** I prefer to finish all of the edges of the garment pieces with a three-step zigzag or three- or four-thread serger stitch before I start to construct the garment. This is the quick way to staystitch and finish raw edges all in one step and keep the shape of the piece while the garment is being made.

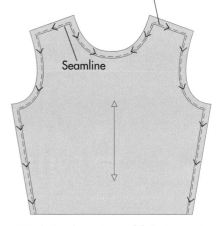

Staystitch just outside seamline

Seamline

Stitch in direction of fabric grain

Fastest **Staystitching with Fusibles** With pinking shears or a rotary-cutter pinking blade, cut ½-inch (1.3-cm)-wide strips of fusible tricot interfacing. Fuse the strips to the seam allowances just inside the seamlines.

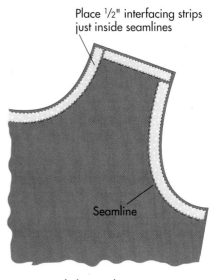

Place ½" interfacing strips just inside seamlines

Seamline

Stabilize edges with fusible interfacing

BASTING

Basting is used to assemble a garment for a trial fit or to hold the fabric in position for construction steps that require accuracy in final stitching.

Basting is time-consuming and can be eliminated or speeded up in most situations. Instead of hand basting, consider pin basting or finger basting—literally "basting" the fabric with your fingers as you sew. With practice, it's a great way to save time sewing.

Fast **Machine Basting** Set your sewing machine for the longest straight stitch of 4, and reduce the top tension until slight loops form on the underside of the fabric when you sew. This will make the stitches easy to pull out later.

Faster **Pin Basting for Fit** Pin baste a garment to try it on for a fitting. (This is a great way to fit slacks and skirts.) Pin with straight pins every few inches. Pull the pins out before getting to them as you sew to avoid stitching a tiny tuck in the top fabric at the pin.

1 Sew all the seams except the side seams, press, and turn the garment right side out.

2 Pin the side seams wrong sides together so the seams are sticking out to the right side and the pins are parallel to the seam allowances.

To mark the seamlines, open the seam allowances, and mark the seamlines on the wrong side with a water-soluble marking pen.

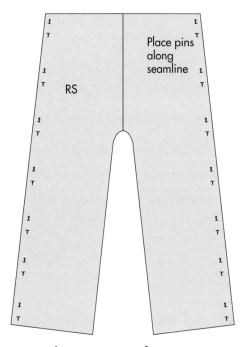

Place pins along seamline

RS

Pin baste garment for trying on

Fastest **Basting Tape** Water-soluble basting tape is a narrow double-sided tape that dissolves in the wash. It is available on the notions rack at fabric stores. It's great for lapped seams, for fabrics that shift, and for basting trims before sewing them in place.

1 To apply trim, peel the paper away from one side of the basting tape, and stick it to the garment where the trim will be sewn.

2 Peel the paper off the other side, and lay the trim on the basting tape. Sew the trim to the garment.

EDGE FINISHES

The purpose of finishing the raw edges in seams is to keep them from fraying or raveling and to help the seam allowances lie flat. Though many pattern instructions suggest finishing seam allowances after the garment is constructed, most often the first thing I do before constructing a garment is finish the edges of each piece of the garment. If I wait until later to finish the edges, it's difficult to get into some areas, and the edges will have already raveled from handling.

Fast Edge Finishes by Machine

Most machines today have a three-step zigzag or a serpentine stitch, which are ideal stitches for finishing the edges of seam allowances. These stitches prevent distortion along the edges of the fabric. Also, they curtail raveling. The three-step zigzag has multiple stitches in each zig and each zag, which produce a sturdy, flat finish. To finish an edge with either of these stitches, use an overcast foot, and sew the edges of each garment piece with the stitch set at a short length of 2 and a width of 4 to 5.

HERE'S WHAT I DO...
to Keep Edges Flat

When using one of the wide zigzag-type stitches along the edge of a single layer of fabric, there's often a problem with the edge of the fabric tunneling under. To avoid the fabric distorting along the edge like this, I use an overcast foot, available for most machines. This foot has a small pin or wire at the right edge, which takes up some additional thread when the needle swings to the right and keeps the stitch from curling the edge of the fabric.

Set the stitch width so the needle just swings over the pin. Then before stitching, test the width setting by turning the handwheel on your machine for one full cycle of the stitch to be sure it does not hit the pin and break the needle. If the fabric still curls under, loosen the top tension slightly.

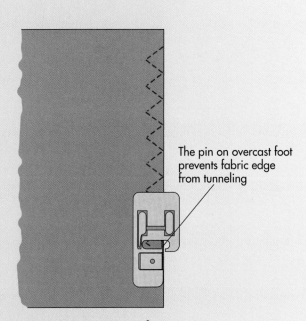

The pin on overcast foot prevents fabric edge from tunneling

Use 3-step zigzag for machine-sewn edge finish

Faster **Zigzag Edge Finishes** A basic zigzag stitch provides a quick edge finish and can be used if that is all that's available. Set the zigzag for an average stitch length of 3 and the width at 4. Sew along the edge of the fabric, allowing the zigzag to fall just off the edge.

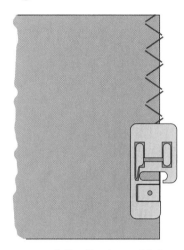

Let zigzag fall off edge of fabric

Fastest **Serged Edge Finishes** A serger definitely gives you the fastest, flattest, and most professional way to finish raw edges. The variety of stitches available on sergers today provides the perfect finish for any type of fabric. As a guideline for selecting the right serger stitch, remember that the more threads used, the bulkier the finish will be.

Use the four-thread stitch to secure the edges on fabrics that are loosely woven. This way, the right-needle safety stitch can help prevent raveling.

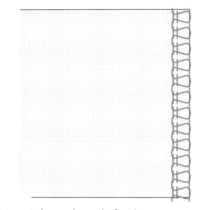

Use 4-thread stitch for loose weaves

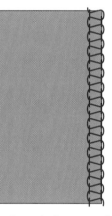

Use 3-thread stitch for most fabrics

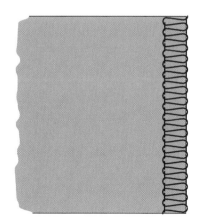

Use 2-thread stitch for lightweight fabrics

on the FAST TRACK...

to Marking While Serging

When serging an edge finish along the outside edges of garment pieces, keep a fabric marking pen or chalk handy to mark any notches or clipped marks that the serger cutter will trim off. This saves you from going back and remarking the garment pieces after the edges have been serged.

LINING AND UNDERLINING

I find that many patterns today do not include lining as a part of the construction. To make a traditional lining pattern when there is none is time-consuming. Yet even if the pattern calls for no lining, I really like lined garments because they hang so much better, wear longer, feel better, and slide on more easily than unlined garments. In some cases, a quick underlining can be substituted for lining even if the pattern calls for no lining. Try these *Fast, Faster, Fastest* lining methods for professional garments made quickly.

Fast Almost Traditional Lining OK,

I admit that lining a garment isn't exactly *fast*. But it's a technique we should all have in our sewing-skills arsenal, and this method is faster than most. This simplified method for a lining works best with simple jacket patterns that do not have collars and lapels.

1 Cut the jacket pieces from the fashion fabric and again from the lining fabric. Traditionally, the back lining piece has a pleat in the center back for wearing ease. But I've found that this isn't necessary on most jackets unless I want some wearing ease through the shoulders. I put ease in the back lining if the design detail of the jacket calls for ease in the lining.

Don't cut the facing pieces from your fashion fabric, but do cut the facing pieces from your interfacing. (Lining does not replace interfacing!)

2 Trim ⅛ inch (0.3 cm) from the edges of the neckline and hemline of the lining pieces for turn of cloth so that the outer edges of the fashion fabric will pull slightly to the wrong side of the jacket. Wait to trim the sleeve lining until you try the jacket on.

3 Interface the jacket, then construct the jacket and the lining separately, leaving a 4-inch (10.2-cm) hole in one of the lining side seams.

4 Pin the finished jacket and the lining with right sides together. Beginning at the center back, sew all the way around the outside edges of the jacket—the back neck, front, bottom edge, and back to the center back. As a general rule, sew with the lighter-weight fabric on top and the heavier-weight one against the feed teeth to prevent the lining from puckering.

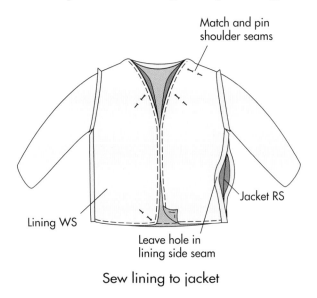

Match and pin shoulder seams

Jacket RS

Lining WS

Leave hole in lining side seam

Sew lining to jacket

5 Trim the seam allowances with pinking shears to eliminate bulk.

6 Pull the jacket right side out through a sleeve. Press the jacket along the lining edges, and topstitch the outside edges if desired.

7 Try on the jacket, and mark the sleeve length. With the jacket right side out, pin the garment sleeve to the lining sleeve with right sides together as they will be stitched together. Leave the lining slightly longer than the jacket sleeve. This allows for a small tuck in the lining for ease.

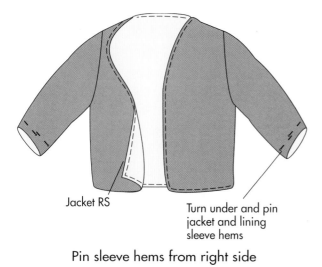

Jacket RS

Turn under and pin jacket and lining sleeve hems

Pin sleeve hems from right side

8 Pull the sleeve out through the hole in the side seam, then stitch the sleeve lining to the sleeve. (This looks like a very strange seam because you are stitching the sleeve to the lining end to end, but it works!)

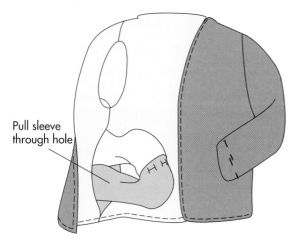

Pull sleeve through hole

Repin and stitch sleeve hems

9 Pull the sleeve back through the side-seam hole to the right side, and topstitch the hem edge and/or tack the lining in place with a straight stitch in the ditch of the sleeve seam.

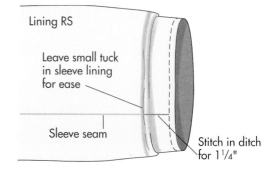

Lining RS

Leave small tuck in sleeve lining for ease

Sleeve seam

Stitch in ditch for 1¼"

Stitch in ditch of sleeve seam

Faster Line with Underlining Underlining is usually added to stabilize the fabric or add warmth to the garment. But it's also a way to attach the lining quickly and professionally by simply underlining with lining fabric. It's my favorite way to line jackets, straight skirts, and slacks. And lining with underlining comes with a bonus. When I hem the garment with a machine-stitched blind hem, the hem stitch catches only the lining fabric so it doesn't show at all on the right side of the garment.

I call this method for lining "save time—underline." You may wonder how a painstaking process like underlining can save time. But since I'm going to finish all the edges on each garment piece on the serger anyway, adding underlining only involves the extra step of cutting out the lining fabric. It is often recommended to trim away some of the seam allowances in the underlining to adjust for the turn of cloth, but I've never found this to be necessary.

This technique, as explained on page 84, is fastest and easiest with a serger, but remember, you *can* substitute a three-step zigzag stitch for the serger stitch. Underlining does not replace

HERE'S WHAT I DO...
to Cut Front Lining and Facings from Fashion Fabric

If you do not want the lining fabric to come all the way to the front edge of a collarless jacket, you can cut the front lining from the fashion fabric as long as it is not too heavy. I have several short jacket styles that have princess seams from the shoulders. Instead of cutting the center front lining piece from lining fabric, I cut it from the fashion fabric.

When cutting the back facing piece for a jacket, instead of using the small back facing pattern piece, cut a second back piece that is cut off at the shoulder blade area for a self-lined look to the back of the jacket. Stitch this back facing to the front facing at the shoulder seams, sew the facings in place, and stitch them together at the armhole edges before setting in the sleeves.

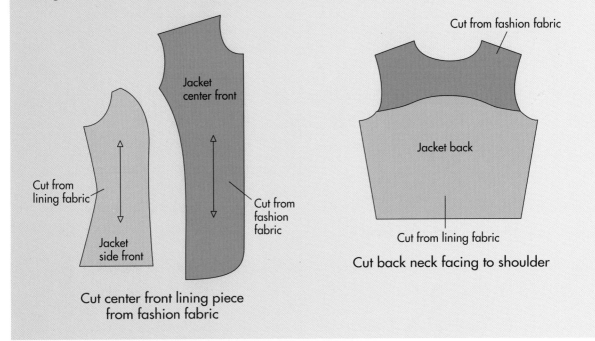

Cut center front lining piece from fashion fabric

Cut back neck facing to shoulder

the interfacing in a garment, so interface before you underline.

1 Cut out the garment, including all of the facing pieces, from the fashion fabric. Cut the major garment pieces from the lining, excluding the facing and pattern pieces for trims. (When the fashion fabric and the lining are the same width, I often lay the lining on top of the fashion fabric, and cut them together.)

2 Cut out any interfacing pieces called for in the pattern, and fuse them to the fashion fabric.

3 Place the fashion fabric pieces with wrong sides together with the corresponding lining pieces, and pin them in each corner. I usually press these to create some static, which makes the layers of fabric stick together. There are also several adhesive basting sprays available at sewing stores that can be used to hold the layers together.

4 Set your serger for a three- or four-thread stitch, and serge the lining to the fashion fabric around the outside edges of each piece. Do not trim the fabric.

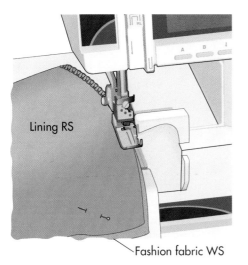

Pin and serge lining to fashion fabric

5 Construct the garment, treating each lined piece just as you would a single piece of fabric.

Fastest Line with Fusible Interfacing
Underlining the entire garment fabric with fusible tricot interfacing is the quickest way to add a type of lining to a garment. The interfacing helps maintain the shape of the garment and makes it easy to slide on and off.

This is also a great way to make a lightweight fabric stable enough to create a more tailored garment. You can cut the pattern pieces for the garment and the interfacing separately, then fuse them together, but it is quicker to fuse the entire piece of fabric and then cut the garment. Whatever you do, be *sure* to preshrink both the fashion fabric and the interfacing before fusing them.

1 Fuse a length of tricot interfacing to the wrong side of the fashion fabric. If the interfacing isn't wide enough, butt the edges together, or overlap them ⅛ inch (0.3 cm).

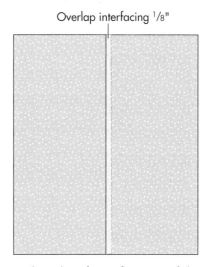

Overlap interfacing ⅛"

Fuse lengths of interfacing to fabric

2 Treat the underlined fabric as a single piece of fabric as you cut out and construct the garment.

HERE'S WHAT **I DO**...
with Darts in Fusible Interfacing

When cutting out the interfacing for any pattern pieces that have darts, I cut the interfacing away from the entire dart along the stitching line of the dart. Then when the interfacing is fused to the fashion fabric, the dart is marked by the cut-out line in the interfacing. Cutting the dart out of the interfacing also eliminates some bulk in the dart.

SEAMS

We can hardly sew without making seams! Yet how often do we stop to think about our choices for the stitch we will use or the type of seam to sew? Before considering speed and convenience, it is important to consider the best stitch for the weight and type of fabric and the style of the garment. Here are some of my favorite *Fast, Faster, Fastest* choices for sewn and serged seams.

Fast **Pinless Seams** One way to speed up sewing seams is to use few or no pins. I generally do not pin straight seams. For one thing, too many pins actually can make it difficult to sew a smooth, puckerless seam because each spot where the pin is placed distorts the fabric slightly. My rule for straight seams is to place pins only where two seams, notches, or dots must match. On curved seams or when one garment piece must be eased into another, I use as few pins as possible.

Never stitch over pins with the sewing machine, because doing so can damage the machine or the fabric (or both) if you hit a pin. Also, hitting a pin always damages the point of the needle and usually breaks it. Pull the pins out as you approach them, which also prevents sewing in the little tuck that forms in the fabric as you stitch up to the pin.

1 To sew long or short straight seams without pins, place the pieces right sides together, put the beginning of the seam under the presser foot, and walk your right hand to the end of the seam to be sure the pieces are the same length. Then hold the seam together about 15 to 20 inches (38.1 to 50.8 cm) from the presser foot with your first finger between the two layers, and start sewing. As you stitch, guide the top layer with your thumb and the bottom layer with your second finger.

It is quite easy to hold the layers at the level of the machine bed and let them feed in evenly. Your left hand is available to support the seam that is coming out of the presser foot, but do not pull or help the machine feed. If one layer tends to feed ahead of the other, reduce the presser foot pressure so there is not as much push on the fabric.

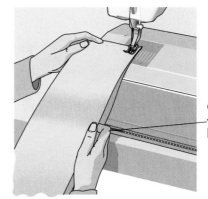

Control fabric with index finger between layers

Use your fingers as "pins"

2 When my right hand nears the presser foot, I stop and take hold of the edges 15 to 20 inches (38.1 to 50.8 cm) down, and continue stitching the seams. Using my fingers as the pins, I sew most seams this way. With practice, finger pinning actually makes sewing many curved seams easier.

HERE'S WHAT **I DO**...

to Press to Perfection

Sometimes we may think that stopping to press seams as we sew just slows down the process. But pressing is one of the most important steps in getting professional-looking results and is worth every extra minute it takes. Pressing makes the seam "disappear" and helps garments, such as skirts made from drapey fabrics, hang better. I press open the seams even on silky and challis-type fabrics on my finer skirts so they hang better.

1 Press the seam flat in the direction it was sewn with the seam allowances together to set the stitches.

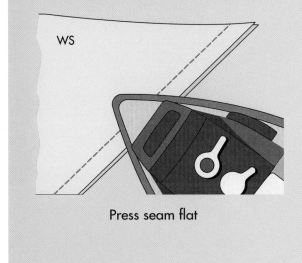

Press seam flat

2 Press the seam allowances open flat from the wrong side.

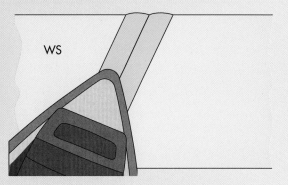

Press seam open from wrong side

3 Press the seam flat from the right side with the seam allowances open. Use a press cloth if needed to prevent shine or scorch. (I find the Titan soleplate on my iron eliminates the need for a press cloth in almost every case.)

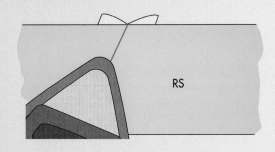

Press seam flat from right side

Faster Seam/Overcast Stitches

Many sewing machines have stitches that allow you to sew the seam and finish the seam allowance edges with an overcast stitch in one operation. I use the stitches to sew along the seamline, then use scissors to trim any excess fabric from the edge of the overcast.

Many machines feature a variety of seam/overcast stitches, but the question is which one to use for which fabric. It is also important to experiment on scraps of your actual fashion fabric before seaming the garment. Try different stitches and different length and width settings. Sometimes a slight adjustment of stitch length or width will make the difference between a stitch that lies flat and stitches a firm, closed seam on the right side and one that does not.

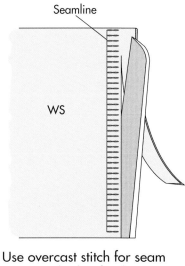

Use overcast stitch for seam
and edge finish

To select a stitch that combines sewing the seam and overcasting the raw edges, use the following guidelines and consult your sewing machine instruction book for more suggestions.

For lightweight knits and wovens, select a stitch that sews *forward motion only,* such as the one shown above. It should sew a straight stitch along the seam with a zigzag-type stitch over the edges of the fabric. For medium-weight wovens, use a stitch with extra overcast stitches to prevent the edges from fraying.

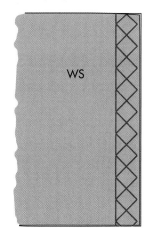

Stabilize medium-weight woven edges
with extra forward and reverse stitches

For medium to heavy knit fabrics, select a stitch with a slant to the overcast stitch to provide more stretch to the seam. This is the stitch that I prefer to use for attaching ribbing.

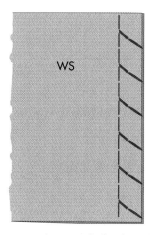

Provide stretch for knits
with slanted stitches

And for heavyweight wovens, select a stitch that has a serged flatlock look to finish the edges firmly.

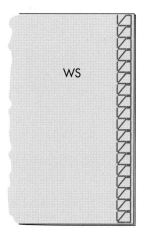

Use stitch with serged flatlock
look on heavyweight fabrics

Fastest Serged Seams If you own a serger, there is no question that serging is the way to sew seams, as long as the final seam allowance can be pressed to one side. (Remember that the edges on any seam

HERE'S WHAT **I DO**...
to Stabilize Seams

Seams that are stitched on the crosswise grain or bias can stretch out after being sewn. Shoulder seams are especially prone to this since most of the weight of the garment is hanging from the shoulders. To prevent seams from stretching or distorting, place a piece of twill tape or narrow ribbon on the seamline, and stitch the seam through the tape.

I use strips of the selvage edge of woven fabrics to tape the seams. This gives me a perfect color match. I also save strips of selvage in a plastic bag to tape future garments.

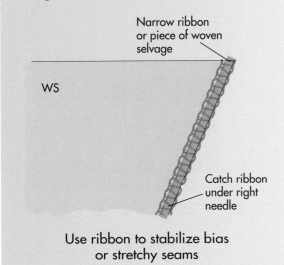

Narrow ribbon or piece of woven selvage

WS

Catch ribbon under right needle

Use ribbon to stabilize bias or stretchy seams

serger stitch that has a two-thread chain stitch, which forms the seam, and a three-thread overcast, which finishes the edges. This is the ready-to-wear industry standard for seams.

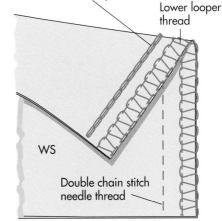

Double chain stitch looper thread

Lower looper thread

WS

Double chain stitch needle thread

Use 5-thread serger stitch on all fabrics

For stable (nonstretchy) knit fabrics, select a four-thread safety stitch. This stitch sews the seam and finishes the edges. The straight stitch created by the serger needle on the right sews a second straight stitch in the overcast portion of the stitch to stabilize it and to prevent fraying in woven fabrics. Use this four-thread safety stitch for woven fabrics when a five-thread stitch is not available.

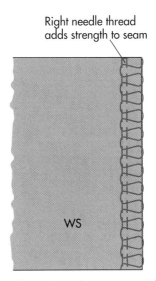

Right needle thread adds strength to seam

WS

Use 4-thread stitch on woven fabrics

that hangs, such as side seams on skirts, pants, and jackets, should be finished first on the serger, then the seam should be stitched on the sewing machine. The weight of the seam allowance helps the hang of the garment.) The serger sews the seam, trims off the excess seam allowance, and finishes the edges in one operation and in half the time of the sewing machine.

For a stable, wide seam allowance on woven fabrics of all weights, select a five-thread

For stretchy knit fabrics, select a three-thread serger stitch. This stitch is not as strong as the four-thread but has more stretch. For additional strength and stretch, thread both loopers with a woolly nylon thread, and reduce looper tensions as needed.

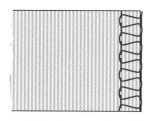

Provide stretch for knits with 3-thread stitch

on the
FAST TRACK...

to Topstitched and Felled Seams

Here's a quick way to create a tailored look and to control seam allowances that will not press flat, such as those in leather and suede. Sew a traditional ⅝-inch (1.6-cm) seam, and press it open. Then topstitch with a straight stitch at a stitch length of 2.5 to 3, sewing from the right side.

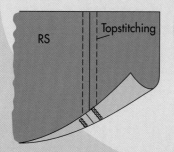

Topstitch from right side of garment

For fast felled and welt seams, you can eliminate the turn-under step to save time and bulk. Serge or machine finish the edge that will be pressed over and topstitched. Sew the seam right sides together, and trim the unfinished seam allowance.

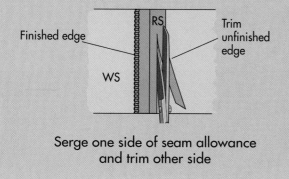

Serge one side of seam allowance
and trim other side

Press the finished seam allowance over it, and topstitch from the right side.

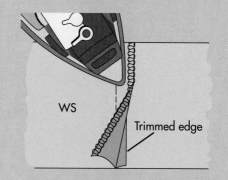

Press seam allowance to one side

For a fast serged and topstitched seam, start by serging the seam with right sides together with a wide three- or four-thread stitch. Press the seam to one side, and topstitch from the right side, stitching parallel to the seam and catching the edge of the seam allowance that is on the underside. You can use an appliqué foot so the wide tunnel on the underside rides over the bulk of the seam. If you want two rows of topstitching, you can topstitch with a 4.0-mm twin needle.

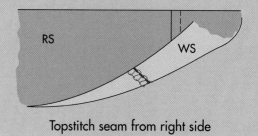

Topstitch seam from right side

DARTS

Darts add fit and design detail to garments. Darts can be moved and their size and shape can be changed to alter the fit of a garment. When dresses and blouses have long waist-fitting darts, I wait to sew the darts until I can try on the garment, then I pin baste the location of the dart.

Fast **Marking Straight Darts** Mark a dart with snips and a dot, then use your thread tails as a stitching guide.

1 To mark darts, clip the dots at the seam allowances, and mark the inside dots with pins or a water-soluble marking pen.

2 Bring the clips together, and fold the dart to the point marked. Press the foldline of the dart, and place one or two pins along the stitching line to hold the fabric in place as you sew the dart.

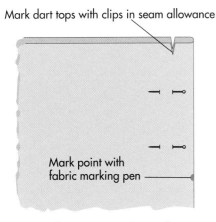

Mark dart tops with clips in seam allowance

Mark point with fabric marking pen

Mark, press, and pin dart

3 Before sewing a straight dart, pull out strands of the top and the bobbin threads longer than the length of the dart. Place the wide end of the dart under the presser foot, and pull the strands of threads to the dart point along the stitching line. These strands will act as stitching guides.

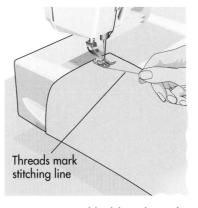

Threads mark stitching line

Use top and bobbin threads as stitching guide

4 Stitch along the guideline created by the strands of thread.

5 Lock the stitch at the dart point. For very lightweight fabrics, hand tie the thread ends to eliminate bulk.

6 Press the dart toward the center of the garment. Clip the dart as needed to eliminate bulk and to keep the dart lying flat.

Faster **Serged Darts** Serged darts are my choice for most knit garments and for wovens that fray. On long, fitted waist darts on dresses and jackets, it is important to clip the dart before serging because it is almost impossible to clip into the dart after it has been serged.

1 Place the pattern piece on one layer of fabric at a time for more accuracy, and fold the dart in place. Trim the excess dart fabric with pinking shears, leaving a ¼-inch (0.6-cm) seam allowance to serge. On the first dart, you are trimming away the fabric and the pattern tissue at the same time.

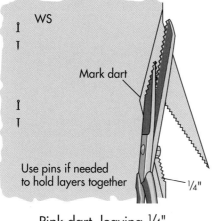

Pink dart, leaving ¼"

2 Begin at the wide end of a waistline dart, and serge to the dart point. Or serge from point to point on a dress dart. Finish the ends by burying the thread chain in the serged stitches.

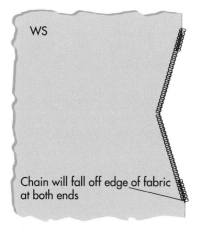

Serge dart

Fastest Eliminate Waistline Darts
Eliminating some or all of the darts in a garment will change the design and fit, but sometimes for the better. For example, because I have a full tummy, I often eliminate the front darts in a straight skirt and ease the skirt front onto the waistband instead. This eases most of the fullness over the tummy area and is a more flattering look for me.

1 Mark the dart with clips in the seam allowance at the fullest part of the dart.

2 Ease stitch with a long straight stitch between these marks, and finish the garment by easing the darted area into the waistband or bodice.

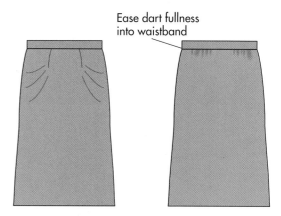

Eliminate pull lines by
easing dart into waistband

HERE'S WHAT I DO...
to Ease Two Fabrics

I let the sewing machine do the work when I want to ease two fabrics that are different lengths. I set the machine for a straight stitch set at a long stitch length of 4 (the longer the stitch, the more fabric is eased). I place the longer of the two fabrics under the shorter fabric and against the feed teeth. Then as I sew, the feed teeth ease the lower (longer) fabric into the top (shorter) fabric.

on the
FAST TRACK...

to Tying Off Serger Threads

The ends of most serged edges are stitched into a hem, waistband, or seam, so there is no need to "tie off" the ends. However, to tie off the serger chain when the serged edge on a seam will be the final end of the seam or the point of a dart, follow these easy steps to secure the stitching.

1 Serge onto the fabric about ⅜ inch (1 cm). Stop sewing, raise the presser foot, and bring the thread tail around to the left of the presser foot and in front of the cutter. Continue to serge, catching the thread tail in the seam and cutting away the excess tail.

2 At the end of the seam or dart, serge just to the edge of the fabric, then raise the presser foot and release the thread tension if possible on your serger. (The tension releases automatically on some sergers and has a release lever on others.)

3 Gently pull the fabric toward the back of the machine, just until the thread is cleared off the stitch fingers. Place it back under the presser foot with the needle about ⅜ inch (1 cm) from the end, and serge off the end of the fabric, catching the threads in the stitching.

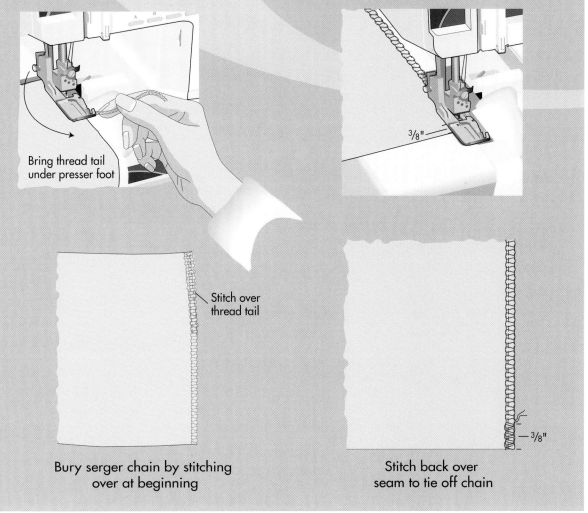

Bring thread tail under presser foot

⅜"

Stitch over thread tail

Bury serger chain by stitching over at beginning

— ⅜"

Stitch back over seam to tie off chain

FACINGS

We all have some part of making a garment that we feel slows us down. For me it is the facings. For that reason I have developed a number of other ways to finish edges. I call them "facing alternatives."

Fast **Facing with Lining** This gives me a bodice that is comfortable to wear and has no facings peeking out to the right side. To face with lining, I eliminate the facing pieces and cut a second bodice from lining fabric instead.

1 Cut the bodice pattern pieces from lining fabric. I like a very lightweight cotton (be sure to prewash it) for summer garments. Trim a scant ⅛ inch (0.3 cm) from the lining edges. The slightly smaller lining will pull the seamed edges just to the wrong side so they cannot be seen from the bodice side.

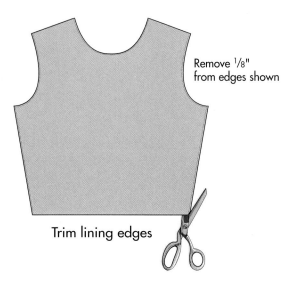

Remove ⅛" from edges shown

Trim lining edges

2 Sew the darts and shoulder seams of the lining and the bodice. Do not sew the side seams now; you will do this later.

3 Place the right sides of the bodice and the lining together, and stitch the bodice to the lining at the neck edge.

4 Trim and turn the bodice and lining right sides out, then press around the neck edge. Understitch the lining to the seam allowance if needed. (I find that accurate cutting, stitching, and pressing eliminate the need for under-stitching with this technique.)

5 If you are making a sleeveless bodice, keep it right side out to sew the armholes. With the side seams still unsewn, rotate the lining and the bodice armhole edges, and pin them right sides together.

Note: If the garment has sleeves, stitch the lining to the bodice at the armholes with wrong sides together before setting in the sleeves.

6 Stitch the armhole edges. It can be hard to get to the shoulder area, so sometimes I sew

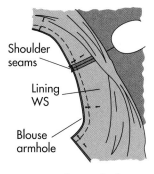

Shoulder seams

Lining WS

Blouse armhole

Stitch armhole

the back from one direction and the front from the other. Try to keep the lining on the top as you sew. Trim the seam allowances, and press.

7 Stitch the side seams of the bodice and lining end to end. Press.

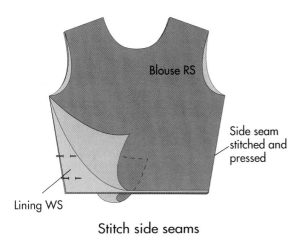

Stitch side seams

8 Complete the garment according to the pattern directions.

Faster Facing from Self-Fabric Binding

I learned this technique from a Stretch & Sew class almost 30 years ago and have used it to finish hundreds of garments in both knit and woven fabrics. Instead of sewing facing, I finish the neck and armhole edges with bands of fabric. This is often called French binding.

This binding is usually made from a fabric strip cut from the same fabric as the garment, but it can be cut from a contrasting fabric, as well. If the fabric is a knit, cut a strip on the crosswise grain, or cut a woven strip on the bias so it has some stretch.

Cut the strip four times the width of the finished binding plus ¼ inch (0.6 cm). For example, I like ⅜-inch (1-cm)-wide binding, so I cut a strip 1¾ inches (4.4 cm) wide and long enough to pull over my head comfortably. Keep in mind that the wider the binding, the

harder it is to keep the edge flat and professional-looking.

When I'm binding the neck and armholes, I cut a long strip, work with the entire strip, and cut off the excess as I go. Before doing this, make sure if you're using a bias strip of woven fabric that it fits easily over your head.

Also, it is important that the fabric of the neck edge supports the weight of this binding. I have had no problem on knits when applying a binding of the same weight. When in doubt, interface the neck edge with fusible tricot interfacing.

To topstitch the binding with a twin needle or a serger cover stitch, I like to sew in the following order so I thread the twin needle or cover stitch only once.

1 Cut a strip of fabric for the binding. Sew only one shoulder seam. Begin at the open shoulder seam, and place the strip with right sides together along the neck edge with the raw edges matching. Stitch the binding strip to the edge with a ⅜-inch (1-cm) seam allowance for a ⅜-inch (1-cm)-wide binding. If you cut the strip for wider binding, sew the seam allowance the desired finished width of the binding. Sew with the binding on top and the garment against the feed teeth of the machine.

The binding can be sewn with a one-to-one ratio of the neck edge to the length of the binding, but I usually pull the binding very slightly to ease the neckline onto it. Do not pull too much, or the neckline will gather onto the binding. This is easy to see as you sew. Cut off the excess strip. Note: If you are binding sleeve edges or armholes, stitch the binding before sewing the sleeves or side seams.

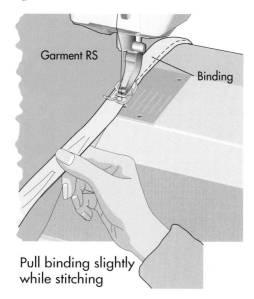

Pull binding slightly while stitching

2 Press the seam allowance toward the binding. Sew the open shoulder seam closed, sewing through the binding as a part of the seam.

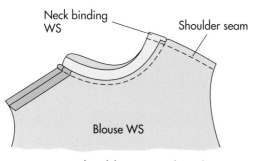

Neck binding WS

Shoulder seam

Blouse WS

Sew shoulder seam closed

3 Turn the garment right side out, and press the binding over the seam allowance to the wrong side of the garment. As you press, make sure that the fold in the binding just touches the edge of the seam allowance.

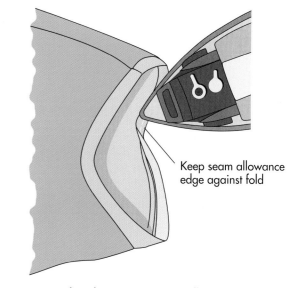

Keep seam allowance edge against fold

Press binding over seam allowance

4 Stitch the binding in place from the right side of the garment. I do not pin this binding but use my fingers to keep it in position as I sew.

5 You can use a single needle, stitch in the ditch with a straight stitch, or sew a decorative stitch. For the most professional topstitching, use a twin needle or a cover stitch on the serger. The twin needle or cover stitch also finishes the wrong side of the binding. Then trim the excess binding from the wrong side.

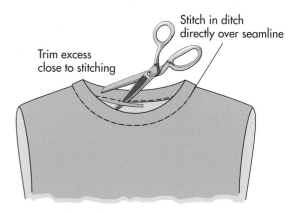

Stitch in ditch directly over seamline

Trim excess close to stitching

Stitch in ditch to secure binding

HERE'S WHAT **I DO**...
to Replace Facings with Ribbing

You can use ribbing to replace neckline, armhole, and sleeve-hem facings on almost any garment. Many designers today are using this attractive finish to add design detail as well as comfort to woven and knit garments.

Use a length of ribbing that matches or co-ordinates with the fashion fabric. Look for ribbing that comes back into its original size and shape after it has been stretched. To determine how wide to cut the ribbing, double the desired width of the band, and add ½ inch (1.3 cm) for seam allowances. (I use ¼-inch [0.6-cm] seam allowances for ribbing.) For example, for a neckband that is 1 inch (2.5 cm) wide, cut the ribbing 2½ inches (6.4 cm) wide, or for a 2-inch (5.1-cm) neckband, cut it 4½ inches (11.4 cm) wide, and so on. Use 6 inches (15.2 cm) for ribbed cuffs and at least 7 inches (17.8 cm) for a ribbed waistband. I usually buy 18 inches (45.7 cm) of ribbing, use what I need, and add the rest to my ribbing collection for future use.

Note: Do not prewash ribbing, because it will change the stretch of the ribbing and the way it sews to the garment.

1 Sew the shoulder seams. Trim the seam allowance of the neck edge to ¼ inch (0.6 cm), then try it on to be sure it pulls over your head. Recut the neckline ⅛ to ¼ inch (0.3 to 0.6 cm) bigger if necessary.

2 Measure the size of the neck opening. To cut a strip of ribbing for this opening, first determine the width of the neckband, as explained above.

3 For most neckline, armhole, or sleeve-hem ribbings, a general rule is to cut the strip two-thirds the measurement of the neck opening. For example, if the neck opening is 24 inches (61 cm), the ribbing strip should be cut 16 inches (40.6 cm) long.

4 Sew the ribbing into a circle by stitching the ends with right sides together. (I usually serge this seam.) Fold the ribbing with wrong sides together lengthwise to create the neckband, and mark quarters with pins or a fabric marking pen.

5 Mark the neck edge in quarters. (In most cases, the shoulder seams will not be at the quarters because the front neckline is lower than the back.) Pin the neckband to the neck edge, matching the quarter marks and placing the seam on the ribbing at the center back.

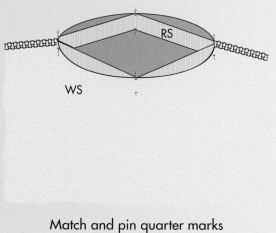

RS

WS

Match and pin quarter marks
on ribbing and garment

6 Stitch the ribbing to the neck edge with a seam/overcast stitch or a three- or four-thread serger stitch. Sew with the ribbing on top, and stretch it as you sew it to the neck edge. On the serger, set the differential feed to 1.25 to 2 to help ease the fabric to the ribbing. Press the seam allowance toward the garment, and topstitch if desired.

on the
FAST
TRACK...

to Sewing Ribbing into a Circle

This tip was shared by a student in one of my workshops who learned it while working in a garment factory.

1 Fold the ribbing strip in half with right sides together.

2 Before sewing the short ends, fold the strip again lengthwise so there are four thicknesses at the short ends.

3 Sew or serge these four short edges together. You will have one layer folded over the others very much like folded socks.

4 Unfold the ribbing, and you have a finished cuff in the round.

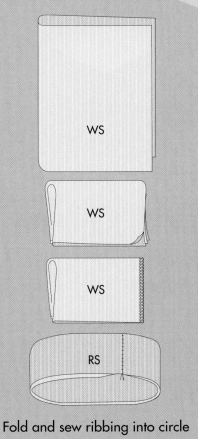

Fold and sew ribbing into circle

Fastest Elastic Facing

I like to replace some neck facings with soft clear elastic. I often use this finish on garments for children and casual tops for myself. The elastic keeps the neck edge stable and prevents it from stretching out with wear and washing.

Use this same technique on the sleeve hems. The elastic keeps the sleeves in place when you push them up and eliminates the stretched-out look when you pull them down.

1 Trim the neck seam allowance to ¼ inch (0.6 cm), and sew only one shoulder seam. Pin the other shoulder seam to try on the neck opening to make sure it pulls over your head.

2 Place a piece of ¼-inch (0.6-cm) clear elastic on the wrong side of the neck edge, beginning at the open shoulder seam. I sew with a length of elastic and cut off the excess after it is stitched in place, which saves measuring time!

3 Stitch the elastic to the neck edge with a zigzag or a three- or four-thread serger stitch sewn along the edge of the elastic and fabric. I sew with the elastic on top and do *not* stretch the elastic. (Sew the elastic with a one-to-one ratio, meaning the elastic and the neck edge are the same length.)

4 Sew the open shoulder seam. Fold the elastic to the wrong side, and topstitch from the right side on a sewing machine with a single or twin needle or on the serger with the cover stitch.

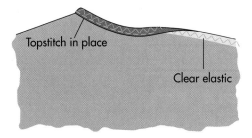

Fold elastic facing to wrong side

EASING

Wearing ease in a pattern is the extra amount of fabric that keeps a garment from fitting skintight. This ease gives "move room" to sleeves and elbows and is a part of the pattern design. Design ease is the amount of ease that is added by a pattern designer for style. Some wearing and design ease can be created with extra fabric. I often add ease to the areas where my garment will need extra fabric to fit over the lumps and bumps on my body.

Always sew with the longer piece of fabric (the one that is being eased) on the bottom against the feed teeth of the sewing machine. The action of the feed teeth will help with any of these techniques.

Fast Crimp Ease
You can use this crimping technique to ease long pieces of fabric. This is my favorite way to ease sleeves.

1 Set your sewing machine for a straight stitch at a long stitch length. To determine the stitch length, remember this rule of thumb: The lighter the fabric and the longer the stitch length, the more the fabric will ease. I use a stitch length of 4 for lightweight fabrics and 2.5 for heavier fabrics. You can always increase the top tension setting for more ease.

2 To crimp the fabric, begin sewing (usually on the seamline) as you place your left index finger behind the presser foot against the fabric

that is coming out from under the foot. Hold the fabric back. (Keep it from moving freely out from under the foot.) When the bulk of fabric builds up so you can no longer hold it back effectively, let go, and place your finger on the fabric just coming out and begin again.

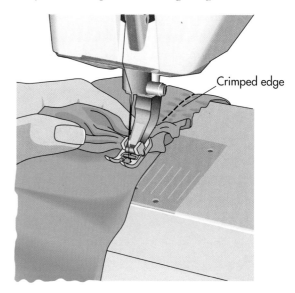

Crimped edge

Delay fabric behind foot
to create crimp ease

3 Place the eased fabric with the shorter fabric with right sides together, and sew with the crimped fabric against the feed teeth.

Faster Easing with Feed Teeth
When there is a small amount of fabric to be eased, let the feed teeth on your sewing machine ease it for you. The basic rule on machine settings is the longer the stitch and the higher the top tension, the more the fabric will ease. This is my favorite way to ease skirts to waistbands, fullness in the bust area, and

elbows and other areas with small amounts of fitting ease. It is definitely the fastest method you can use on the sewing machine because you sew the fabric that is being eased to the shorter fabric all in one step.

1 Set your sewing machine for a straight stitch at a long stitch length of 4 (6 to 6.5 spi). Place the longer piece to be eased on the bottom against the feed teeth and the shorter piece on the top.

2 Stitch the two layers with right sides together, holding the top layer back as needed to force the feed teeth to ease the bottom layer to it. This takes a little practice but is a great time-saving technique.

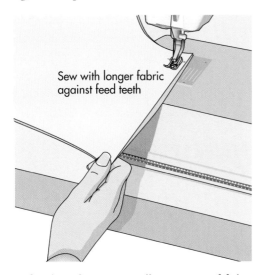

Sew with longer fabric against feed teeth

Let feed teeth ease small amounts of fabric

Fastest Easing with the Serger

I love to ease using the differential feed on my serger for circular and A-line hems because they can be eased and edge finished all in one step. Differential feed is perfect for seams and edges that need to be eased only in certain areas, because you can set the differential feed to ease or not ease at any time as you are serging. This is a great way to finish

HERE'S WHAT I DO . . .
to Ease Heavy Fabrics

When your fabric is very heavy or stiff and will not ease with the normal methods, let narrow clear elastic do the easing for you.

1 Cut a piece of ¼-inch (0.6-cm) clear elastic to the finished length you need. For example, if it is a sleeve cap you want to ease, place the elastic along the armhole that the sleeve will be sewn into without stretching it, and cut the elastic to that length.

2 Mark the elastic in half or in quarters, and also mark the piece to be eased. Pin the elastic to the piece, matching the markings.

3 Stitch the elastic to the piece to be eased just outside the seamline, stretching the elastic as you sew. I sew with a long straight stitch or a long narrow zigzag stitch.

the shirt-tail hem of a blouse because you can set the differential feed at normal (1) for most of the hem but move it to 1½ to serge around the curved tails. On most sergers the differential feed can be set between 1 and 2.

1 Set your serger for a three- or four-thread stitch at a stitch length of 3 to 4. Set the differential feed to 1½ to 1¾. The higher the setting on the differential feed, the more the fabric will be eased.

2 Serge the fabric edge, adjusting the differential feed as needed for more or less ease. When serging two layers of fabric, place the longer fabric against the feed teeth and adjust the differential feed as needed.

GATHERING

When it comes to gathering, most pattern instructions suggest sewing two or sometimes three rows of long straight stitches, then pulling on the bobbin threads to draw up the threads to create the gathers. This can be time-consuming, especially if one of the threads should break, which often happens. There are much easier and more reliable ways to gather fabric. Next time, try one of these gathering techniques.

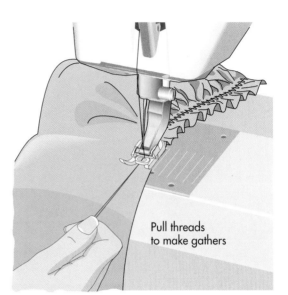

Pull threads
to make gathers

Stitch over top and bobbin thread tails
to create gathers

Fast Gathering over Top and Bobbin Threads I love this method because I do not have to look for heavy thread or cord. Also, the starting end of the thread to be pulled is anchored automatically, so there is no danger of its pulling out and having to start over!

1 Pull out strands of top and bobbin thread as long as the fabric piece to be gathered (but don't cut them). Lay the strands on the fabric along the line you would sew the stitches to be gathered.

2 Set your machine for a zigzag stitch at a medium width and medium length, 3. Zigzag over the top and bobbin threads using a braiding guide foot if you have one. I hold back the threads that are being zigzagged over, creating the gathers as I sew. With practice, you can judge just how much to hold them back for even gathers.

3 Adjust the gathers as needed, and anchor the ends around a straight pin.

Faster Gathering with Special Feet To sew even gathers, use a gathering foot for light- to medium-weight fabrics and a ruffler for heavier fabrics. With these two feet, the fabric can be gathered and attached to a second flat piece of fabric all in one step. However, once the gathers have been sewn into the fabric, they cannot be adjusted.

When using a gathering foot, plan a fullness ratio of two or three to one on lightweight fabrics (the fabric being gathered is two or three times longer than the flat piece it is being sewn to). Plan less fullness for heavier fabrics. I usually cut the piece to be gathered longer than needed.

Sew a sample length of gathering to determine the amount of fullness the foot will sew.

Begin with a straight stitch set at the longest stitch length. Place the fabric to be gathered under the foot against the feed teeth of the sewing machine. Mark a length on your fabric. I usually sew 18 to 24 inches (45.7 to 61 cm). Be sure to sew along the same grainline on your test piece as you will be sewing on the garment piece. (I usually sew a part of the piece to be ruffled as my test, then pull it out.) Stitch, then measure the gathered piece. If your piece is half as long, you have two-to-one fullness. If it is a third as long, you have three-to-one fullness. You can change the stitch length and the top tensions to adjust the amount of gathering. The longer the stitch length and the tighter the top tension, the more the fabric will gather.

1 When you are satisfied with the way the fabric is gathered in your test piece, set the machine at the desired stitch length and thread tensions. Place the fabric to be gathered under the gathering foot and the flat fabric in the slot in the foot. Move the needle to the left position.

2 Sew, letting the bottom fabric move freely as it is gathered onto the flat piece.

Fastest **Gathering on the Serger**

You can gather a fabric and finish the edges at the same time with the differential feed on your serger. Many sergers have an accessory foot that has a slot for the flat fabric so you can gather one fabric and attach it to a flat fabric all in one step. When the differential feed is set to 2, the front feed teeth feed twice as fast as the back. When this happens, the fabric is pushed under the needle faster than it is fed out.

To adjust the fullness to the desired look and the length you have cut, you have three variables—the longer length, the setting of the differential feed, and the top tension. The higher each of these settings is, the more the fabric will gather. You can adjust the finished differential feed gathering by pulling on the needle threads.

1 Set your serger for a three- or four-thread overcast stitch at a long stitch length. Set the differential feed on 2.

2 Place the fabric to be gathered under the serger presser foot, and serge.

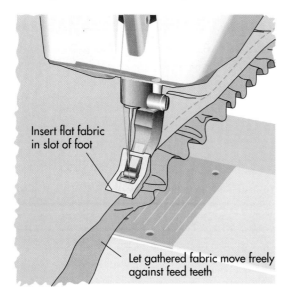

Insert flat fabric in slot of foot

Let gathered fabric move freely against feed teeth

Gather bottom piece and attach to top piece with gathering foot

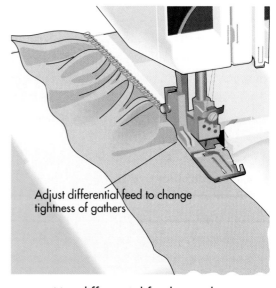

Adjust differential feed to change tightness of gathers

Use differential feed to gather and edge finish in one step

RUFFLES

Ruffled, pleated, ruched, and frilled fabrics add feminine detail and romance to any garment. They come and go in fashion trends but are always in style for party and bridal dresses and lingerie. Add length to a skirt with a ruffle, add elegance to a neckline, placket, or cuff with a ruffle set into the seam, or create a romantic look with a lace-ruffle collar and cuffs.

The main difference between ruffles and ruching is the way the gathered fabric is attached to the garment. I think of ruffles and frills as gathered strips that are sewn into a seam or hem to produce fullness. Ruching is strips of fabric gathered along both edges or down the middle and topstitched to a garment or set between flat fabrics. Ruching has evolved to a wearable-art technique, with gathered strips sewn onto and into wearable-art garments. One top designer covered a vest and jacket with strips for a Carmen Miranda look.

Ruffled strips and ruching are quick to make. Cut strips to the desired width, seam end to end, and finish the raw edges. Ruffle or gather down the middle of the strip. There is a limit to how wide a strip will fit into the ruffler without removing the guide flange, so a gathering foot may be the best choice for these ruched strips.

Many sewers dread patterns with ruffles because they envision hours of drawing up threads (only to have one break) and adjusting fullness before stitching ruffles to a garment. It can be easier!

Create ruffle, then sew to fabric

Gather edges, then sew between two fabrics

Sew ruching to right side of fabric or insert edges into seams

Ruffle Basics

Ruffles are either straight or circular. Straight ruffles are made from strips of fabric and are easy to cut without pattern pieces. Circular ruffles are made from a circle of fabric cut from pattern pieces.

When cutting straight ruffles, it is easy to eliminate the pattern pieces that might come with the garment pattern and instead cut strips of fabric with a rotary cutter. Bias strips will give the softest ruffle; crosswise grain is second choice. As a general rule, the wider the finished ruffle and/or the lighter the fabric, the more fullness is desired.

Cut ruffles from light- to medium-weight fabrics. Heavy fabrics do not ruffle well. Cut straight ruffles two to three times the length of

to Make a Ruffle with a Heading

For a ruffle with a heading, cut ruffle strips, and seam them end to end. Finish both raw edges with a narrow rolled hem on the sewing machine or a rolled edge on the serger. Place the strip between the ruffler separator blades with the header of the ruffle to the right. Ruffle the strip, and topstitch it to the flat fabric.

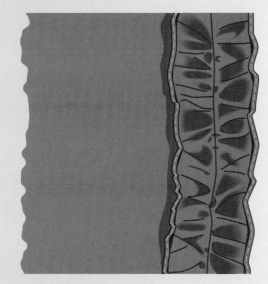

Stitch ruffle with header

the piece they will be joined to. In the case of a very lightweight or sheer fabric, the ruffle may even be four times longer than the flat piece.

Using a Ruffler

Ruffles can be created with the techniques explained in "Gathering" on page 101, but regardless of which *Fast, Faster, Fastest* ruffle you make, the ruffler attachment for your sewing machine is the key to fast, easy, even ruffles.

Almost all sewing machines have a ruffler available. Years ago they were included with every sewing machine, but today most companies sell them separately. Ask for a demonstration when you purchase your ruffler so you know just where and how to adjust the fullness.

The ruffler can stitch even-gathered or pleated ruffles instantly on light- to medium-weight fabrics. With practice you can join the ruffle to the flat fabric in one sewing step. The ruffler looks quite intimidating, but don't let that stop you. Practice on scraps until you are comfortable with the attachment.

To put the ruffler on the machine, remove the standard presser foot and the ankle or the shank. Raise the needle to the highest position, and place the ruffler on the machine with the fork on the ruffler over the needle clamp screw. The up and down movement of the needle clamp screw is what makes the ruffler work. It is important to tighten the presser foot screw well because the ruffler creates movement and vibration as you ruffle.

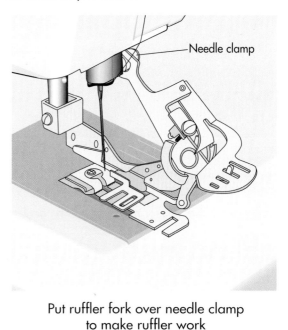

Needle clamp

Put ruffler fork over needle clamp
to make ruffler work

Be sure to set your sewing machine for a straight stitch. The ruffler has a single round hole for the needle, and any zigzag-type stitch will mean the needle hits the foot. Set the stitch length between 2.5 and 3 and the top tension at normal. If you desire a denser ruffle after using the adjustments described in "Adjusting the Fullness of the Ruffle," below, try setting the length and the top tension to a slightly higher number to increase the amount of ruffling. Use care when setting the top tension because if it is too tight, the top thread will break.

Cutting the Ruffle

Determine the width and length of the finished ruffle. Add hems and seam allowances. (For a double ruffle, cut the strip twice the width of the finished ruffle plus seam allowances.) Cut bias or crosswise-grain strips that when seamed together end to end will equal two to three times the length of the finished ruffle. It is best to cut extra and have a little left over when working with the ruffler.

Seam the strips end to end with ¼-inch (0.6-cm) seam allowances, and press the seam allowances open to eliminate bulk as the strip feeds through the ruffler. (I trim my seam allowances with pinking shears before pressing to eliminate even more bulk.) Ruffler attachments do not feed well over bulky seams.

Placing the Fabric

Place the fabric to be ruffled between the two black blades. The ruffling blade moves back and forth, pushing the fabric into the pleat or ruffle so the needle can stitch it in place, and the separator blades separate the fabric that is being ruffled from the feed teeth.

When ruffling fabric and attaching it to flat fabric at the same time, the fabric to be ruffled is placed wrong side up between the separator blades, and the flat fabric is placed right side up under the separator blades against the feed teeth. (The fabrics will be sewn right sides together.)

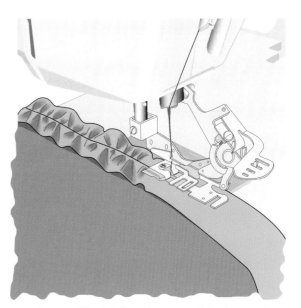

Place ruffled fabric between blades and flat fabric under blades

Adjusting the Fullness of the Ruffle

The fullness of the ruffle can be varied by changing the stitch length and the settings on the adjusting lever. At the front, the ruffler has numbered slots—1, 6, 12, and 0 (or a * on some rufflers). When this lever is set on 1, a ruffle will be formed by the ruffling blade each time the needle takes a stitch. This setting will produce a more gathered look. When it is set on 6, the ruffle will be formed every sixth stitch, and on 12, the ruffle will be formed on every twelfth

HERE'S WHAT **I DO**...
to Keep My Ruffler Running

The ruffler has many moving parts. To keep it in good working order, when I have finished ruffling, I place a drop of sewing machine oil at each place where the ruffler moves as it sews. I store the ruffler in a small plastic bag, and I wipe the oil off before using it the next time.

stitch. In other words, the higher the number set, the farther apart the ruffles will be. When set on 0 or *, no ruffles will be made; the sewing machine will just sew a standard straight stitch. If you need to join strips or do other basic sewing, there is no need to remove the ruffler attachment; simply set the adjusting lever to 0 or *.

While the adjusting lever determines the distance between the times the ruffling blade pushes the fabric into a small pleat, the adjusting screw determines how *much* fabric is pushed into a pleat each time. This screw is located on the top of some rufflers and on the side of others. Loosening and tightening the screw increases and decreases the fullness of the ruffle. A trick for remembering which way to turn the screw is "right is tight and left is loose." The more the screw is tightened, the more fabric will be pleated. For a softer gathered effect, loosen the screw.

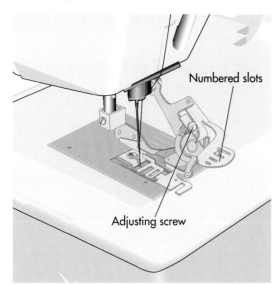

Change spacing and fullness of ruffles by adjusting numbered slots and adjusting screw

To determine the amount of fullness the ruffler will stitch, cut an 18-inch (45.7-cm)-long scrap strip of the same fabric to be ruffled, or

HERE'S WHAT **I DO**...
to Ruffle Sheer Fabrics

Some fabrics do not work with the ruffler as well as others do. One of my sewing teachers years ago suggested that ruffling a very lightweight or sheer fabric can be made easier by running a moist sponge or cloth along the edge to be placed into the ruffler and ruffling it while the edge is still damp. Double ruffles of specialty fabrics can also be a challenge. If the sewing machine skips a stitch, a tiny pleat is lost. To solve this, I use a Schmetz 90/14 stretch needle and increase the presser foot pressure.

measure 18 inches (45.7 cm) of the ruffle and mark it so you can stitch to that point. Place the strip in the ruffler, and stitch. Measure the ruffled piece. If the piece is 9 inches (22.9 cm) long, your ruffler is set for two-to-one fullness, which means the finished ruffle will be half the size of the ruffle strip you started with. A 6-inch (15.2-cm) ruffle means your ruffler is set for three-to-one fullness, and the ruffle will be one-third the size of the strip.

Sewing Seams with Ruffles

When you use any of the *Fast, Faster, Fastest* methods for ruffling, you will place the ruffle to the fabric and the ends of the ruffle will be unfinished. When possible, leave a seam open in the garment, and begin and end the ruffle at the open seam. The ends of the ruffle can be stitched together when the seam is sewn. If possible, taper the ruffle at each end so it will be caught in the seam allowance of the garment.

To finish the ends of the ruffle, begin stitching the ruffle in place several inches from the end of the ruffle, and stop sewing before meeting the beginning point. Trim the excess ruffle away, leaving adequate seam allowances, and open the ruffle at each end to sew the ends together. Gather the edge, and stitch the ruffle in place.

One of my struggles when sewing ruffles into seams or between the garment and the facing has been catching bits of the ruffle in the seam, especially at corners. To prevent this, I pin the ruffle in place, then tape the ruffle securely to the garment so it cannot shift between the layers of fabric as I sew. It is easy to remove the tape once I have turned the garment right side out.

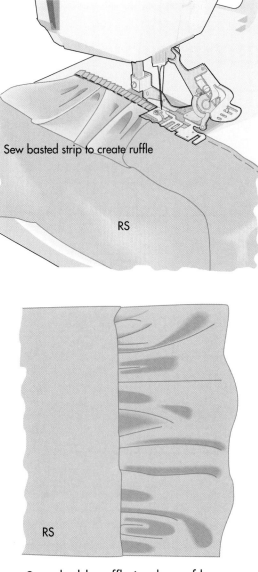

Sew basted strip to create ruffle

RS

Sew double ruffle in place of hem

Fast Ruffles in Place of Hems Adding

a double ruffle eliminates the need to finish the edge of the ruffle or hem the garment. Double ruffles are reversible and add body to the edges they are sewn to.

1 Cut the strips to be ruffled twice as wide as the desired width of the finished ruffle plus two seam allowances.

2 Fold the ruffle strip in half lengthwise with wrong sides together. Press the folded edge for a crisp-looking ruffle edge, or do not press the edge if you prefer a softer look.

3 Machine baste the raw edges together along the seamline along the length of the ruffle strip. This step is needed to keep the edges from shifting as they are ruffled.

4 Place the flat fabric against the feed teeth and the folded strip between the separator blades of the ruffler, and sew. Test and adjust the fullness.

Faster Ruffles with Rolled Hems

A ruffle with a narrow-rolled-hem finish on the sewing machine is made from a single thickness of fabric.

1 Cut the ruffle strips, and seam them end to end to make one long strip.

2 Finish the hem edge using the narrow-rolled-hem foot on the sewing machine. (See "Here's What I Do to Sew Rolled Hems" on page 171.)

3 Place the raw edge of the ruffle between the separator blades, and test and adjust the fullness.

4 Sew to create a ruffle. To stitch the ruffle and attach it to a flat fabric in one step, place the fabrics right sides together with the fabric to be ruffled between the blades and the flat fabric under the ruffler against the feed teeth.

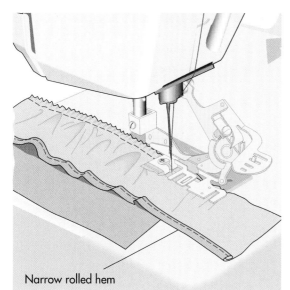

Narrow rolled hem

Make single ruffle with
narrow rolled hem

Fastest **Serged Ruffles** To create serged ruffles, use the gathering foot (called a separator foot or shirring foot by some serger manufacturers).

1 Cut ruffle strips, and seam them end to end to make one long strip.

2 Finish the hem edge with a rolled-edge serger stitch (or create a double ruffle).

3 Replace the regular foot on the serger with the gathering foot, and insert the fabric to be ruffled under the foot. Set the serger for a four-thread stitch, length 4, differential feed 2, and

sew. Most serger gathering feet have a slot for flat fabric so the ruffle can be attached to flat fabric as it is being sewn.

Three factors will adjust the amount of ruffling—the stitch length, the differential feed, and the needle tensions. Change one setting or a combination of the three. It is best to stitch a practice length with the same fabric to determine the fullness of the ruffle before ruffling the entire length of fabric.

on the
FAST
TRACK...

to Cut Ruffle Strips

For real time savings and accuracy, cut your strips with a rotary cutter, mat, and ruler. Lay the fabric on inch marks for the desired width along the edge. Right-handed people will place the fabric to the right and left-handed to the left. (This little tip has saved me a great deal of thinking on many occasions.) Cut the ruffle strip across the entire piece, then cut the length to size.

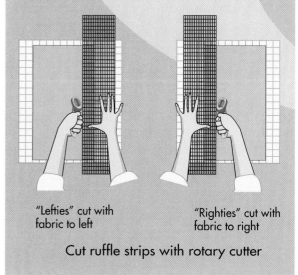

"Lefties" cut with
fabric to left

"Righties" cut with
fabric to right

Cut ruffle strips with rotary cutter

Ruffled Flower Pin

A quick and simple flower pin in matching or contrasting fabric can dress up any garment.

A flower pin is a wonderful fashion accessory made from fashion fabric that matches or coordinates with a garment. Here's an easy way to make this accessory.

1. Cut a strip of fabric approximately 3 by 45 inches (7.6 by 114.3 cm). I love to use soft challis and silky-type fabrics. For a really luxurious flower, cut the strip on the bias.

2. Fold the strip in half lengthwise with wrong sides together.

3. Press along the fold for a crisper flower, or do not press for a softer, fluffier flower.

4. Taper the ends from the raw edges to the fold to eliminate bulk at the center and end of the flower.

5. Gather the long raw edge of the strip. My favorite technique is to use the differential feed on my serger because it finishes the edge and gathers all in one step.

6. Begin at one end, and roll the strip to create the flower. Try a tighter and a looser roll for different looks.

7. Stitch the raw edges together, and stitch on a pin back or safety pin. I do this by machine, with a zigzag over the edges and a zigzag over the safety pin at the same time, which is a little tricky but fast!

Back of rose

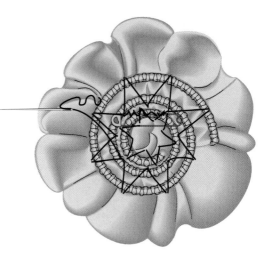

Stitch raw edges and bar of safety pin

PLEATS

Pleats differ from gathers because the fabric is actually folded into a tuck to form the pleat. Pleats can result in a flatter or less full look than gathers, especially for medium- to heavy-weight fabrics. I often replace the gathers in a skirt with several pleats, which can be tiny or large, depending on the pattern style.

Fast Pleat As You Sew

There is no need to pin pleats before you sew them. To save time, I fold the pleats at the sewing machine as I baste them in place.

1 When cutting the pattern, mark pleats at the waistline with a snip in each pleat marking. I make longer snips into the seam allowance on the lines that the pleats are to be folded to. Mark the direction of the pleats in the seam allowance.

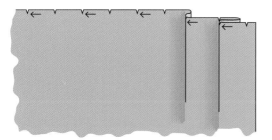

Mark direction of pleats with arrows

2 Set your sewing machine for a straight stitch, and place the piece to be pleated under the presser foot.

3 Fold the pleats in place as you approach the markings. Stitch the pleats.

Faster Pleat with a Fork

Use a fork to make the pleats at the sewing machine as you baste them in place. Husqvarna Viking educator Patti Jo Larson taught me this technique. The size of the fork determines the size of the pleats—a large fork makes large pleats, and a tiny fork makes tiny pleats.

1 Do not cut the piece to be pleated to size. Instead, cut a larger piece, pleat it up, then cut it to the size needed for the pattern. In the case of a skirt, cut two full lengths of 45-inch (114.3-cm) fabric, seam them together at the side seam, and pleat the fabric. Then try on the skirt, and cut off the excess pleated fabric on each side.

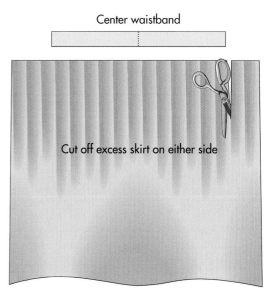

Center waistband

Cut off excess skirt on either side

Pleat skirt first, then cut to fit waistband

2 Set your sewing machine for a basting stitch, and place the piece to be pleated under the presser foot.

3 Slide the fork along the edge of the fabric so that the two outside tines of the fork are on top of the fabric and the two (or more) middle tines are under the fabric. Then form a pleat by twisting the fork in the direction you desire the pleat to go. Without disturbing the pleat, slide the fork out off the edge of the fabric and machine baste the pleat in place.

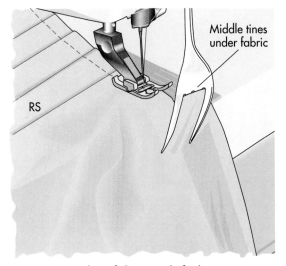

Pleat fabric with fork

4 Continue forming pleats with the fork and basting them. You can position the pleats right next to each other or you can space them as far apart as you desire. Measure an equal space between each pleat.

Fastest **Pleat with a Ruffler** For perfect tiny pleats that look more like little gathers, use the ruffler accessory on your sewing machine. (See "Using a Ruffler" on page 104 for more information on this attachment.) This technique is limited to lighter-weight fabric types.

1 Place the ruffler on your machine. Experiment with different settings on scraps of the same fabric to see which ruffler pleat style you prefer. Set the ruffler at 1 if you want a ruffler pleat formed at every stitch, 6 if you want a ruffler pleat formed only every sixth stitch, and 12 for a ruffler pleat formed every twelfth stitch. Change the stitch length and adjust the gathering screw on the ruffler for tiny pleats that are farther apart or closer together. The longer the stitch length, the bigger the ruffler pleats. Once you've selected a setting, sew a sample strip of fabric, as explained in "Gathering" on page 101, to determine the amount of fabric that will be ruffle-pleated (the ratio of pleated fabric to the unpleated fabric you started with).

2 Place the fabric to be pleated between the metal flanges on the ruffler, and pull it into the flanges far enough that the needle will stitch into the fabric when you begin sewing.

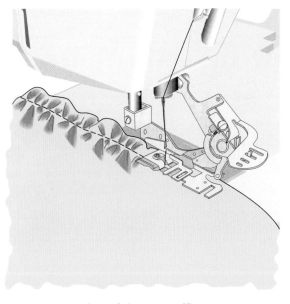

Place fabric in ruffler

3 As you sew, the tiny ruffle pleats will be formed by the foot.

Fast Faster Fastest

GARMENT DETAILS

When we sew, we all have our favorite and least favorite garment details. Usually our least favorite details are the ones that are time-consuming or tricky in some way. To save time and maybe some frustration on your next sewing project, take a look at the techniques for garment details in this chapter, and use the ones that make your sewing faster and more enjoyable.

COLLARS

Too often a well-made garment can be ruined by a collar that looks homemade. That is why I suggest to sewers that it is very important to sew professional-looking collars. Here are some of my favorite techniques for making quick, good-looking collars.

Fast Traditional Collar This is the collar found in many patterns, but the instructions here are easier and faster than the ones in the pattern guide sheets.

1 To prepare the upper collar, mark a fold line by straight stitching the upper collar along the neck edge with a ½-inch (1.3-cm) seam allowance, and press the seam allowance to the wrong side. With right sides together, sew the upper collar to the undercollar.

Sew the collar in two steps, beginning at the center back of the collar and sewing to the front edge. Repeat this two-step process for the other side. If the collar tip is pointed, stop one stitch before the point with the needle in the fabric, and pivot to sew two stitches across the point on the diagonal. Pivot again and continue to sew the collar.

2 Trim the seam allowances around the sewn edges of the collar with pinking shears, and turn the collar to the right side.

To turn the points, use a point turner. (I prefer the bamboo-type point turner because you can press the corners of the collar to sharp points with the turner in the collar.) Press the collar well.

3 Stitch the undercollar to the neck edge of the blouse with right sides together, and trim the seam allowance with pinking shears.

4 Bring the folded edge of the upper collar to the inside of the neck edge, and baste with fabric glue, or pin it in place. Try the garment on to be sure the collar lies flat.

Topstitch the collar in place. Depending on how the blouse will be worn, you can top-stitch from either the undercollar or upper collar side. If the collar will be worn up, sew it from the undercollar side. Topstitch from the upper side if the collar will be worn open. Topstitch around the outer edges of the collar if desired.

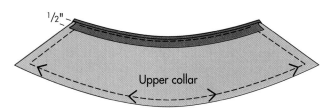

Stitch collar from both sides

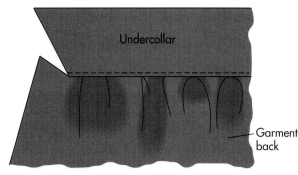

Topstitch close to seamline

Faster **Decorative Collar** One of the fastest ways to sew a collar to a garment is to start with a collar that is already finished around the edges. You can finish the collar edges with a satin decorative stitch on the sewing machine. This technique creates a collar with a designer look for any basic pattern.

1 Cut out the upper and lower collar pieces and the interfacing, and interface the collar. Pin the upper collar and the undercollar with wrong sides together. Baste the collars together by straight stitching along the seam allowance.

2 Stabilize the edge of the collar with scraps of tear-away stabilizer. Select a satin stitch or other decorative stitch such as a scallop stitch or wing-needle hemstitch. Satin stitch around the collar edge at the seamline, stitching over the basting stitch.

3 Treat the edge of the stitching with a fray-stopping liquid, and let it dry. To do this, place a light bead of the fray-stopping liquid on the fabric just outside the satin stitching (in the seam allowance). The liquid will seep or wick to the edge of the stitching, sealing it from fraying if the threads are accidentally cut. Trim the excess seam allowance close to the stitching.

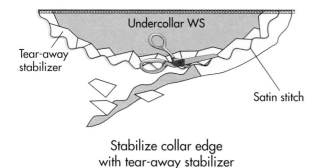

Tear-away stabilizer

Undercollar WS

Satin stitch

Stabilize collar edge with tear-away stabilizer

4 Eliminate the back-neck facing piece. Straight stitch the upper collar and undercollar together on the edge that will be sewn to the neck. Pin the collar to the neck edge of the garment. Pin the front facing over the collar on each side, and serge through all thicknesses to stitch the collar in place and finish all edges at the same time, as shown in Step 4 for the *Fastest* collar on page 117.

Note: A purchased finished collar or knit collar can be sewn in using just this step.

Fastest **Serged Collar** In this technique, you can utilize your serger to construct a traditional collar with pointed corners, eliminating the need to trim the seam allowances before you turn the collar points. You can eliminate the step of cutting and sewing a back-neck facing because you serge the collar to the garment, which creates a finished edge where the facing would be.

1 Cut and interface the collar. Place the upper collar and undercollar with right sides together.

2 Set a three- or four-thread stitch, and serge the long outside edge of the collar.

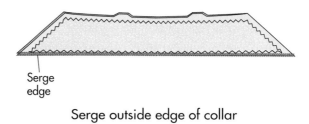

Serge edge

Serge outside edge of collar

3 Fold the serged seam toward the collar, and serge the seams at the ends of the collar, catching the seam in the folded position. Turn the collar right side out, push out the points with a point presser, and press the collar. It is

Interchangeable Lapels

I make interchangeable lapels from artificial suede for my quick collarless jackets.

I make most of my jackets without a collar or lapels because it saves sewing time and I like the look. These jackets can be dressed up with lapels that button on and off. Soft, artificial suede fabrics are perfect for these interchangeable lapels. Many jacket patterns have views with and without lapels, so the lapel pattern can be used as a cutting guide. Once you have a favorite lapel shape, you can use it to make interchangeable lapels in many different colors and fabrics.

1. Finish the outside edge of the lapel on the seamline with a decorative scallop stitch. If your fabric ravels, dab the edge with a seam sealant, and let it dry. Instead of using a woven fabric, choose a beautiful faux suede or leather, which does not require edge finishing.

2. Trim away the excess fabric around the scallop stitching.

3. To hold the lapel in place, sew three or four buttonholes in the seam allowance of the lapel edge that will tuck into the jacket. Try the jacket on with the lapel, and mark the button placement. Sew backer buttons (thin clear buttons) inside the jacket edge.

amazing how the fold-over seam allowance fills the collar point. This is the easiest and best collar point ever.

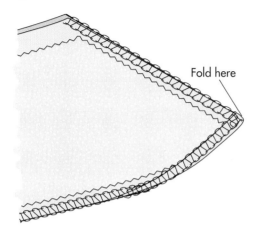

Fold seam allowances in, and serge end

4 To attach the collar to the garment, pin the front facing over the collar on each side. To stitch the collar in place and finish all of the edges in one step, serge through all thicknesses of the collar and the garment neckline and front facing.

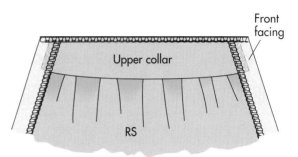

Serge collar to neckline

HERE'S WHAT **I DO**...
to Interface Collars

The key to giving a collar the shape and stability you want is to add just the right amount of interfacing. If you prefer a very crisp collar, consider interfacing both the upper collar and undercollar pieces (and band, if there is one).

Try using a crisper interfacing on the undercollar than you use on the upper collar. This gives the collar firm support without making it look stiff.

1 Cut fusible interfacings with pinking shears along the seamline so there is no interfacing in the seam allowance. This allows for flat edges around the collar and sharp points at the corners.

2 Trim the undercollar piece about ⅛ inch (0.3 cm) smaller than the upper collar all the way around.

3 Stretch the undercollar slightly to sew it so the edges meet.

The shorter undercollar will pull the upper collar slightly to the wrong side. (I cheat by pulling the undercollar slightly outside the edges of the upper collar as I sew to eliminate the trimming step.)

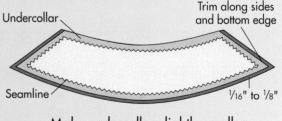

Make undercollar slightly smaller than upper collar

POCKETS

I used to eliminate the pockets in a garment to save time, but too often an important design detail was lost, so I came up with quicker ways to make pockets. Now instead of eliminating pockets, I often add pocket details to garments when the patterns do not call for them. Here are three different quick pockets.

Fast **Patch Pockets** Patch pockets are an easy way to add detail and function to any garment. But be careful with the placement, and reposition the pockets as needed to avoid calling attention to problem areas in your figure. Regardless of where the pattern places the pockets, I suggest trying on the garment (or pinning the garment piece to your body) with the pockets pinned in place and checking in a mirror before sewing them to your garment.

As a general rule, patch pockets cut from matching fabric are the most flattering. Contrasting patch pockets create design detail but call the eye to the area of your body where they are sewn. I have found that a hip patch pocket that is larger and sewn into the side seam along one edge can be more flattering than a patch pocket right on the tummy/hip area. Look for this type of pocket in your pattern choice, or experiment with different sizes using fabric scraps before sewing the pocket.

1 Cut the patch pocket from a pattern piece, or cut a rectangle 5½ inches (14 cm) wide by 7 inches (17.8 cm) long for a breast pocket or

8 inches (20.3 cm) wide by 8 inches (20.3 cm) long for a hip pocket. Both cut sizes include ⅝-inch (1.6-cm) seam allowances and a 1-inch (2.5 cm) hem to fold to the wrong side of the pocket along the top edge. Create a cutting line for curved bottom corners by placing a jar lid at the one corner and tracing around it. Cut the other corner to match. Mark the top foldline 1⅝ inches (4.1 cm) below the top edge with snips in the seam allowance.

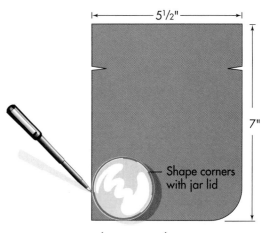

Cut breast pocket

2 Cut a piece of interfacing the size of the finished pocket, and fuse it to the wrong side of the pocket. Cut a piece of lining the width and length of the pocket piece, but do not worry about the curves or shape yet.

3 With right sides together, straight stitch the lining to the pocket along the top edge. As you stitch, change to a basting stitch length of 4 for 2 inches (5.1 cm) in the middle of the seam, then stitch around the rest of the pocket. Trim the seam allowance, and press it toward the

lining. Remove the basting stitches to create a hole for turning the pocket right side out.

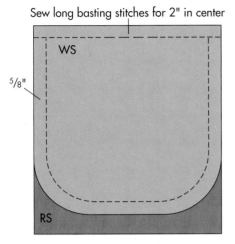

Sew long basting stitches for 2" in center

WS

5/8"

RS

Stitch pocket to lining

4 Keep the pocket and lining right sides together, folding the top edge of the pocket along the snips that mark the fold-down for the top edge. Trim the lining to be a smidgen smaller than the pocket, taking about ⅛ inch (0.3 cm) off the lining edges.

5 Straight stitch around the pocket side and bottom edges with a ⅝-inch (1.6-cm) seam allowance. Trim the seam allowance with pinking shears, and turn the pocket right side out through the hole in the lining/top hem edge seam.

6 Press well, then slipstitch the hole, or fuse it closed with a strip of fusible web.

7 Baste the pocket in place with a fabric-glue stick or fusible web. Stitch the pocket to the garment.

Faster Fake Welt Pockets You can create the design detail of a pocket with an easy topstitched welt that has no pocket attached. This technique is often used on ready-to-wear vests.

HERE'S WHAT **I DO**...

to Sew a Lined Patch Pocket

I like the new fusible web called Steam-A-Seam II (sold in ½-inch [1.3-cm] width) because it is tacky until you fuse it in place. Stick a strip of the web on the garment at the pocket marking. Then remove the top paper layer and place the pocket on the garment. Because the web can be moved around before pressing, the pocket can be repositioned as needed. Press to fuse the pocket, and topstitch it in place. For a hand-stitched look, use monofilament thread. (The straight stitch of the blindhem stitch will be just off the edge of the pocket, and the zigzag will jump onto the pocket.)

1 Mark the placement of the bottom of each welt on the garment. Cut a piece of fabric the same size as the welt piece in the garment pattern. If there is no welt pattern, cut a fabric piece 2½ inches (6.4 cm) wide by 6 inches (15.2 cm) long for each welt, which includes ⅝-inch (1.6-cm) seam allowances. You may want to cut a larger or smaller welt depending upon the placement of the welt and the style of the garment.

2 Fold each welt piece with right sides together, and sew a ⅝-inch (1.6-cm) seam at each end. Trim the seam, and turn the welt right side out. Press and stitch the raw edges together.

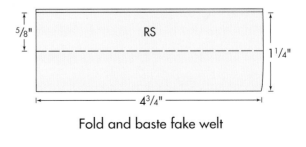

5/8"   RS   1¼"

4¾"

Fold and baste fake welt

3 Place the raw edges of the welt at the welt location of the garment ⅝-inch (1.6 cm) above the marked placement line, with the raw edges toward the top of the garment.

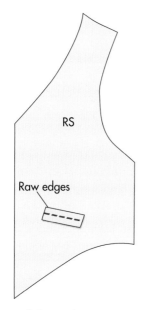

Pin fake welt to garment

4 Stitch the welt along the raw edges with a ⅝-inch (1.6-cm) seam allowance. Trim the seam allowance to ¼ inch (0.6 cm). Press the welt up, and topstitch through all thicknesses at each end.

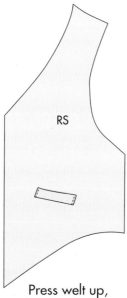

Press welt up,
and topstitch in place

Fastest **Welts from Trim** By using a length of braid or trim, you can create the design detail of a welt pocket without all the work of sewing a welt. Consider using the same braid or trim for the binding to tie the look of the garment together.

1 Cut a 4-inch (10.2-cm) strip of trim for each welt. If needed, add enough to the length to turn under the ends.

2 Topstitch the trim in place onto a vest or jacket at the welt or pocket location.

Sew trim to garment where
welt pockets would go

SUE'S SNIPPETS
WE'RE ALL EXPERT RIPPERS

Years of sewing and teaching have made me an expert ripper. When demonstrating techniques, I often rip a sleeve out in my hotel night after night only to demonstrate setting it in at a sewing demonstration the next day. I love the saying "As ye sew, so shall ye rip!"

WAISTBANDS

The traditional methods of making waistbands for skirts, shorts, and slacks take extra time for cutting, fitting, and finishing. Substitute one of these *Fast, Faster, Fastest* methods to save time and create a comfortable waistband that will grow or shrink as you do.

Fast Waistband with a Hook and Eye

For a comfortable waistband with a hook-and-eye closure, cut the waistband with some extra ease, and interface it with nonroll elastic.

Do not take time to cut the waistband from the waistband pattern piece. Instead, use the rotary cutter, mat, and ruler to cut a strip of fabric across the grain of the fabric. (The best part is that you do not measure your waist.) The width of the waistband is a matter of personal preference and depends on the width of the elastic you will use inside.

1 Cut the waistband to a width twice the width of the elastic plus 1½ inches (3.8 cm) for seam allowances and roll factor. I use 1-inch (2.5-cm) elastic, so I cut my waistband strip 3½ inches (8.9 cm) wide.

2 Finish one long edge of the waistband with a three- or four-thread serger stitch or a three-step zigzag on the sewing machine. This edge finish eliminates bulk because there is no need to turn under the edge on the inside of the waistband.

3 To determine the length of the waistband, put it around your waist comfortably while you are seated. Mark the length, and add 3¼ inches (8.2 cm) for seam allowances and the overlap for the hook and eye. If you are making a skirt with a pocket extension, such as the one in the Quick Skirt on page 22, you will need extra length in the waistband. (I usually mark the waist size on the waistband strip, which is cut the width of the fabric, and do not cut any excess off the strip until it is stitched to the garment.) Mark the length of the waistband, not including the hook-and-eye overlap or seam allowances, into quarters to match to the front, back, and side seams.

4 Pin the waistband to the garment at the center front, back, and side seams. I like to have extra fabric in the garment to ease to the waistband because then the garment does not fit so tightly over my tummy and hip area.

5 Straight stitch the waistband to the garment with the garment against the feed teeth. The longer the stitch, the more the garment will ease onto the waistband.

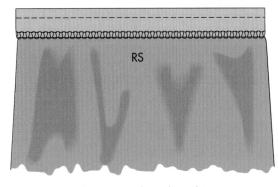

Sew waistband to skirt

Trim the extra length of the waistband. Try the skirt on, and pin the waistband closed to be sure the garment lies flat on your body. Also check that the skirt hangs straight at the hem since a slight variance in the seam allowance when attaching the waistband can make one side longer than the other. Trim bulky seam allowances to ⅜ inch (1 cm).

6 Mark a piece of nonroll elastic to a snug but comfortable fit around your waist, and add 2 inches (5.1 cm) for the hook-and-eye extension.

7 Place the garment under the presser foot of the sewing machine with the seam allowances to the right and the waistband and the garment to the left. Mark the elastic in quarters, and pin it at the skirt front, back, and side seams for equal ease. Place the elastic on the seam allowances with the left edge of the elastic at the waistband stitching line and the elastic on top of the seam allowances. Zigzag stitch the elastic to the seam allowances with a width of 4 and length of 3. Stretch the elastic as needed to fit the waistband.

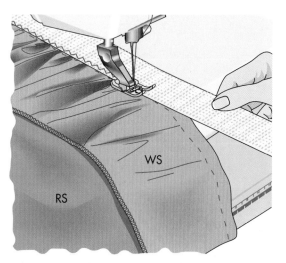

Sew elastic to seam allowance

8 To finish the ends, fold the waistband with right sides together at each end, and stitch

the ends, catching the elastic in the stitching. Trim the excess seam allowance and elastic.

9 Turn the waistband right side out. Pin the waistband in the ditch from the right side, catching the serged edge of the waistband on the inside of the garment.

10 Topstitch the waistband in the ditch from the right side. An edge foot will guide you.

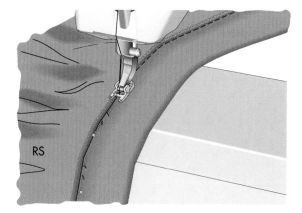

Stitch in ditch to finish waistband

HERE'S WHAT I DO...
to Divide a Waistband into Four Parts

Most bodies cannot be divided into equal quarters! The first time you mark the quarters for a waistband, wrap the waistband around your body and mark the sides of your body. Use these marks in place of the quarter markings. I take ¾ inch (1.9 cm) from the back waistband and use it in the front because my front is broader than my back. Once you determine where you need to add or subtract, you always mark the waistband the same until you gain—or hopefully, lose!

Faster Elastic-Casing Waistband

A standard waistband with a hook and eye or with a button closure can be replaced with an elastic-casing waistband on just about any garment as long as the garment can be pulled on over the head or hips. This method will create gathers at the waist, so it is best to use on knits where no ease is added at the waistline of the skirt. But this waistband can also be used for light- and medium-weight wovens.

1 Before cutting the garment, increase the width of the waistline to fit over your hips. To do this, stretch the yardage around your hipline comfortably, then mark and measure to determine the needed measurement. Extend the side-seam edges so the total measurement is your hip measurement plus 4 to 6 inches (10.2 to 15.2 cm) of ease. On a knit garment, the knit will usually have enough ease so the width of the garment at the waist can be equal to the hip measurement or even 2 to 3 inches (5.1 to 7.6 cm) less for knits that are stretchy on the crosswise grain.

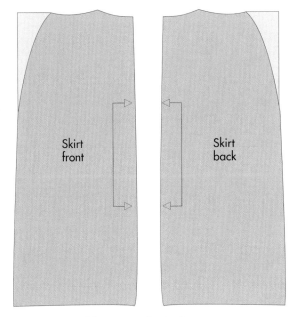

Add to waistline of pattern

2 Use the rotary cutter, mat, and ruler to cut the waistband strip. The strip should measure two times the width of the elastic plus two seam allowances by the hip measurement plus approximately 2 inches (5.1 cm) of ease for knit fabric to 4 inches (10.2 cm) of ease for woven fabric. For example, for 1-inch (2.5-cm) elastic with ⅝-inch (1.6-cm) seam allowances, cut the waistband 3¼ inches (8.2 cm) by your hip measurement plus ease.

3 Sew the side, front, and back seams of the garment. Then prepare the waistband with right sides together, joining the ends of the waistband. Cut a piece of nonroll elastic to fit your waist comfortably, and stitch it into a circle.

4 Place the elastic on the wrong side of the waistband, fold the waistband lengthwise with wrong sides together, matching the raw edges, and mark equal quarters.

5 Pin the waistband quarter markings to the garment quarter markings with right sides together, positioning the waistband seam at the center back. Stitch the waistband to the garment with the garment on the bottom against the feed teeth to ease the garment to the waistband.

on the
FAST TRACK...
to a Quick Elastic Casing

This quick one-piece waistband is often called the casing/hem-fold technique because the same sewing steps are followed to sew a band-style hem. This is often used for hems on short sleeves in fine ready-to-wear. I used to think the manufacturers had added a band, but actually the hem was folded as for a blind hem and sewn with a serger, catching the fold of the edge as the hem was sewn.

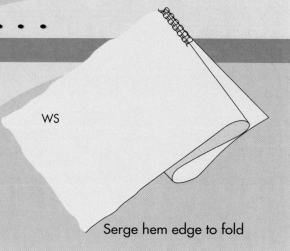

WS

Serge hem edge to fold

I usually stitch with a straight stitch first, then finish the edge with a four-thread serger stitch, sewing through all layers, but not the elastic, and trim the seam allowances to ¼ inch (0.6 cm). If you do not own a serger, trim the seam allowances to ¼ inch (0.6 cm) first, then finish the edge with a three-step zigzag stitch.

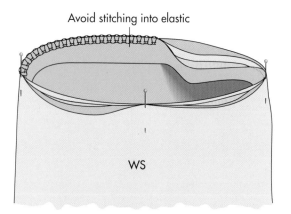

Avoid stitching into elastic

WS

Stitch waistband to garment

6 To even up the elastic gathers, grasp the waistband at the side seams, pull it firmly to stretch it, and then let go. Pin the waistband through the elastic at the sides, and topstitch horizontally through all the waistband layers at the center back and sides.

Fastest **One-Piece Waistband** I realized serveral years ago that the elastic casings on many ready-to-wear garments were not separate waistbands, as explained in the *Faster* method on page 123, but instead were cut as part of the garment. This fast waistband can be added to any pattern where an elastic waistband is desired.

1 Before cutting out the skirt, create a casing by adding two times the width of the elastic to the top edge of each skirt piece. For example, for 1-inch (2.5-cm) elastic, add 2 inches (5.1 cm) to the top edge of a skirt pattern. That's all you need to add since the seam allowance is already on the pattern. Remember, if the pattern does not call for an elastic waistband, you must also add ease to the waistline of the skirt, anywhere from 2 to 6 inches (5.1 to 15.2 cm), so you can pull the skirt over your hips.

2 Sew the side, front, and back seams of the skirt. To create the casing, press one elastic width plus seam allowance to the wrong side of the garment. Pin the casing with several pins as you would pin for a blind hem.

3 Fold the casing to the right side of the garment just as you would fold a blind hem. Sew along the fold, catching all of the layers with a four-thread on the serger or with a seam/overcast stitch. For best results, sew from the casing side, removing the pins as you sew. Stop stitching just before you reach the place you began sewing to leave a hole to insert the elastic.

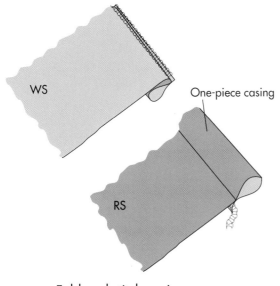

WS

One-piece casing

RS

Fold and stitch casing

4 Use a safety pin or bodkin to pull a piece of elastic into the casing. (I usually start with a piece of elastic that is longer than I'll need.) Before closing the waistband casing, try the skirt on and adjust the elastic to fit. The elastic should fit comfortably at the waist and still stretch long enough to slip over your hips. Trim the excess, and stitch the ends together. Serge over the hole to close it.

on the
FAST
TRACK...

to Make a No-Band Waistband

The wide, colored elastics are a very quick way to add a waistband to a skirt. I have used the 2-inch (5.1-cm) and 3-inch (7.6-cm) widths in navy, black, white, and off-white.

Many people ask me how much elastic to buy. The easiest way to determine the length you need is to take the roll of elastic (I do it at the cutting table of the store) and stretch it around the fullest part of your hips. This is the amount you need, because you have to pull the skirt on over your hips or head.

1 Sew the short ends of the waistband elastic with right sides together to make a circle. I use a four-thread serger stitch or a seam/overcast stitch.

2 Mark the quarters on the elastic circle and on the top of the skirt. If the skirt is very full, gather the top of it to fit the stretched elastic.

3 Lap the elastic over the top edge of the skirt. Topstitch with a narrow zigzag along the lower edge of the elastic, stretching slightly as you sew and catching the skirt in the stitching. In place of a zigzag, you can also use a twin needle to topstitch on the sewing machine or a cover stitch on the serger, which gives built-in stretch to the topstitching.

ZIPPERS

Too often I find that sewers avoid patterns with zippers. The following techniques can simplify any zipper application.

Fast **Center-Lapped Zipper** The center-lapped zipper is stitched into a seam with equal laps of fabric on each side. It is popular for center back seams in skirts and dresses.

1 Cut a small snip in the seam allowance to mark the desired position of the bottom of the zipper.

2 Beginning at the end of the seam below the zipper opening, sew the seam with a straight stitch to the place marked with a snip, then lockstitch and cut the thread. Machine baste the zipper opening closed.

3 Press the seam open from the wrong side and then from the right side.

4 Center the zipper right side down over the wrong side of the basted zipper opening. Position the stopper bottom of the zipper at the snipped marking. If you are using a zipper that is longer than the garment opening, the top of the zipper will extend above the top of the garment.

5 Hold the zipper in place with transparent tape across the zipper, or bartack over the teeth at 1½-inch (3.8-cm) intervals. To bartack,

HERE'S WHAT **I DO**...
to Simplify Zippers

Purchase a zipper longer than the placket opening so the zipper pull can be extended above the placket during zipper insertion. With a zipper that is longer than the placket opening, you do not need to sew around the zipper pull. For example, purchase a 9-inch (22.9-cm) zipper for a 7-inch (17.8-cm) placket. After sewing the zipper in place, be sure to have the zipper pull at the bottom, and stitch across the top before cutting off the excess zipper.

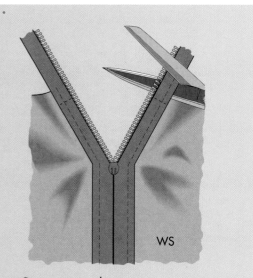

WS

Open zipper, then trim away excess

lower the feed teeth, and select a zigzag stitch wide enough to stitch over the zipper teeth. Place one bartack at the top and bottom of the zipper and a few in between.

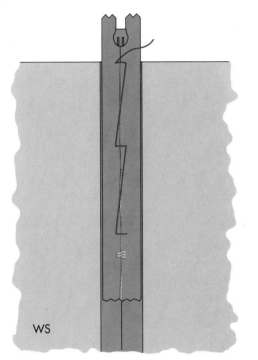

WS

Bartack zipper in place

6 Turn the garment over, and straight stitch from the right side. Try using a standard presser foot, sewing with the edge along the teeth and adjusting the needle position to stitch close to the zipper. If your machine does not have needle position adjustment, use a zipper foot.

For best results, begin sewing across the bottom of the zipper, sew up one side, then sew across the bottom again for strength. Sew up the other side, adjusting the needle position of your sewing machine to the opposite side. (On a computerized machine, use a side-to-side mirror image to move the needle to the precise position on the opposite side.) Sewing each side in the same direction will prevent shifting and distortion.

HERE'S WHAT I DO...
to Stabilize Zippers

When inserting a zipper into a bias edge, I fuse narrow strips of fusible tricot interfacing to the seamline on the wrong side of the garment in the zipper area. This prevents stretching and distortion as you insert the zipper.

7 Remove the tape or bartacks and the basting. Before trimming away the excess zipper, *be sure* to unzip the zipper and stitch across the top edge of the teeth on both sides of the open zipper. I only *once* made the mistake of cutting off the excess with the zipper pull still attached to it!

Faster **Invisible Zipper** The key to an invisible zipper is the presser foot. You can buy this type of foot in a package. However, most sewing machines come with a presser foot that will actually work better than the invisible zipper foot, because a foot designed specifically for your machine will feed better and stitch better. Look among your sewing machine accessories for a foot with two tiny grooves on the underside. Often this is the buttonhole foot. These grooves guide the satin columns of a buttonhole as it is sewn, but they will also guide the teeth of an invisible zipper.

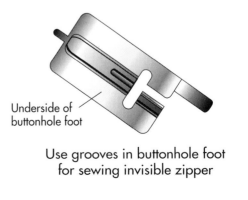

Underside of
buttonhole foot

Use grooves in buttonhole foot
for sewing invisible zipper

HERE'S WHAT **I DO**...
to Stitch Zippers in Place

As I travel, I find many sewers are unhappy with the new zipper feet that come with their machines because they are quite wide. Because contemporary sewing machines have wide zigzag and decorative stitches, the feed teeth are much farther apart to allow for the swing of the needle.

Presser feet must ride directly on the feed teeth for the best feeding result. Zipper feet often ride on only part of the feed system, which results in uneven feeding. This is why I suggest using the standard presser foot and adjusting the needle position to the right and left. Not only does the foot ride the feed teeth perfectly, but if you use the edge of the foot as a guide along the zipper teeth and/or seamline, your stitching is also more accurate. Please try this; many people have said this tip has been a tremendous help to them.

1 Unlike regular zippers, you will not sew the seam below the zipper opening until after sewing in the zipper. Sew the invisible zipper into the seam before sewing the garment seam. Start by pressing the zipper flat, as directed in the zipper instructions. Press from the tape side, being careful not to touch the iron to the teeth of the zipper.

on the ⅝-inch (1.6-cm) seamline and the top point of the teeth ¾ inch (1.9 cm) from the top edge. At the top of the zipper, place the zipper teeth in the left groove on the underside of the presser foot. If needed, adjust your needle position so the needle sews right next to the zipper teeth to the bottom of the zipper until the zipper pull stops you.

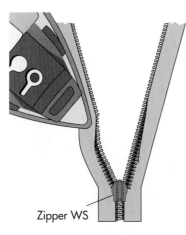

Zipper WS

Press zipper coils
flat from wrong side

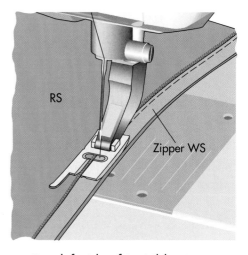

RS

Zipper WS

Sew left side of invisible zipper

2 With the buttonhole foot or invisible-zipper foot on your machine, place the left side of the zipper to the left side of the garment piece with right sides together, with the zipper teeth

3 To check the placement on the other side of the garment (and to avoid twisting the zipper), close up the zipper, and pin the top of the unsewn side of the zipper tape to the top

edge of the right side of the garment. Unzip the zipper.

4 Place the right teeth of the zipper in the right groove on the underside of the foot. Again, readjust the needle position to the other side so it will stitch right along the edge of the zipper teeth as needed.

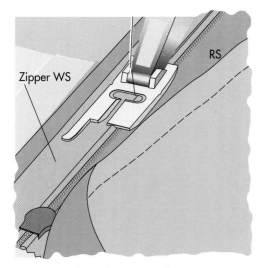

Sew right side of invisible zipper

5 To prepare to stitch the seam in the garment at the bottom of the zipper, put on the zipper foot that came with your sewing machine.

6 Close the zipper. Place the garment pieces right sides together, pull the zipper end out of the way, and place the needle in the fabric just above the end of your zipper stitching and just outside the stitching line. The zipper foot should ride along the edge of the zipper, so adjust the needle position as needed. Lockstitch or tie off threads by hand at this beginning point to avoid bulk. Stitch the seam for several inches until you have cleared the zipper. For best feeding, change to the standard presser foot, and sew the rest of the seam.

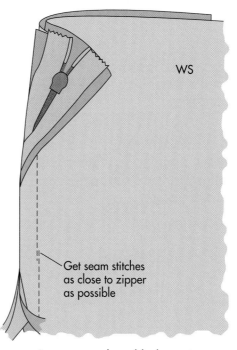

Sew seam closed below zipper

SUE'S SNIPPETS
ZIPPERS WITH A DIFFERENCE

I love invisible zippers! They are very easy to sew in place and are beautiful to look at. Plus, the top designers use them! I often use them in skirts, but invisible zippers are especially nice for dresses and special-occasion wear. Do you notice the zippers in the backs of bridesmaid gowns? I once attended a wedding where I noticed that one bridesmaid's zipper was center lapped, another was lapped, and a third was invisible. I'm sure no one else noticed, but the invisible zipper is virtually "invisible" down the center back of a dress. The only thing that shows is the tiny pull. Sometimes it is impossible to find a perfect color match in a zipper, and the invisible zipper is a great solution. I have found the pulls blend in even if they aren't the perfect color, or they can be "painted" with permanent markers or nail polish!

Fastest **Zipper as Piping** The fastest way to insert a zipper is to stitch it as you would stitch piping. Most sewing machines and sergers have a piping foot available as an accessory. This foot has a groove on the underside to guide the piping. The plastic teeth of standard zippers can be guided by this groove also. For heavier metal zippers, use a standard presser foot with the edge of the foot against the teeth as you sew.

Groove in piping foot fits over zipper teeth

This technique works well on exposed zippers such as on jacket fronts and in applications where the zipper will be a decorative detail.

1 Open the zipper, and place one side of the zipper on the garment, right sides together. Place the teeth in the groove of the piping presser foot (or place the teeth against the edge of the standard foot and adjust the needle to stitch close). Stitch in place with a straight stitch.

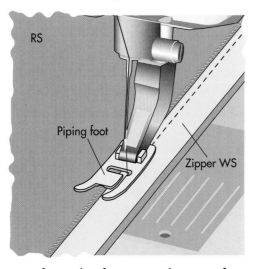

Sew first side of zipper with piping foot

2 Zip the zipper closed, and pin the other side of the zipper to the garment, right sides together. Unzip, and repeat the sewing steps.

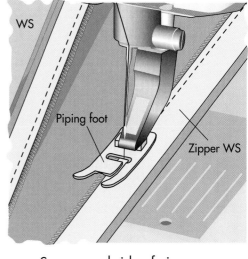

Sew second side of zipper
with piping foot

3 Press the seam allowance away from the zipper, and topstitch from the right side. (A lap of fabric over the zipper can be pressed and topstitched.)

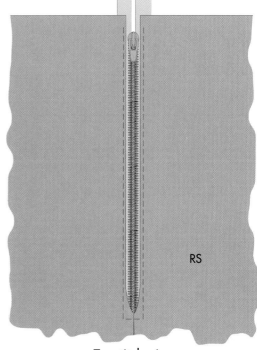

Topstitch zipper

SLEEVE PLACKETS

One of the details that can slow me down when I am making long sleeves is the sleeve placket. Sometimes the placket technique can take as long as the rest of the blouse, so I always use one of the following methods. No one has ever inspected my plackets and noticed that I did not do them the way shown in the pattern instructions.

Fast **Bias Strip Plackets** In this quick method, you will serge or stitch the placket in place, then topstitch it from the right side of the sleeve.

1 Cut a bias strip of fabric 1½ inches (3.8 cm) wide by at least 8 inches (20.3 cm) long. (Longer plackets require longer strips.) Use a rotary cutter for quick cutting. Fold the strip lengthwise with wrong sides together, and press. Staystitch the length of the folded strip ¼ inch (0.6 cm) from the raw edges.

2 With a short stitch, 2 to 2.5, staystitch the V of the placket to mark and stabilize it. Cut the V open to the point.

3 Matching the staystitching on the bias strip with the staystitching on the placket opening, sew the strip to the placket opening with right sides together. Pull the V of the placket to make a straight line to sew. It can be tricky at the point, but just keep the original stitching lines matched as closely as possible. It is actually easier if you do not pin this step!

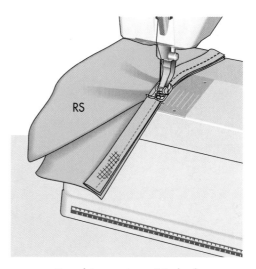

Sew bias strip to V-placket

4 Press the seam allowance toward the bias strip. Press the folded edge of the bias strip over the seam allowances to the wrong side of the placket.

5 Pull the V of the placket straight again to topstitch the placket from the right side, catching the fold of the strip on the underside.

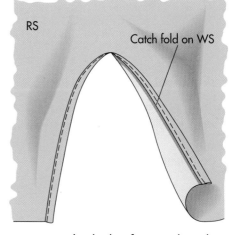

Topstitch placket from right side

6 Hold the sleeve up to your arm to determine front and back. (If the right and wrong sides of your fabric are not obvious, be sure to mark the fronts of both sleeves so you don't end up with two left or two right sleeves.) Pin and press the placket strip to the wrong side of the placket opening on the front side of the sleeve, and leave it extended on the back side of the sleeve.

7 Baste the front placket strip to the wrong side, and stitch across the top of the placket strip from the fold to the top of the V at the top of the placket.

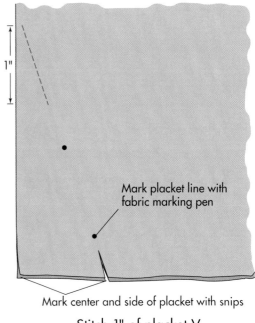

Mark placket line with fabric marking pen

1"

Mark center and side of placket with snips

Stitch 1" of placket V

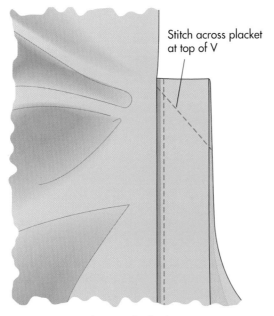

Stitch across placket at top of V

Stitch top of placket

Faster **Darted Plackets** Instead of cutting the placket all the way open, sew a short dart at the top of the placket, then finish the edges with a narrow hem.

1 Mark the placket from the pattern tissue onto the fabric. Fold the sleeve with right sides together, matching the placket markings as you would sew a dart. Begin stitching at the point of

the V of the placket, and sew about 1 inch (2.5 cm) just inside the placket markings. Lockstitch at both ends.

2 Slit the placket open, and fold and press a double turn of fabric along the raw edges to form a narrow hem.

3 Topstitch the narrow hem from the wrong side of the sleeve.

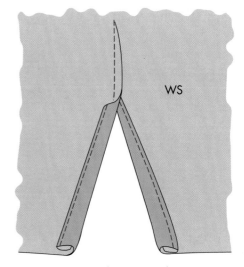

WS

Topstitch narrow hem

Fastest **Serger Plackets** Look for this placket finish in ready-to-wear. The placket opening is serged instead of being hemmed.

1 Mark the placket from the pattern tissue. Slit the placket to the V.

2 Begin at one edge of the placket, and serge along the placket markings with a three- or four-thread serger stitch, trimming the excess fabric.

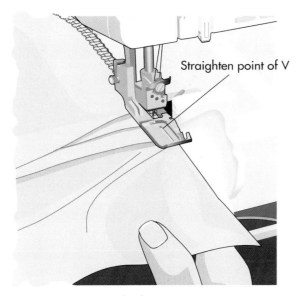

Straighten point of V

Serge placket opening

3 As you approach the V, pull the fabric to create a straight edge to serge at the V of the placket. Continue to serge to the other edge. Remember, because the cutter is in front of the needles on the serger, it is important to pull the placket edge straight before the cutter reaches the fabric of the V.

4 Press and topstitch the serged edge to the wrong side of the sleeve.

SUE'S SNIPPETS

BE WILLING TO TRY SOMETHING NEW

Some years ago at Husqvarna Viking we brought in a teacher to help train our educators in the correct ways to sew. She taught us to set sleeves in with the sleeve on top and the garment down against the feed teeth of the sewing machine.

When I asked her about this and explained how much easier it is when you let the feed teeth of the machine work for you, easing the fabric along, she replied, "You *must* have the sleeve on the top." I asked why, and she responded, "Because the textbooks say so." Soon after this, I was with another sewing expert who presented the sleeves on top in a slide presentation. When I talked to her about having the sleeves on the bottom, she said, "That makes sense; I'll try it," and she did.

I'm glad she decided to break away from the textbook to try new ideas. That is how we keep learning and improving how we sew.

Few, if any, of the *Fast, Faster, Fastest* techniques in this book are ever shown in commercial pattern guide sheets. Some of the techniques have been borrowed from the ready-to-wear garment industry. But most of them came from inventive home sewers looking for better ways to do things.

I like to tell sewers that there is no one right way to do things. If it works, it's right!

CUFFS

Cuffs come in many different sizes and types. They can be a functional way to hold a long sleeve closed or a decorative element on the garment. Depending on the style of the garment and fabric you are sewing, there are a number of quick ways to add cuffs to sleeves. You will not find most of these techniques in the commercial pattern instructions. Don't be afraid to change the style of the cuff or the method used to sew it to a sleeve.

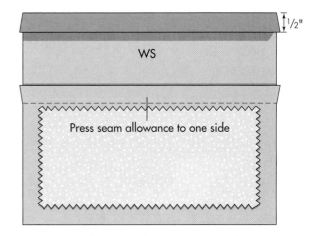

Press facing edge to wrong side

Fast Cuffs Sewn "in the Flat" Here is a fast way to sew traditional top-stitched cuffs. The cuff is sewn to the sleeve after the sleeve seam is stitched but before the ends of the cuff are finished.

1 Prepare the sleeve by sewing the placket, if any, and the sleeve seam.

2 Cut the inner and outer cuff pieces and interfacing piece. Interface the outer cuff, then sew the two cuff pieces together only along the lower edge of the cuff. Do not stitch the ends of the cuff before sewing the cuff to the sleeve.

3 Press ½ inch (1.3 cm) to the wrong side of one of the long edges of the facing side of the cuff. This will be the cuff-facing edge. I like to straight stitch at the ½-inch (1.3-cm) seam allowance, then press the edge to the wrong side along the stitching line.

4 Pin and stitch the other long cuff edge to the sleeve edge with right sides together, matching the markings from the pattern tissue. Use the free arm of your sewing machine.

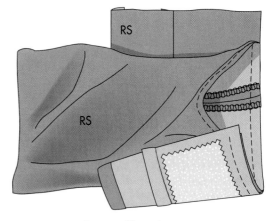

Sew cuff to sleeve

5 Trim the seam, and press the seam allowance toward the cuff.

6 Fold the cuff and cuff facing (can be one piece) with right sides together, and stitch across the cuff ends. Trim the seam allowances.

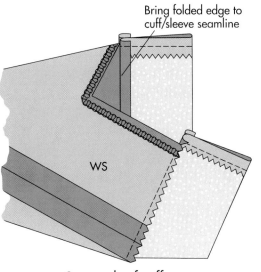

Bring folded edge to cuff/sleeve seamline

WS

Sew ends of cuff

7 Turn the cuff right side out. Press and pin the cuff edge in the ditch from the right side, catching the cuff facing.

8 Stitch the cuff in the ditch from the right side, catching the cuff facing in the stitching.

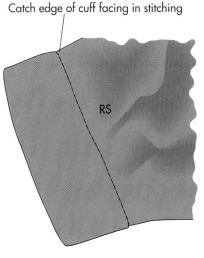

Catch edge of cuff facing in stitching

RS

Stitch cuff in ditch

Faster **Serger Cuffs** Try sewing cuffs completely on the serger, as they do in ready-to-wear. You can stitch the placket on the serger using the *Fastest* technique in "Sleeve

Plackets" on page 133, but do not topstitch the serged placket before putting on the cuff.

1 For a two-piece cuff, serge the cuff and cuff facing with right sides together with a four-thread serger stitch along the long edge. Fold the serged seam toward the cuff, and serge the seams at the ends of the cuff, catching the seam in the folded position.

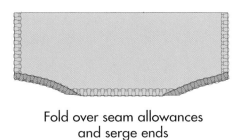

Fold over seam allowances and serge ends

2 Turn the cuff right side out, and press. Basting the raw edges of the cuff pieces together is optional.

3 Pin the raw edge of the cuff to the sleeve edge with right sides together, matching the markings from the pattern tissue. Fold the serged edge of the placket over the ends of the cuff to the facing side of the cuff. Serge the cuff to the sleeve.

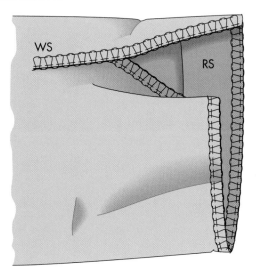

WS

RS

Serge cuff to sleeve

4 Serge the cuff to the sleeve edge with a four-thread serger stitch.

Fastest Pleated "Cuffs"
My favorite quick way to finish a sleeve is to eliminate the cuff and create the effect of a placket by using a button and buttonhole or a decorative snap in a placket pleat.

1 When cutting out the garment, eliminate the cuff, and cut the sleeve straight down from the elbow. Also cut the sleeve longer to make up for the length of the cuff that you're eliminating. To figure out how much longer to cut the sleeve, add the width of the cuff plus a 1½-inch (3.8-cm) hem to the sleeve length. Mark the location where the placket would have been placed.

2 Sew the sleeve underarm seam. Try on the garment, and hem the sleeve.

3 Try the sleeve on again, and pinch and pin a pleat at the placket marking. Bring the pleat toward the back of the sleeve to a comfortable and attractive sleeve width at the wrist. Mark the pleat. Remember that the pleat should button toward the back of the sleeve.

4 Stitch a buttonhole in the pleat, and add a button to the sleeve.

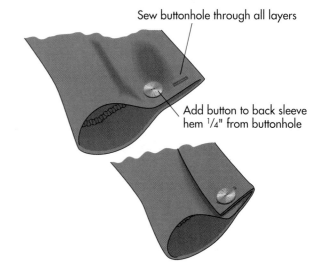

Sew buttonhole through all layers

Add button to back sleeve hem ¼" from buttonhole

Sew buttonhole and button

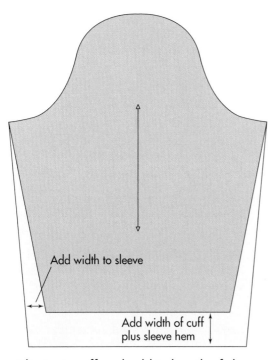

Add width to sleeve

Add width of cuff plus sleeve hem

Eliminate cuff and add to length of sleeve

SLEEVES

Professional-looking sleeves are essential to a fine sewn garment. Try the following speedy methods for perfect-looking sleeves that are quick and easy.

Sleeve Basics

Accurate marking is the first step in sewing a sleeve that hangs correctly and fits well. Mark the notches and dots when cutting sleeves and the corresponding markings on the garment. These are essential so that the front of the sleeve (one notch) is in the front and the back (two notches) is in the back and the correct amount of fullness is eased into each area of the sleeve cap. Be sure to take special note on patterns where the shoulder seam is not matched to the top of the sleeve.

No Tucks, No Puckers

Tucks or puckers in the sleeve cap are dead giveaways of a home-sewn garment. I'm not talking about sleeves that are designed to have gathers at the cap; I mean sleeves that have not been eased properly. Most of us were taught to ease a sleeve with two rows of gathering stitches that are drawn up, creating gathers in the cap, and then to use as many pins as possible to pin baste the sleeve into the armhole before sewing.

I have found that these two steps actually contribute drastically to causing tucks and puckers when the sleeve is sewn in. The sleeve is already gathered, so it is difficult not to sew the gathers in, and every time you ap-proach a pin, a little tuck forms against the pin as you sew. I ask students to take an oath that they promise to try setting in their next sleeve with the three-pin method—one at each notch and one at the top of the sleeve—and let the feed teeth ease in the sleeve cap as described in "Crimping to Ease," below. Many of them have come back to say they cannot believe how well this works. I am so excited that it has become an easy technique for them.

Crimping to Ease

To ease sleeve caps quickly and easily, use this crimping technique. Instead of sewing two rows of gathering stitches, straight stitch with your standard sewing foot from the front notch to the back notch along the ⅝-inch (1.6-cm) seamline.

The key to crimp gathering is to hold your finger behind the foot of the machine and press against the fabric as it tries to feed out from under the foot. This holds back the feed of the fabric and creates little crimps in the seam allowance. When fabric builds up, let go, then begin holding it back again. Use a stitch length of 4 for light- to medium-weight fabrics and longer, if your machine has it, for heavier-weight fabrics.

If you cannot lengthen the stitch enough, increase the top tension for more gathering. When you have finished, shape the sleeve cap over your hand. You can adjust the crimp gathers slightly, but there is usually no need. More fabric can be eased if necessary while the sleeve is being set into the garment.

Once you have crimp eased a sleeve, try the *Fast* two-step sleeve method below for perfect, professional-looking set-in sleeves.

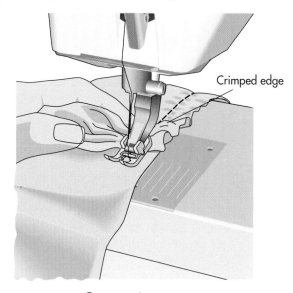

Create crimp ease

Fast **Two-Step Sleeves** Here is my favorite way to sew traditional tailored and other set-in sleeves with high sleeve caps. The secret to getting the best "hand" and fit quickly is to sew the sleeve to the garment in two separate steps. This method combines the best of both worlds. First, you sew the part of the sleeve that requires the most easing "in the flat" before the side and sleeve seams are stitched. Then you sew the rest of the sleeve "in the round" after the other seams are sewn.

1 Sew the shoulder seams of the garment. Crimp ease the sleeve cap between the notches, as described in "Crimping to Ease" on page 137. After crimping, if there is still quite a bit of fullness to ease, select a basting stitch, and baste the sleeve in before the final stitching. Pin the sleeve in place using only three pins, two at the front and back notches and one at the shoulder.

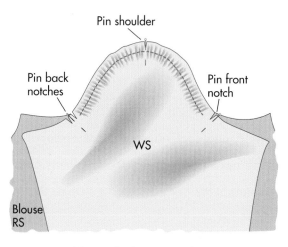

Use only 3 pins in sleeve

2 Do not begin sewing the sleeve at the edge; instead, begin sewing the sleeve to the garment at the notch. Place the sleeve down against the feed teeth of the machine with the garment on top. Trust me! When the sleeve is on the underside, the feed teeth will help ease in the fullness. If the sleeve is on the top, you can watch all the tucks get caught in the stitching. Stitch from notch to notch over the sleeve cap. The longer the stitch, the more easily the sleeve is eased. Hold back the top garment layer for even more easing in areas where needed.

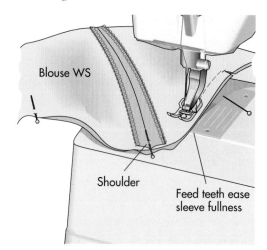

Place sleeve against feed teeth

3 Steam press the seam allowance from the sleeve side to ease out any minor crimps.

4 Sew the garment side seam and sleeve seam. You now have a hole in the underarm area.

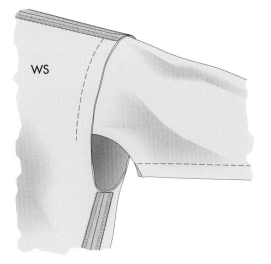

Sew garment side seam and sleeve seam

5 Pin the sleeve to the garment with one pin where the garment side seam and the sleeve underarm seam match. Stitch the sleeve into the garment from notch to notch, closing the underarm hole. Because the underarm area is stitched in the round, the sleeve hangs better.

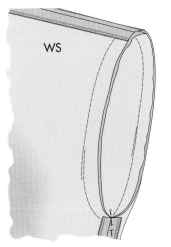

Sew sleeve underarm

6 Finish the sleeve seam allowance with a three- or four-thread serger stitch or three-step zigzag on the sewing machine. Trim the seam allowance to ¼ inch (0.6 cm) in the un-derarm area from notch to notch, and taper the seam allowance to the full ⅝ inch (1.6 cm) over the sleeve cap. Press the sleeve cap seam allowance toward the sleeve.

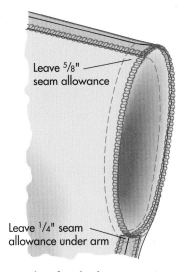

Leave ⅝" seam allowance

Leave ¼" seam allowance under arm

Edge finish sleeve seam

SUE'S SNIPPETS
EMBELLISHING
IN ALL THE RIGHT PLACES

One of the most important considerations when embellishing a garment is the placement of the embellishment. It's always tempting to "individu-alize" a blouse by embellishing the sleeve hems or the cuffs, but before you do, think about how it will look on the overall garment. Be sure to mark the location of the embellishment on the garment and try on the garment or hold it up to you in front of a mirror before sewing.

The mirror will reveal if the embellishment calls attention to parts of your body you would rather not emphasize. I suggest keeping most embellishments near the top of a garment to call attention to the face rather than the chest, waist, or hips. It always amazes me to see an appliqué on the midriff of a shirt instead of on the yoke area. "Better too high than too low" is my motto.

Faster **Sleeves on a Serger** On casual clothes and knitwear with flat sleeve caps, let the differential feed on your serger ease the sleeve cap for you.

1 To crimp ease with the serger differential feed, set the serger to a three- or four-thread stitch, with a stitch length of 3 to 4 and the differential feed set at 1.5 to 2. To predict how much ease you will get, remember that the higher the differential feed number, the longer the stitch length, and the lighter weight the fabric, the more fabric will be eased. Experiment on scraps until you get to know how much fabric the different settings on the differential feed on your serger will draw up. Then it will be quick to set. You can let out some of the fullness after stitching or ease in more fullness by pulling on the needle threads.

2 Pin the sleeve to the garment with right sides together, matching markings. Use only three pins—one at each notch and one at the top of the sleeve cap.

3 Place the sleeve down against the feed teeth of the serger, and stitch the sleeve into the garment from notch to notch, allowing the feed teeth to ease the sleeve into the garment.

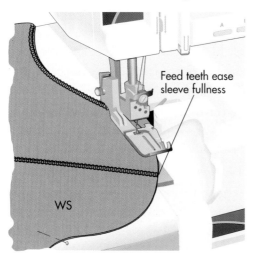

Place sleeve against feed teeth

4 Sew the garment side seam and the sleeve seam. You now have a hole in the underarm area.

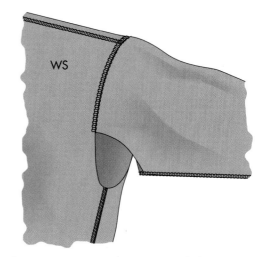

Serge garment side seam and sleeve seam

5 Finish the sleeve seam allowance with a three- or four-thread serger stitch. Trim the seam allowance to ¼ inch (0.6 cm) in the underarm area from notch to notch, and taper the seam allowance to the full ⅝ inch (1.6 cm) over the sleeve cap. Press the sleeve cap seam allowance toward the sleeve.

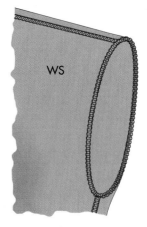

Serge sleeve seam

Fastest **Sleeves "in the Flat"** Many casual and knitwear garments have flatter sleeve caps, which do not require leaving a great deal of ease in the sleeve cap.

You can set in these sleeves "in the flat" before the garment side seam and sleeve underarm seam are sewn, letting the feed teeth of the sewing machine or the differential feed of the serger do the easing for you.

1 Sew or serge the shoulder seams in the garment.

2 Pin the sleeve to the garment at the shoulder seam and notches.

3 Place the sleeve down against the feed teeth of the sewing machine or serger, and stitch as follows.

On the sewing machine, set for a straight stitch and a length of 4. Hold back the top garment layer as needed so the feed teeth can ease the sleeve into the garment. The longer the stitch length, the more the fabric will be eased.

On the serger, set a four-thread stitch at a stitch length of 3 and a differential feed of 1.5 to 2. Serge. The differential feed will ease the sleeve to the garment. The higher the differential feed number, the more fabric will be eased.

4 On each side sew the side seam of the blouse and the underarm seam on the sleeve in one step.

HERE'S WHAT **I DO**...
to Make French-Bias Piping

French-bias piping that matches or contrasts the garment fabric is a good way to add design detail to necklines.

1 Cut a bias strip 2 inches (5.1 cm) wide by the desired length. Fold it in half lengthwise with wrong sides together, and press.

2 Lay a piece of small cable cord on the center of the double layer of bias, and fold the bias again, wrapping it around the cable cord and bringing the lengthwise raw edges of the bias strip to the folded edge.

3 Place this strip under the piping foot so the cording rides in the groove. Straight stitch. Trim the raw edges close to the stitching.

4 Place the piping on the right side of the garment with the trimmed edge of the bias against the right side of the garment and the folded edge to the raw edge of the neck-

line. Place the piping into the groove in the piping foot, and straight stitch over the previous stitching. Clip and trim the blouse neckline edge. (But *don't* trim the folded edge of the bias!)

5 Press the bias and the seam allowance to the wrong side. Topstitch the piping in place, sewing in the ditch from the right side.

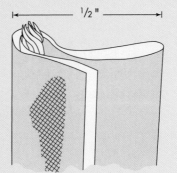

Wrap cord with folded bias strip

YOKES

okes add design details to otherwise plain blouses, dresses, and jackets. There are a few ways to make yokes even more of a design statement on your garments.

I love to cut the yoke in a direction that adds detail to the garment. For example, on a striped fabric, cut the yoke with the stripe going in the opposite direction from the rest of the garment.

Consider cutting the yoke on the bias, especially when the fabric is a plaid or print that would require matching. Cutting the yoke on the bias eliminates the need to match the stripes, plaid, or print, which saves cutting and sewing time and adds design interest to the garment. For a yoke cut on the bias, fuse the yoke with tricot interfacing to prevent stretching and to add body.

Another suggestion is to cut a yoke from a compatible but different fabric. Or embellish a yoke with decorative stitching.

Fast Rolled Yoke This is a fast way to sew a yoke to any garment. You can use this method for back yokes, as shown here, or for front/back yokes. This method is quick and eliminates the hand finishing usually required in sewing a yoke.

1 Cut two back yokes. One is the outer yoke, and the other is the yoke facing. Interface the outer yoke as needed.

2 Stitch the front and back garment pieces to the yoke, with right sides together. Trim the seam allowances, and press them toward the yoke.

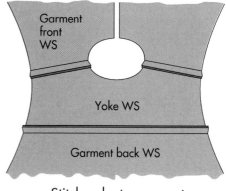

Stitch yoke to garment

3 Pin the right side of the back yoke facing to the wrong side of the garment back. Then stitch through all layers.

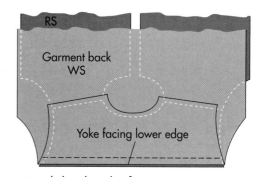

Stitch back yoke facing to garment

4 Roll the garment, and wrap the yoke facing completely around it so the lower edge of the yoke facings can be pinned to the garment fronts. Pin the right sides of the yoke facings to the wrong sides of the garment fronts. Then stitch through all layers.

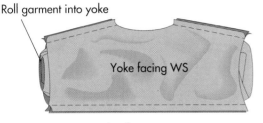

Sew yoke facings to garment

ditch from the right side, removing pins as you sew.

5 Pull the garment right side out through one armhole, and press.

6 Stitch the armhole edges together, and complete the garment.

Faster Topstitched Yoke

This topstitched yoke is easy for beginners to make and a perfect way to add design detail to a simple blouse.

1 Cut the yoke and yoke facing pieces. Press ½ inch (1.3 cm) to the wrong side along the bottom edge of the yoke facing only.

2 Stitch the yoke shoulder seams, and repeat for the yoke facing. Press the seams open from the wrong side, then the right side.

3 Stitch the yoke to the garment front and back pieces with right sides together. Trim the seam allowances, and press them toward the yoke.

4 Pin the right sides of the yoke facing to the wrong sides of the garment front pieces. Stitch through all layers, then trim the seam allowances with pinking shears, and press them toward the yoke.

5 Bring the yoke facing over the shoulders to the back yoke seam, and pin the seams in place from the right side. Topstitch in the

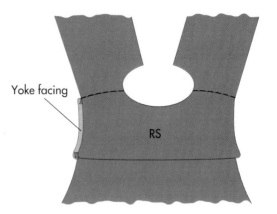

Topstitch front yoke facings in ditch

Fastest Faux Yoke

You can eliminate cutting a yoke and create the illusion of a yoke instead with topstitching or decorative stitches.

1 If the pattern has yoke pieces, pin the yoke pattern pieces to the garment pattern pieces, matching the seamlines so the fronts and backs of the garment can be cut as one.

2 Use a fabric marking pen to mark lines along the previous yoke/garment seamlines for stitching that will give the illusion of a separate yoke.

3 Place tear-away stabilizer under the fabric, and create the yoke illusion with stitching.

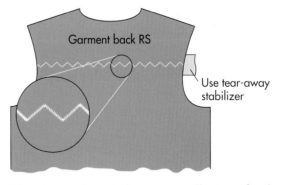

Use decorative stitch to create illusion of yoke

FastFasterFastest

FINISHING TECHNIQUES

Way back when I learned to sew, all the finishing work on a garment was sewn by hand. Once the seams, facings, and zippers were sewn, I took several evenings to hand sew the buttonholes, hems, buttons, and so on. Now I do most of that finishing work on my sewing machine with its many features that save hours of time finishing a garment. I hope this chapter will inspire you to get out your sewing machine instruction book and discover these timesaving features as well as others that will help you add new details to your creations.

BINDING

Binding is a very classic (and classy!) finish for the edges of just about any garment, but I especially like it for vests, jackets, and coats. Because binding eliminates the need for a facing, it is especially suitable for heavyweight and textured fabrics.

Binding Basics

Be sure your fabric is stable enough to support the weight of the binding. A fabric will usually support a binding made from the same or a similar weight fabric. If not, before cutting, use fusible tricot interfacing to stabilize the entire piece of fabric that you intend to add the binding to. Use the same fabric as the garment when the bound edge is not the focal point, or use a contrasting fabric to make the binding a design detail.

Staystitch the edges to be bound to prevent them from stretching as you apply the binding and to help the garment hug your body at the armholes and neckline. At armholes and other curved edges, place your finger behind the foot, and hold the fabric against the foot to crimp ease the edge slightly. When a garment pattern does not show binding, staystitch at the seamlines, then trim away the seam allowances on the edges to be bound.

Fast **Binding from a Bias Tape Maker** To make binding from any light- to medium-weight fabric, you can use a bias tape maker, which folds perfect binding strips. Then you can use fusible thread to "baste" the binding to the garment.

1 Use the 25-mm bias tape maker for 1-inch (2.5-cm) binding that folds to create ½-inch (1.3-cm) binding on the garment. (There are other sizes of bias tape makers available for wider and narrower bindings.) Cut strips 1⅞ inches (4.7 cm) wide on the bias or on the crosswise grain of the fabric. The bias will give more flexibility and add design interest when a plaid or stripe is used. The crosswise grain has less stretch and flexibility but is suitable for most fabrics and requires less yardage than bias-cut strips.

2 To join the strips, place one strip vertically and the other horizontally, then sew on a diagonal. (Joining the strips diagonally eliminates bulk from the seam when you stitch the binding to a garment.) Trim the excess.

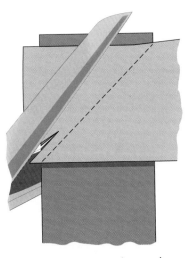

Join strips at right angles

3 Cut one end of the strip to a point to make it easier to insert into the bias tape maker. Insert the fabric strip with the wrong side up (toward the handle) into the wide end of the bias tape maker, and work the fabric out the narrow end with a straight pin inserted in the slot on the top of the bias tape maker.

4 At the ironing board, pull the strip through the bias tape maker. The edges of the strip will be folded to the wrong side as it comes out the narrow end of the bias tape maker. Press the strip as you pull it through, taking care not to distort the strip by pulling on it or giving it too much steam or pressure.

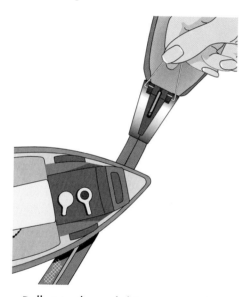

Pull strip through bias tape maker

5 Wind a bobbin with fusible thread. Use regular sewing thread in the needle. Leave about a 2-inch (5.1-cm) tail of the binding to make it easy to finish the ends later, and begin sewing the binding to the garment in an inconspicuous place such as the back neck or underarm.

To sew it onto the garment, unfold one edge of the binding, and place the right side edge of the unfolded binding strip to the edge of the wrong side of the garment. Do not bother to pin the binding in place; simply work with a length of binding as you stitch. Straight stitch the binding to the edge, sewing in the crease where the binding was folded and working with the binding on top so the fusible thread is on the right side of the garment.

Use fusible thread in bobbin

6 To finish the ends of the binding, fold back and press the ends of the binding on the bias where the ends will meet, cut the binding, and seam the ends together at the pressed crease.

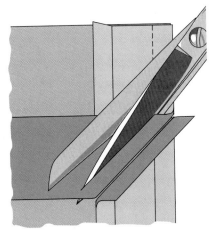

Finish binding where ends will meet

7 Replace the bobbin with a bobbin wound with regular sewing thread. Fold the binding strip to the right side, and press it in place, fusing the folded edge of the binding to the fusible thread.

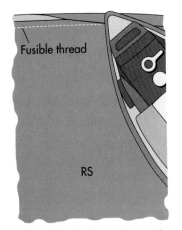

Fold binding to right side, and press

8 Topstitch the binding from the right side of the garment with your choice of plain or decorative stitches. A narrow zigzag or decorative stitch, such as a featherstitch, is more forgiving than a straight stitch—if a straight stitch is sewn slightly crooked, it is very obvious. My favorite decorative stitch for finishing sewing on binding is the heirloom appliqué stitch, which looks like a hand-picked stitch along the edge. I use a transparent embroidery foot for more visibility, and sew with the straight stitch in the ditch where the binding joins the fabric and the small zigzag jumps just onto the edge of the binding. If you do not have a special stitch for this use, try a blindhem stitch. Experiment with different stitch lengths and widths.

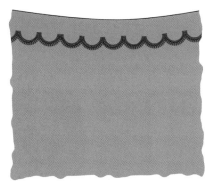

Use decorative stitch to sew binding

Faster Binding That Doesn't Fray
Make your own binding from a fabric that does not fray and has stretch. Some of the neatest bindings have been made from Lycra swimwear fabrics, knits, velours, and artificial leathers and suedes.

1 Determine the desired width of your finished binding. A good size is ½ to ¾ inch (1.3 to 1.9 cm). Your seam allowance will be the same measurement as your finished binding. Cut the binding strips across the stretch of the fabric four times the width of your finished binding. For example, for ½-inch (1.3-cm) binding, cut 2-inch (5.1-cm) strips, and use a ½-inch (1.3-cm) seam allowance.

2 Seam strips end to end with a ¼-inch (0.6-cm) seam, and press the seams open.

3 Place the right side of the binding to the right side of the garment. In an inconspicuous place on the garment, begin sewing 2 inches (5.1 cm) from the end of the binding. (This leaves an allowance for finishing the ends of the binding when they meet.) Stitch the binding in place, sewing with the binding down against the feed teeth of the sewing machine. This helps prevent the garment from inching ahead of the binding, causing a rippled edge along the binding, especially on the curves.

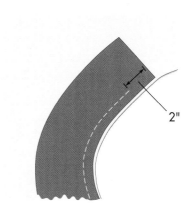

Begin 2" in from end of binding

HERE'S WHAT **I DO**...

to Miter Corners

Here's an easy way to stitch a mitered corner in a bias-bound edge. The trick is in the way the corner is stitched and the way fusible thread is used.

1 To miter the corner, put fusible thread in the bobbin and the binding on top, sew toward the corner, and stop with the needle down one binding width from the end of the edge.

2 Raise the presser foot. Pivot the point edge, and stitch diagonally right to the corner.

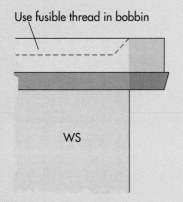

Use fusible thread in bobbin

WS

Stitch diagonally to corner

3 Cut the threads, and fold the binding back on the diagonal stitching until a fold is created at the edge. Then line up the binding along the new edge. Begin sewing where the diagonal fold is under the binding. Do not catch the fold in the stitching.

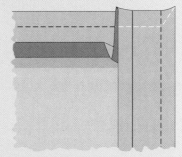

Continue stitching from fold

4 Fold the corner to the right side, creating a mitered fold, and press it to the fusible thread.

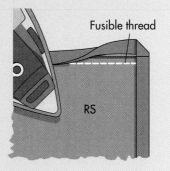

Fusible thread

RS

Press corner to fusible thread

4 Fold the binding to the wrong side of the garment, and pin in the ditch on the right side. Use the edge/joining foot on your sewing machine, and stitch in the ditch from the right side.

5 Trim away the excess binding from the wrong side of the garment.

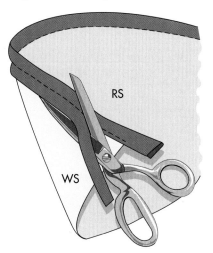

Stitch binding in ditch and trim

Fastest **Serger Binding** A three-thread–wide overlock stitch is used to create serger binding.

1 With standard sewing threads and a balanced three-thread stitch at normal stitch length of 2, serge around the edges of the garment, trimming the edges to the binding-edge line. Engage the differential feed slightly (1.2 to 1.5) at the curves to keep their shape.

2 Place heavy decorative serger thread in the upper looper and normal sewing thread in the lower looper and needle. Set tensions for a balanced stitch. As a general rule, the heavier the thread, the lower the tension. Begin sewing on scraps, and reduce the upper looper tension one number at a time until the stitch looks good. Set a short stitch length for a satin stitch binding look.

3 Begin at an inconspicuous place, and serge around the edges of the garment. Overlap several stitches at the start, and weave the thread tails into the stitch with a tapestry needle.

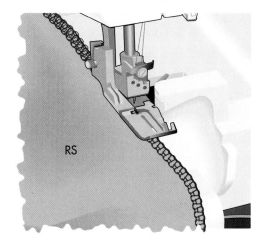

Serge second layer with decorative thread

on the
FAST
TRACK. . .

to Bias Strips

Here's a quick way to make bias strips for binding. Begin with about a yard of fabric. Lay it flat, and fold the selvage edge to the crosswise raw edge to form a triangle. The fold is on the bias. Cut along this folded edge with your rotary cutter and ruler. Fold the bias edge in half. (The folded edge is now double.) You can fold it one more time if desired. Use your rotary cutter to trim away the fold, then cut the binding strips along this bias edge.

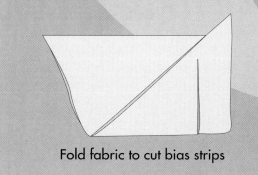

Fold fabric to cut bias strips

BELT LOOPS

When I see that a pattern calls for belt loops, I am sometimes tempted to leave them off. But belt loops are a finishing detail that must not be forgotten. I sew the two loops on the side of the garment, then in order for a belt really to stay in place, I add a loop near the center front, which is hidden by the buckle. This keeps the belt in place at the tummy.

Fast **Self-Fabric Belt Loops** As a rule, I prefer to put inconspicuous self-fabric belt loops on skirts and pants.

1 Cut a crosswise grain fabric strip about ⅞ inches (2.2 cm) wide.

2 If you have a bias-binder foot for your machine, put the fabric strip into the foot, and stitch with a twin needle. If you do not have a binding foot, make a folded bias strip with a bias tape maker, then stitch it with a twin needle.

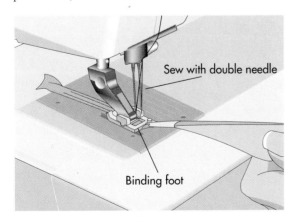

Make belt loops from folded bias strips

3 To make one belt loop, cut a length of the sewn strip the width of the belt plus 1 inch (2.5 cm) for ease and seam allowances.

4 Press ¼ inch (0.6 cm) to the wrong side on each end of the strip, then position the strip on the garment and bartack it in place. For a quick bartack, lower the feed teeth, set your machine for a wide zigzag, and stitch back and forth over the belt loop end.

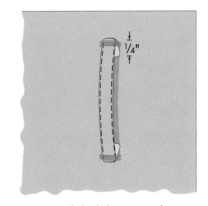

Bartack belt loop in place

Faster **Serged Self-Fabric Belt Loops** Use a flatlock stitch to make quick belt loops.

1 Cut a crosswise grain strip of fabric twice the desired width of the belt loop. For example, to make a finished belt loop ½ inch (1.3 cm) wide, cut a 1-inch (2.5-cm) strip.

2 Fold the strip lengthwise with wrong sides together. Set your serger for a three-thread flatlock stitch. (The usual settings for a flatlock stitch are needle tension 0, upper looper tension normal, and lower looper tension increased slightly.)

HERE'S WHAT **I DO**...

to Get Even Flatlock Serging

If your serger has a blindhem foot or multipurpose foot, use it for flatlock. Adjust the flange guide so when the edge of the fabric is against it, the stitches will loop slightly off the fabric edge. This results in a very flat finished stitch because there is some space for it to lie flat.

3 Flatlock stitch along the raw edge of the belt loop strip, letting the stitch loop fall slightly off the edge of the fabric. Pull the strip so the stitch lies flat.

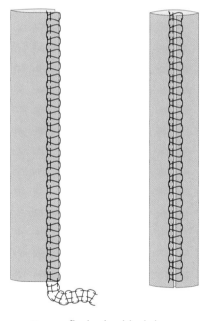

Serge flatlocked belt loop

4 Press the belt loop strip with the flatlock seam at the back side. Then trim the length of the flatlocked strip to the width of the belt plus ease and ½ inch (1.3 cm), and bartack the belt loop to the garment.

Fastest **Serger-Chain Belt Loops**

You can create thread-chain belt loops with the rolled edge on your serger.

1 Set your serger for a three-thread rolled edge, and thread with the color you need for your belt loops.

2 Serge a long chain of stitching with no fabric under the presser foot.

3 Cut the chain into belt loop lengths, and knot each end with an overhand knot. Stitch the chains into the seams of the garment as it is constructed, or hand stitch the chains in place.

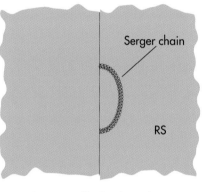

Serge rolled-edge chain

HERE'S WHAT **I DO**...

to Stock Up on Extra Lengths of Serger Chains

Since I am always looking for ways to save time when I sew, I like to stock up in advance whenever I can. So every time I have my serger set for a rolled edge, I serge off about 24 inches (61 cm) of thread chain, and put it into my belt loop box. Then when I need belt loops for a dress, I often have just the right color in the box.

BUTTON LOOPS

Button loops eliminate the need for buttonholes and add design detail. They are most often used when center front or center back pieces meet rather than overlap, but you can add interest to any garment by adding buttons and button loops to pockets and cuffs. Also, the keyhole opening at the back of a blouse usually requires at least one button loop to close it.

Fast Fabric-Tube Button Loops I usually make fabric tubes for button loops from the same fabric as the garment. The Fasturn tube turners make this easy. (See "Sources" on page 203 and "Sue's Snippets: A Success Story" on this page.) You can make flat tubes, or you can make padded loops by filling a fabric tube with cord or yarn as you turn it. You can also make great knotted buttons from padded tubing.

1. Use the Size 1 or Size 2 Fasturn cylinder (depending on the weight of the fabric) for a finished tube of $\frac{3}{16}$ inch (0.5 cm) in diameter. Cut a crosswise-grain or bias fabric strip 1 inch (2.5 cm) wide.

2. Set your machine for a straight stitch at a short stitch length of 1, and sew the fabric strip with right sides together with a $\frac{1}{4}$-inch (0.6-cm) seam allowance. Use a tiny zigzag or lightning stitch so the stitch has a little strength and stretch when you turn the tube. (See "Sources" on page 203 for the Fasturn sewing machine foot, which actually folds and guides the fabric for perfectly straight stitching.) Trim the seam allowance to $\frac{1}{8}$ inch (0.3 cm).

3. Pull the fabric tube over the Fasturn cylinder, folding the end of the fabric over the end of the tube.

4. Insert the corresponding wire into the tube, and twist the spiral point of the wire into the fabric. Twist the wire to the right to bring the

curly end through the fabric, which is folded over the end of the cylinder.

5 Spread open the seam allowance of the tube with your fingers as you begin to pull the handle of the wire, pulling the fabric tube into the cylinder. Magically, the seam allowance will open flat as it is pulled through. Continue pulling the tube through the cylinder until it is completely turned right side out. If you want to make a padded loop, place a piece of cord or yarn at the tube opening before pulling the fabric back through the tube. (It will get sucked into the tube with the fabric.)

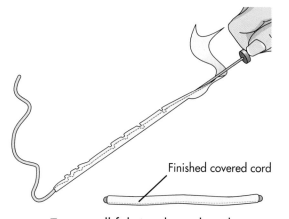

Finished covered cord

Turn small fabric tube right side out

6 Press the fabric tube flat, placing the seam allowance in the center of the back or along one edge.

7 To make one button loop, measure a length of tube that will make a loop large enough to go over the button or knot, add seam allowances, and cut. Stitch the loops into the seam as you apply the garment facing or lining, or stitch them to the garment by hand.

Faster Loops from Satin-Stitched Cord For quick button loops guaranteed to match your garment, make a thread-

covered cord by satin stitching over rat-tail cord, gimp cord, or yarn. The size of the cord depends on how large you want the loops to be.

1 Thread your sewing machine top and bobbin with thread the color and type desired for the loops. For decorative detail, I love to make loops from decorative rayon thread in a color that complements my garment.

2 Use a sewing machine presser foot that has a tunnel on the underside to allow the cord to pass through. Many machines have a braiding foot for this purpose, but a buttonhole, piping, or pintucking foot will do.

3 Set a satin stitch zigzag at a width just wide enough to sew the zigzag over the cord.

4 Satin stitch over the cord as you guide it under the presser foot.

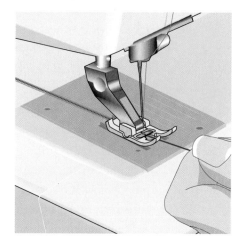

Satin stitch over cord

5 Cut lengths of satin-stitched cord long enough to go over the buttons easily plus seam allowances. Put fray-stopping liquid on the stitches on each end of the cords, and stitch the cords into the seam, or stitch them in place by hand.

on the FAST TRACK...

to Serged Button Loops

Create satin-stitched covered cord even faster on your serger. Thread your serger for a three-thread stitch at a width that will serge over the cord.

Set a stitch length short enough to cover the cord without the stitches bunching up. Serge over the cord, guiding it so the needle swings over the cord without stitching into it. Many sergers have a hole in the presser foot to guide the cord right into the stitch.

Fastest Round-Elastic–Thread Loops Elastic-thread loops are perfect for button loops that are functional rather than decorative. You can simply cut a length of round-elastic thread long enough to go over the button plus seam allowances, and stitch it in place in the seam as the facing is sewn on. If you are creating a row of button loops, you can also zigzag a length of elastic thread along the finished edge of the garment.

1 Set your machine for a long zigzag stitch of 4, lay the elastic along the seamline on the right side of the garment (before the facing is sewn in place), and stitch the elastic with the swing of the zigzag jumping over the elastic thread.

2 When you have sewn the entire edge, end the zigzag stitching, but do not cut off the end of the elastic until you have formed the button loops.

3 Match the elastic-thread edge to the button edge of the garment, and pull the elastic thread away from the edge to create loops the right size to go over the buttons. Many times if the buttons are small, the elastic in the thread is enough to stretch over the buttons without having to pull out excess loops.

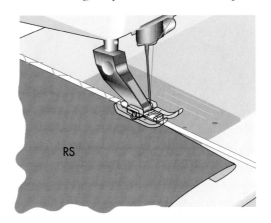

Zigzag elastic thread into seam

4 Once you are satisfied that the elastic button loops are the correct length, finish the ends by tying them off and/or hand stitching them in place. Secure them at the ends so they don't slip. To do this, sew the facing to the garment with the elastic-thread loops facing toward the garment. Be careful not to cut the thread when trimming the seam. In most garments, you can usually catch the ends in a hem and facing later.

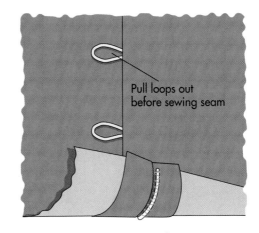

Pull loops out before sewing seam

Sew loops into facing

Nancy's Scarf

Using less than a yard of loosely woven fabric, you can make this warm winter accessory in about 30 minutes.

At the first meeting for this book, my previous editor, Nancy Fawley, put on her coat to leave for the day and slipped on a warm scarf she had hand knit. I was immediately intrigued by a large loop at one corner. She pulled the scarf through the loop for a warm, comfortable, and attractive look that stayed in place. I insisted that we make the scarf in fabric and share it in this book.

1. To create Nancy's scarf in fabric, cut a 20-by-28-inch (50.8-by-71.1-cm) piece of any loosely woven fabric in a wonderful fiber, such as silk, mohair, or lightweight wool. This scarf also works well in knit fabrics. Finish the edges with an edge appropriate to the fabric type, or fringe the edges.

For the scarf shown here, I fringed a few threads from each edge of my tweed weave, then stitched around the edges with a blanket-type stitch on my sewing machine, which gave the fringe a tied look.

2. To make the loop, you will need a finished tube of fabric 10 to 12 inches (25.4 to 30.5 cm) long. Make the strip shorter for silk and lightweight fabrics and longer for wool so the loop will be long enough for you to pull the scarf through easily but short enough to hold the scarf without slipping. I cut the loop from the selvage. A piece of ribbon or trim would work, too.

3. For a self-fabric loop that is 12 inches (30.5 cm) long, cut a strip of the same fabric 1¼ inches (3.2 cm) wide and 16 inches (40.6 cm) long, fold it lengthwise with right sides together, and straight stitch along the long edge of the strip with a ¼-inch (0.6-cm) seam allowance. (I like to use my forward-and-reverse-motion straight-stretch stitch for strength.)

4. Trim the seam allowance with pinking shears, and turn the tube to the right side with a Fasturn tube turner. (See "Sources" on page 203.)

5. Tuck the raw ends into the fabric tube, and stitch the fabric tube as a loop in one corner of the scarf.

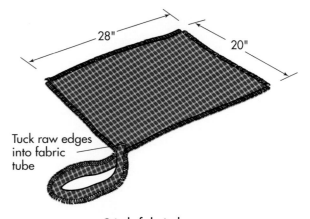

Stitch fabric loop
in one corner of scarf

6. When wearing the scarf, place the loop on your shoulder, slip the scarf through the loop, and adjust it at your neck. The loop keeps your scarf from sliding around or falling off.

BUTTONS

Buttons and snaps are so quick to stitch on the machine that I rarely ever sew them by hand anymore. Recently I was in a hotel room finishing a blouse and had no sewing machine. It took me 20 minutes to sew buttons that I could have sewn in 2 minutes by machine!

Fast **Hand-Sewn Buttons** Occasionally it is easier to sew a button on by hand than by machine, as in the case of shank-style buttons. It's also handy to have some quick tricks when the final finishing steps on a garment are going to be completed in the car or on an airplane.

HERE'S WHAT I DO...
to Remove New Buttons from Cards

Recently I was with a student while she was trying to take the buttons off the button card. I showed her a simple trick, and she said, "Be sure to include that in your book." When buttons are stapled onto a card, put a straight pin through the staple on the wrong side of the cardboard, and pull the button off from the right side. The pin keeps the staple from pulling out of the cardboard with the button. (The pin usually has to be thrown away because it is bent by the time all the buttons are off, but what a time-saver!)

1 To cut the sewing time in half, thread a hand-sewing needle with a double thickness of thread. To do this, pull a length of thread off the spool, take hold of it in the middle, and fold it to make two equal lengths. Take the tiny loop formed at the middle, and thread it through the needle. Pull the loop of the thread even with the thread ends, and knot the loop and the ends together. Now you can sew the buttons on with four strands at once.

2 Stitch the button in place with the four thicknesses of thread. This should require taking only two stitches.

3 If the button does not already have a shank, you can create a thread shank by bringing the thread to the right side under the button. Wrap the thread around the stitches that are holding the button in place several times to form the shank.

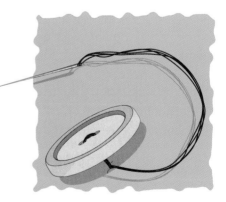

Create thread shank

4 Bring the thread to the wrong side, and stitch in place from the wrong side to knot off the thread.

HERE'S WHAT **I DO**...
to Mark Buttons and Snaps

To mark the placement of the buttons easily, I like to stitch and cut the buttonholes first. Then I overlap the buttonholes over the button area, and mark button placement with a fabric marking pen right through the buttonholes. This is a very fast and accurate way to mark.

To mark snap and hook-and-eye placement, lap the garment pieces to the correct placement, and stick a straight pin through both layers. Mark at the pin on both pieces with a fabric marking pen.

Faster **Buttons and Snaps Sewn by Machine**
One very fast way to attach a button is to sew it on by machine. Snaps, hooks and eyes, and skirt hooks are just as easy to machine sew as buttons. The advantage of sewing any of these fasteners by machine is that they will be much stronger than when sewn by hand. Many people think machine-sewn buttons will be like those done by manufacturers that pull off the minute a thread is loose. Quite the contrary. When sewn by machine at home, the fastener is actually sewn with a lockstitch, and the stitch is tied off at the end.

1 To place the buttons, use a fabric-glue stick to put a dab of glue on the bottom of each button, and stick the button to the garment. You can also tape the button in place with transparent tape. (Use the frosty type or a piece of pressure-sensitive web. I find that you can stitch right into the frosty tape, but the old-fashioned clear kind will stick to your needle.)

2 Set your sewing machine for a medium zigzag stitch width of 3, drop the feed teeth (or cover them), and change to a button-sewing presser foot. (Often, because the feet on my machine snap off of the shank, I just use the shank. Then when I lower the presser foot, the shank comes down on the button and holds it in place.)

3 Place the button under the needle, and walk the machine through one complete zigzag stitch *with the handwheel* to be sure the needle drops into the holes of the button. If the needle hits the button, adjust the width of the stitch, and/or reposition the button as needed.

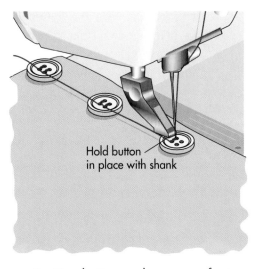

Hold button in place with shank

Position button under presser foot

4 Zigzag about six times to stitch the button on. If you have a tying-off function on your computerized machine, use this function to tie off the stitches. Otherwise, set the machine for a straight stitch, position the button so the needle is over a hole, and stitch in place several times to lock the threads. Move to the next holes or to the next button. I don't cut the thread tails, but carry my threads instead until all the buttons have been sewn in place. It is faster!

HERE'S WHAT **I DO**...

to Make Designer Buttons

Once I was looking for toggle-type buttons for a casual-style jacket and could not find the right color or type of button. So I decided to make my own one-of-a-kind matching toggle buttons with self-fabric. I call them "butterhorn-roll" buttons because my parents loved to make this type of roll on holidays, and the steps to roll the button are the same.

You can use fabric scraps from the garment, or you can create a design detail with a contrasting or color-coordinated fabric. Cut a triangle of fabric about 2 inches (5.1 cm) at the base and 3 inches (7.6 cm) on the other two sides. Finish all the edges with a serger stitch or satin stitch, or hem as desired. Roll the triangle beginning at the 2-inch (5.1-cm) base edge and rolling toward the point. Secure with hand stitching, and stitch in place as a toggle button.

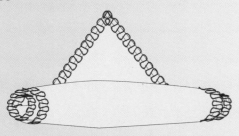

Tack point of triangle to back side

Make "butterhorn-roll" button

Fastest **Programmed Stitches** If you have a programmable computerized sewing machine that doesn't already have a built-in button-sewing program, you can create your own program to make sewing on buttons by machine fly by in a flash. Then save the program in memory for the next time.

1 Consult your sewing machine instruction book on programming.

2 In the program mode, enter six zigzag stitches at a width of 3, then enter a stop or finishing stitch.

3 To sew buttons on, simply bring up the button-sewing program, drop the feed teeth, place a button under the needle, test the button placement and the stitch width by taking one stitch with the handwheel, and sew. If you don't mind taking a little extra time, sew buttons on with a decorative detail. You can actually make the stitching look like flowers and leaves. I use contrasting thread colors to create a design in the holes in the buttons.

Embellish buttons with contrasting thread

BUTTONHOLES

Buttonholes can make or break a garment. Whether they are supposed to stand out as a design focal point or are meant to be inconspicuous like the buttonholes on a workshirt, they need to be uniform and well sewn. If making buttonholes is right up there on your list of necessary evils (alongside washing dishes), this section may help you turn a dreaded task into an opportunity for fun and creativity.

Buttonhole Basics

When considering a new sewing machine, be sure to see what kinds of buttonholes the machine offers. Take samples of fabric to the sewing machine dealer, and stitch several types of buttonholes as a test. Try a bartack buttonhole for tailored shirts, blouses, and dresses and a round-end buttonhole for less tailored

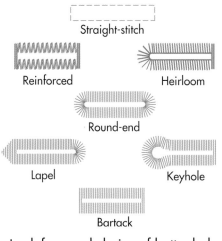

Straight-stitch

Reinforced · Heirloom

Round-end

Lapel · Keyhole

Bartack

Look for good choice of buttonholes

garments. A keyhole buttonhole is best for coats and suit jackets. Specialty hand-look buttonholes for heirloom garments, reinforced buttonholes for heavy-duty and stretch fabrics, straight-stitch buttonholes for leather, and patch-method bound buttonholes are all nice features to look for in a sewing machine.

Stability First

Always stabilize buttonholes! In most cases, buttonholes are stitched in a part of the garment that has already been interfaced. But this is not always enough. To add some extra stability to ensure the buttonhole doesn't stretch or sag, it never hurts to place a piece of tear-away stabilizer under the buttonhole. On napped fabrics, use a piece of water-soluble stabilizer on top as you are stitching the buttonhole. On dark fabrics where the white leftover of the tear-away stabilizer is noticeable later, place water-soluble stabilizer on both sides. Using these additional stabilizers helps your stitches in satin-stitched buttonholes lay up out of the fabric.

Stitch Away

When sewing a buttonhole, stitch away from the bulky edge of the garment so that the column of the buttonhole that stitches toward you comes toward the faced edge or other bulky area of the garment.

Reduce the top tension for a satin-stitched buttonhole. When there is less pull on the top thread, it is pulled slightly to the underside of the fabric, which creates a prettier satin stitch.

SUE'S SNIPPETS

BUTTONHOLES THAT EMBELLISH

I sometimes make buttonholes the focal point and the design detail on a garment. Buttonholes stitched on the diagonal or decorative motifs added to the ends of buttonholes are special effects that are often featured on designer garments.

Designer Valentino calls his buttonhole design detail "ribbon edging." In his ready-to-wear collections, his bright blue cashmere-blend jacket with green lapel accents and a matching slim skirt carries a price tag of $3,160. But not if you sew!

Patti Jo Larson, one of our Husqvarna Viking educators, calls it the "buttonhole jacket" and recreated the look with ⅝-inch (1.6-cm) buttonholes evenly spaced every ⅝ inch (1.6 cm) along the front edge of a Chanel-type jacket. Weave a ⅝-inch (1.6-cm) ribbon or strip of artificial suede through the buttonholes, and change the ribbon for the occasion or season.

There is really no special formula. You set the tone by the width of the ribbon, the spacing between the buttonholes, and the distance the buttonholes fall from the edge of your jacket. What a unique and stylish way to update a favorite outdated jacket or to add a designer touch to a yet-to-be constructed jacket.

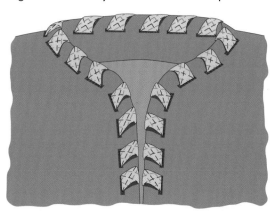

Use buttonholes as design detail

Stitch away from
bulk of garment

Go for a Clean Finish

After stitching a buttonhole but before cutting it open, use a toothpick to place a bead of fray-stopping liquid down the center of the buttonhole. Let the liquid dry, then place a pin at each end of the buttonhole before cutting it open. The pins prevent cutting beyond the ends of the buttonhole. Better yet, use a buttonhole chisel and mat, which is a relatively inexpensive notion you will appreciate over and over.

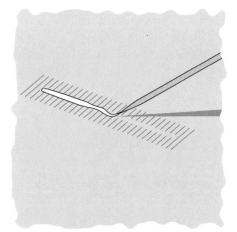

Lock in buttonhole threads with
fray-stopping liquid

Fray-Free Buttonholes

Rhonda Chaney, who chairs the Fashion Design Program at La Cañada College in California, brought a great tip when she was a guest on my "America Sews" television program. To prevent the threads in a buttonhole opening from fraying, place fusible web strips on the top and on the underside of the fabric at the buttonhole markings so the buttonhole will be sewn right through the fusible web. (Do not press it yet!)

After the buttonhole has been stitched, tear away the excess fusible web. Place a nonstick press sheet or a sheet of paper under and on top of the buttonhole to absorb any excess web, and press the buttonhole with an iron. The fusible web melts into the stitching, which strengthens the buttonhole and traps the fibers in the buttonhole opening.

Fast **Bound Buttonholes** Bound buttonholes can really make a garment special. And this patch method makes it easy to create the lips of the buttonhole in a contrasting fabric for a real designer look. If you practice making several of these easy buttonholes, you will want to add them to your next jacket for sure. If you have a straight-stitch buttonhole on your sewing machine, these bound buttonholes will go even faster because the first step is sewn automatically by the straight-stitch–buttonhole machine stitch. Even the old buttonhole attachments have a template for a straight-stitch buttonhole that works.

Use straight-stitch buttonhole

Bound buttonholes should be made at the first stage of garment construction, right after the interfacing has been fused to the wrong side of the garment front. If no interfacing is called for, interface at least in the area of the buttonhole with fusible tricot or weft-insertion interfacing before beginning the buttonholes.

1 Mark the buttonhole placement on the right side of the garment. Be sure to mark the length accurately.

2 Cut one 3-inch (7.6-cm)-wide strip of fabric on the crosswise grain. Cut the strip into one rectangle for each buttonhole lip, cutting a length 2 inches (5.1 cm) long for a buttonhole up to 1½ inches (3.8 cm) long. Add another inch for a larger buttonhole.

3 Press a crease lengthwise across the center of the rectangle, then place the crease at the buttonhole marking with the right side of the rectangle to the right side of the garment. Pin the rectangle in place, and mark the buttonhole length with pins.

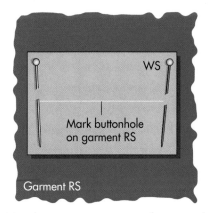

Match crease in center of rectangle to buttonhole on garment RS

4 Stitch a straight-stitch buttonhole on the rectangle, or with a short stitch length of 1, sew a box around the buttonhole marking with about ¼ inch (0.6 cm) between the marking

and the stitching on both sides. It is important that these rows be the same distance above and below the buttonhole marking line because this will form the lips of the bound buttonhole.

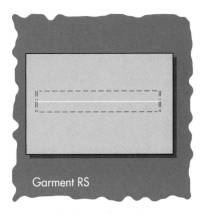

Stitch buttonhole box

5 Cut the center of the buttonhole along the marking line, stopping when you get to ¼ inch (0.6 cm) from each end. Make short cuts from the end of the center to each corner on the diagonal, as illustrated below. You can do this with small scissors, but for very accurate, easy cutting that gives cleanly finished buttonholes, I prefer to use a buttonhole chisel and board.

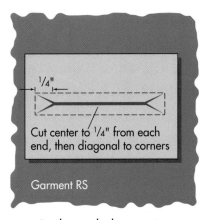

Cut buttonhole opening

6 Press open the seams of the fabric rectangle. (As shown in the illustration, press only the seams of the rectangle, but not the seams of the buttonhole cut in the garment.) And press the triangles at the ends of the rectangle away from the buttonhole.

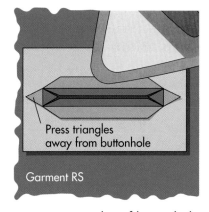

Press open sides of buttonhole

7 Pull the rectangle through the opening to the wrong side of the garment. Fold the rectangle so the lips of the bound buttonhole are formed and an inverted pleat that meets at the center of the buttonhole opening is formed on the wrong side. Press.

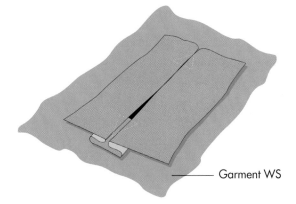

Pull rectangle to wrong side, and press

8 From the right side of the garment, fold back the end of the buttonhole to expose the triangle. With a short stitch length of 1.5 to 2, stitch across the base of the triangle, catching the pleat of the rectangle to secure

it. Be careful not to stitch into the garment fabric.

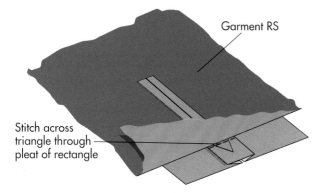

Garment RS

Stitch across triangle through pleat of rectangle

Stitch across triangle

9 When the garment is completed, match the facing to the buttonhole, and slit the facing just at the buttonhole. Fold back the raw edges of the facing slit, and slip stitch the facing edges to the back side of the bound buttonhole.

Faster **Corded Machine Buttonholes** Whatever the age or make of the sewing machine you have, it probably makes buttonholes. If so, it will also make corded buttonholes with a little help from you. A corded buttonhole is stronger and won't stretch out as you button and unbutton through it. You can use pearl cotton, topstitching thread, or any heavy gimp for the cord. Match the fabric color if possible. Some machines have special ways to make corded buttonholes, so check your instruction book for information.

1 Mark the buttonhole placement on the right side of the garment.

2 If your buttonhole foot has a special finger for cord, loop the cord over it. Otherwise, put the needle into the fabric, and wrap the cord around the needle. As you begin to sew, guide the cord into the satin stitch column on the underside of

the buttonhole foot. Begin sewing at one end of the buttonhole. Once it is started, the column will sew right over the cord without guidance.

Note: It is always easier to sew the buttonhole away from you because you can see the starting point as you come back to it. On most sewing machines that sew forward first, you can select the order of the satin columns to sew backward first. Try it!

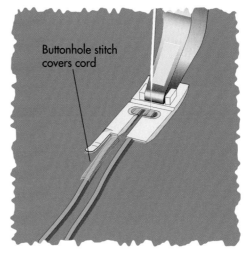

Buttonhole stitch covers cord

Couch cord under buttonhole stitching

3 When the buttonhole reaches the correct length, catch the cord in the bartack at the end of the buttonhole, and guide the cord into the other satin column.

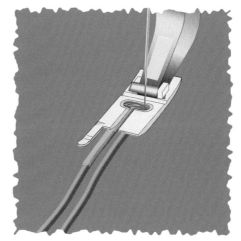

Catch cord in bartack (shown in pink for clarity)

4 At the final end, stop sewing with the needle in the fabric, and cross the ends of the cord in front of the needle. Stitch the bartack over the cord. Use a tapestry needle to pull the cord ends to the wrong side of the buttonhole, and tie them off.

Stitch bartack over loose ends of cord (bartacks shown in pink for clarity)

Fastest Computer Buttonholes

If you are a serious sewer, a computerized sewing machine can save you a great deal of time and frustration in many areas of sewing. Buttonholes are one major reason to make the investment in a quality computerized sewing machine. A sensor buttonhole foot plugs in to the machine and senses (actually measures) the length of the buttonhole as you stitch it, telling the machine when and where to start and stop sewing. Because each buttonhole is measured (instead of counting stitches), the buttonholes will all be the same length even if there are different thicknesses of fabrics to sew over, which require varying numbers of stitches.

1 Mark the starting point of the buttonhole on the garment. Install the sensor buttonhole foot on your machine. Enter the type and the length of your desired buttonhole into the machine.

2 Begin sewing. The sensor foot will do the rest. The buttonhole is sewn and tied off automatically. Now continue making as many identical buttonholes as your heart desires and the garment requires.

HEMS

In traditional sewing, hems were stitched by hand. Today we can sew the hems on most garments by machine. The only trouble is, we have so many quick sewing machine and serger hem options that it is sometimes hard to choose which one to use!

To finish the edge of the hem allowance before stitching the hem, see the options in "Edge Finishes" on page 80. When finishing the hem allowance on a serger, you can use the differential feed on the serger to ease full hems to fit.

Fast **Machine Blind Hem** Today most sewing machines have two blindhem options, one for wovens and one for knit or stretchy-type fabrics. The woven blind hem is a series of straight stitches with a zigzag every fourth stitch or so that actually catches the hem.

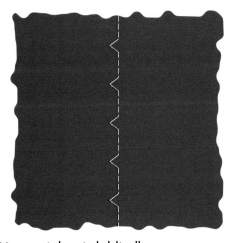

Use straight-stitch blindhem on wovens

The stretch blind hem has one wide zigzag and a series of tiny zigzag stitches in place of the straight stitches in the regular blindhem stitch. These extra stitches provide "give," making this a good stitch for hemming knits and stretchy fabrics.

Use stretch blindhem stitch on knits

The key to an invisible blind hem is a blindhem foot. This foot has a flange or guide. You can position the fabric in the machine so the guide rides along the fold of the hem. Then you can adjust the width of the zigzag so it catches only a few threads of the fold. Check your sewing machine instruction book to see if you have a blindhem foot. Most machines come with this type of foot. Or visit your sewing machine dealer to buy one; they are available for all machines that have a blindhem stitch.

1 Press the hem to the wrong side of the garment as you normally would. Pin the hem with the pins perpendicular to the hem and with the first "bite" of the pin ¼ inch (0.6 cm)

from the hem edge. (You will fold the hem back along this ¼-inch [0.6-cm] pin edge.)

2 Fold the hem to the right side so that a ¼-inch (0.6-cm) edge of the wrong side of the hem extends.

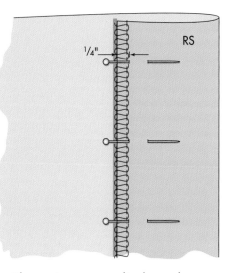

Place pins perpendicular to hem

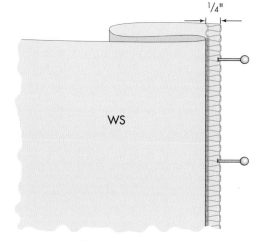

Fold hem to right side

on the
FAST TRACK...

to Rolled Hems

It can be frustrating and often impossible to sew a rolled hem on curves. That's where the serger rolled edge comes in handy as a quick, easy substitute for a rolled hem—on curves as well as on straight hems.

The serger rolled edge has revolutionized edge finishing. I call it an edge because the hem is right on the edge of the fabric. Because you see only the upper looper thread on a serger rolled edge, thread the upper looper with a decorative thread such as rayon embroidery thread for a shiny look or wooly nylon for a fuzzier look, or try invisible thread so the edge doesn't show. You can use the rolled edge to finish ruffles, scarves, blouses, and more—in a flash.

1 Consult your instruction book on how to set your serger for a rolled edge. As a general rule, increase the lower looper tension to pull the upper looper threads around the edge to the wrong side of the fabric, creating a roll in the fabric.

2 Place the fabric with the hemline at the cutter. Any excess fabric will be trimmed away by the cutter.

3 Serge the rolled edge, adjusting the stitch length as desired. Traditionally, the rolled edge has a short satin stitch length of 1 or less, but I really like the picot length of 1.5 to 2 for many projects, especially scarves.

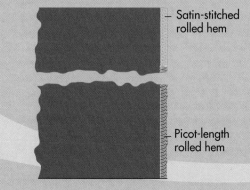

Satin-stitched rolled hem

Picot-length rolled hem

Serge narrow rolled hem on curves

3 Set your machine for the blindhem stitch at a length of 1 and a width of 3 to 4. (See Step 5, below, for how to fine-tune the width adjustment.)

4 Place the ¼-inch (0.6-cm) extension with the wrong side up under the presser foot and with the fold of the hem against the guide on the presser foot.

5 Stitch along the ¼-inch (0.6-cm) extension so the wider zigzag just catches the fold of the fabric. Remove the pins as you approach them. Adjust the width of the stitch so that just a few threads of the fold are caught.

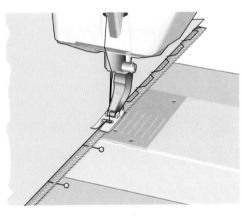

Catch fold with zigzag

HERE'S WHAT **I DO**...
to Erase Hem Crease

A hem crease can often be re-moved by mixing 1 part white vinegar and 9 parts water in a spray bottle. Mist the crease, then press it flat. (This mixture also helps set creases and pleats.)

If all else fails, experiment with putting a design detail, such as piping or decorative stitching, over the crease. Sew several rows so the purpose of the thread is not to hide but to embellish.

on the FAST TRACK...
to Serged Hems

When a blouse will be tucked in, I never turn the hem. I simply serge around the bottom of the blouse with a four-thread balanced stitch at normal tension and stitch length for a hem that adds no bulk.

Faster **Topstitched Hem** For a quick topstitched hem, I like to use a single or twin needle. The trick that makes this finished hem look professional is to sew with the hem on the underside and the garment on top. With the fabric in this position, if the hem is slightly curved, the feed teeth will ease any extra fullness at the edge of the seam allowance.

My favorite is the twin-needle topstitched hem, which must be stitched from the right side of the garment. There are several different spacings between the two needles. I like the 4.0 and 6.0 needle for hemming because it creates two rows of topstitching up to ¼ inch (0.6 cm) apart and the rows are perfectly straight (with each other). There are several types of twin needles. The universal will sew most fabrics. For stretch fabrics, use a stretch twin needle to avoid skipped stitches. And for denim and other tightly woven fabrics, use the jeans sharp-point twin needle. Because there is only one bobbin picking up both of the needle threads, a zigzag is formed on the underside of the garment, lending more stretch to the hem of the garment. Sew with a longer stitch length and a reduced tension when using wooly nylon because the thread is thicker and actually has stretch.

1 Finish the raw edge of the hem allowance. Press to the wrong side, and pin as needed from the right side.

2 Place a twin needle in the machine. Topstitch the hem by sewing from the right side. This takes some getting used to, but because the feed teeth move the hem evenly with the garment, it produces the best results. Usually you can actually see the ridge of the hem on the right side. If not, with accurate hem measuring, you can follow the correct seam guide on the machine needle plate.

Topstitch hem with twin needle

HERE'S WHAT **I DO**...
to Hem Lightweight Fabrics

I call this hem a floating blind hem because I use it on garments made from very lightweight fabrics. Some of the threads in the stitch actually float off the fabric.

Press and pin the hem, as explained in the *Fast* blindhem technique on page 167, but fold it back so the edge of the hem is even with the fold. Sew just off the edge of the fabric, letting the zigzag stitch catch the fold of the fabric. This is an easy hem to remove later because there are only a few stitches to snip, so use it on garments that may require future alterations in length.

Fastest **Hem with a Serger Cover Stitch** The cover stitch found on top-of-the-line sergers today is probably the most desired stitch of the last few years. It is the same stitch used in ready-to-wear for hems, swimwear elastic, knit ribbings, and many other finishes. The right side resembles the twin-needle topstitch described in the *Faster* technique on page 169 because it has two (or three in a triple cover stitch) rows of straight stitch. The underside has a sturdy flatlock-type stitch that has a great deal of elasticity. The serger blade is not used with the cover stitch, so the fabric is not trimmed as you sew.

1 Press the hem to the wrong side of the garment.

2 Consult your instruction book to set your serger for the cover stitch.

3 Serge the hem using a cover stitch with the right side of the garment up.

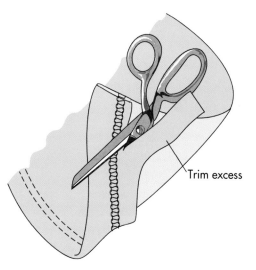

Trim excess

Topstitch hem with serger cover stitch

4 Trim away any excess hem fabric from the wrong side of the garment.

HERE'S WHAT **I DO**...
to Sew Rolled Hems

No section on hems would be complete without mentioning some of the specialty hems that can save time and give garments that ready-to-wear designer look. The narrow rolled hem is perfect for ruffles, sleeve edges, and other garment pieces with straight edges that require a narrow hem.

This fast double-turned hem is stitched with the narrow-rolled-hem foot, which is available for all types of sewing machines. Most sewing machine companies make several different feet that sew different widths of narrow rolled hems. There is a groove in the bottom of the foot that indicates the finished width of the hem. The wider the groove, the heavier the fabric you can hem, but this foot is really designed for light- to medium-weight fabrics.

A very tiny groove means a fine roll will be created on sheer fabrics. If the hem edge is on the bias or loosely woven and fraying, straight stitch around the hem edge first to stabilize it. Then use a tiny zigzag stitch to give the edge a scarf-type hem.

1 Put a narrow-rolled-hem foot on the machine, and set the machine for a straight stitch. (You can also sew with a narrow zigzag or decorative stitch if your narrow-rolled-hem foot allows for the swing of the needle.)

2 Start with a clean cut or torn edge at the hem. Stitch into the fabric at the starting point, and pull the top and bobbin threads out so you have long thread tails.

3 Use the thread tails to pull the starting point of the edge into the funnel on the foot.

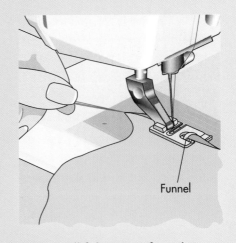

Funnel

Pull fabric into funnel

4 Lower the presser foot, and begin sewing. The fabric edge will roll into the funnel and be stitched. Do not try to help it roll—the foot does the work.

PIPING

Piping adds designer detail to any garment and is fast and easy to apply. It also keeps edges crisp and facings or reversibles from peeking to the right side.

Fast **Covered Cable Cord** Piping is the trim that results when cable cord is covered with fabric. Piping can be stitched into seams for detail, or it can be used to eliminate facings. Cable cord comes in a variety of diameters and has more flexibility than craft cord has.

Cover your cording with a matching fabric to give your garment a tailored look, or use a contrasting fabric to cover it, which adds more design detail. The possibilities are endless when you cover the cord yourself.

A regular sewing machine foot will not stitch closely along the edge of cording or piping, so it is important to use a zipper foot or a special piping foot. A piping foot is a worthwhile addition to your collection of sewing machine feet if you think you will be sewing piping even occasionally. The disadvantage of a zipper foot is that it is somewhat difficult to sew exactly straight along the edge of the cording because the foot wants to move away from the cord. Also, because a zipper foot does not ride on the entire feed teeth system on a zigzag sewing machine, it will not feed as straight. The piping foot is usually the same shape as the standard sewing foot, so it rides on the entire feed teeth system. The

piping lies in a groove on the underside of the foot and is fed perfectly straight.

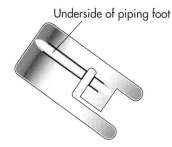

Underside of piping foot

Groove in piping foot fits over cord

1 To make piping from self- or contrasting fabric, purchase cable cord, and cut strips of fabric on the bias or crosswise grain. Cut strips wide enough to cover the cord plus 1¼ inches (3.2 cm) for seam allowances.

2 Put a piping foot on your machine. Wrap the cable cord with the fabric strip right side out, and lay the cable cord into the groove on the underside of the foot. With a straight stitch, sew through both layers of fabric next to the cord.

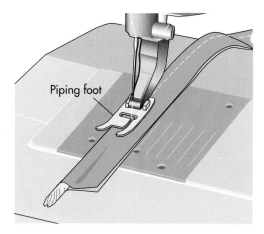

Piping foot

Stitch with cording in groove of foot

3 To set piping into seams with corners and curves, trim the piping seam allowances with a wavy or pinking rotary cutter blade or pinking shears before beginning to set it into the seam. This serves the same purpose as clipping into the seam allowances of the piping seam, but without running the risk of the fabric fraying.

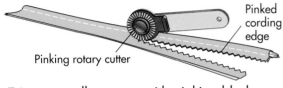

Trim seam allowances with pinking blade

4 To sew the piping into a seam, place it on the right side of the garment on the seamline. Stitch it in place with the piping in the groove of the piping foot. To go around corners and curves smoothly, clip into the piping seam allowance if you haven't pinked the piping, as shown above.

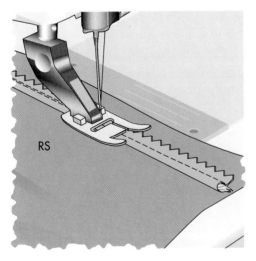

Sew piping to garment

5 Place the other garment piece over the first with right sides together. Stitch the two garment pieces together with the piping in the groove of the piping foot. If you can adjust the needle position on your sewing machine, adjust the needle position one step closer to the piping to be sure none of the first stitching shows on the right side.

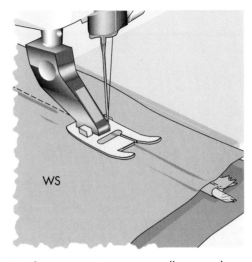

Stitch over piping one needle step closer

6 Trim the seam allowances to eliminate bulk. A quick way to trim is with a pinking rotary cutter.

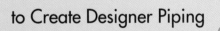

HERE'S WHAT **I DO**...

to Create Designer Piping

For effects seen in designer wear, try decorative stitches over piping. Before setting it into the seam, place the piping under the piping foot and stitch over it with decorative rayon thread. I like to sew several zigzag stitches over the piping.

Embellish piping with decorative stitches

173

Faster **Flat-Fabric Piping** Piping with no filler cord inside is a popular technique used by ready-to-wear designers to define seams and add design lines to a garment.

1 Decide how wide the finished flat piping strips will be, double that width, and add

two seam allowances. I like to make flat piping a little wider than filled piping for added detail on gored skirts and yoke seams. A good guideline for cutting strips for fairly wide, ½-inch (1.3-cm) flat piping with ⅝-inch (1.6-cm) seam allowances is to cut the strips 2¼ inches (5.7 cm) wide. For a narrow flat piping (¼ inch [0.6 cm]

HERE'S WHAT **I DO**...
to Finish Piping Ends

When sewing piping into most garments, you will usually sew in a circle, ending up back where you started with two ends to join. The quick way to finish the ends is to lap them at an angle into the seam allowance, and sew over them.

I prefer to finish the ends with the cable cord trimmed out of the fabric so the ends butt, with one end of the fabric turned under on the bias, then overlapped over the other end.

1 Begin sewing the piping about 1 inch (2.5 cm) from the end, and when you reach the starting point, stop sewing about 1 inch (2.5 cm) from the end.

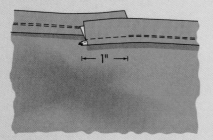

Leave 1" unsewn on each end

2 Lay the piping along the unsewn edge, and mark the point where the ends should meet. Pull some of the cable cord out of each end of the fabric covering it, then cut the cord so both ends of the cord meet exactly at the starting (and ending) point.

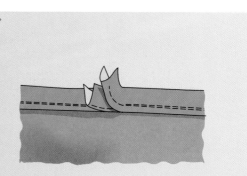

Pull filler cord out of both ends

3 Trim the fabric cover at one end even with the cord, and leave an inch or so of fabric beyond the other end of the cord. Fold this edge of the piping fabric under to the wrong side (on an angle to eliminate bulk), and overlap that end over the raw end.

Trim fabric cover

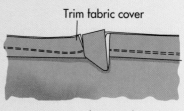

Overlap ends

4 Place the piping along the edge, and finish stitching it down.

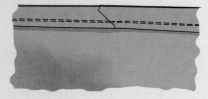

Finish stitching piping in place

wide), cut strips 1¾ inches (4.4 cm) wide. Cut strips for the piping on the crosswise grain (or bias for design detail with stripes and plaids) the length of the seam.

2 Fold and press the strip wrong sides together.

3 Place the strip between two garment pieces with raw edges matching. Sew the seam. No special foot is needed.

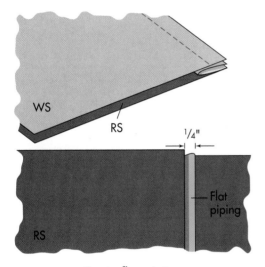

Set in flat piping

4 Clip curves and corners as you sew, or trim the seam allowances of the strip with pinking shears or a pinking rotary cutter blade.

Fastest **Ready-Made Piping and Trims** There are different types and colors of piping available in the notions department of fabric stores, including packaged maxi piping. And don't overlook the home decorator department for additional piping options. I often pick up piping in my favorite colors—black, navy, and gold—when I see it on sale. Four yards (3.7 m) will finish most jackets.

Insert ready-made piping using the *Fast* technique on page 172.

on the FAST TRACK....

to Serger Piping

You can make piping on your serger by making the thread on the upper looper the piping.

1 Cut a crosswise-grain strip of self-fabric 1½ inches (3.8 cm) wide and the length you need for your finished piping.

2 Fold the crosswise-grain strip lengthwise with wrong sides together, and press.

3 Set your serger for a three-thread rolled edge, and set a short stitch length for a satin finish and the widest cutting width possible for the rolled edge. Thread the upper looper with decorative thread. The color of your thread will be the color of your piping. I like to use two spools of decorative rayon thread on the upper looper for good coverage.

4 Serge the rolled edge along the raw edges of the strip.

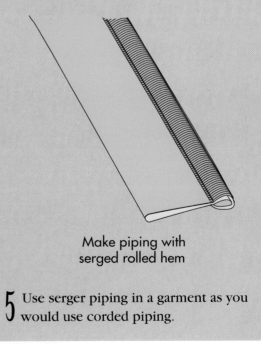

Make piping with serged rolled hem

5 Use serger piping in a garment as you would use corded piping.

TOPSTITCHING

opstitching has become the signature of many designers. It gives garments a classic tailored look and controls the edges of garments at the same time. Topstitching in a color that contrasts the garment fabric lends a casual look to a garment. Matching thread adds sophistication, while topstitching in a shiny rayon or metallic thread adds a touch of fun to an evening garment. Topstitching is traditionally sewn with a straight stitch, but today's machines offer many decorative stitches that are perfect for creative topstitching.

Traditionally, buttonhole twist was the topstitching thread of choice, but there are many new decorative threads on the market that are perfect for topstitching. One of my favorite choices is to use two decorative rayon threads on the top, threaded as one. They both go through the eye of one needle and give a heavier stitching. Both heavy threads and double thread will sew trouble-free when a Schmetz topstitching sewing machine needle is used. This needle features a larger, longer eye and a deeper groove in the front of the needle so it will sew with heavier threads without fraying or breaking.

For more pronounced topstitching, select a triple straight stitch, and make it as long as the sewing machine will allow. This stitch, often called a straight stretch stitch, sews one stitch forward, a second back over the first, and a third

forward over the first two. For very textured fabrics, place a piece of water-soluble stabilizer on top of the fabric before topstitching. This keeps the stitch from sinking down into the fabric.

Topstitch textured fabric

Single-Needle Topstitching Most new machines today come with a special foot for edge stitching and topstitching. The foot has a built-in guide that helps you topstitch quickly and accurately.

1 Thread a topstitching needle with decorative or heavy thread.

2 Use an edge-stitching guide foot. Most machines have this type of foot available. It features a flange guide along one side so the edge of the fabric rides along the flange for perfect straight stitching.

3 Adjust the position of the needle so the row of topstitching is exactly the desired distance from the edge.

4 When more than one row is desired, adjust the needle position for the second row.

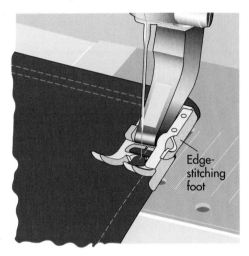

Use edge-stitching foot
to guide fabric

Topstitch with twin needle

Faster Twin-Needle Topstitching

Twin-needle topstitching is a fast, easy way to create neat rows when you will see only the top side of the garment. The top side has two parallel rows of straight stitching, while the bobbin side looks something like a zigzag. A twin needle can be used in virtually any zigzag sewing machine that threads from front to back. I like the 4.0 or 6.0 width between the needles for two rows of topstitching that are up to ¼ inch (0.6 cm) apart.

1 Thread a twin needle as directed by your sewing machine instruction book. (It is necessary to pay attention to how the threads are guided through the top tension disks, which determines which needle to thread.)

2 Topstitch as desired. Place a stabilizer underneath lighter-weight fabrics to prevent the fabric from tucking up between the two rows of stitching. Lockstitch at the beginning and the end to prevent the ends of the twin-needle topstitching from pulling out.

Fastest Cover-Stitch Topstitching

The serger cover stitch is used for the topstitching that you see on most knit and some woven ready-to-wear garments. It creates two rows of straight stitches on the right side of the garment and flatlock-type stitches on the wrong side.

1 Consult your serger instruction book on how to thread the serger for the cover stitch.

2 Topstitch as desired. It is important to tie off the ends of the cover stitch to keep it from pulling out later. I usually stitch farther than needed, carefully pull the stitch back to the desired point, then hand sew the ends in place with a large needle.

Tie off ends of serged cover stitch

Fringed Shawl

A simple piece of challis becomes an elegant shawl when you flatlock a decorative border near the fringe.

I have a fringed shawl scarf made from a beautiful paisley imported cotton. When I wear it with my old tan trench coat, people stop me to compliment me on my great coat! It is the shawl that makes the coat look so good!

This shawl can be a square or a rectangle—it's your choice. A word of caution, however, about this fabulous fast accessory—before you select a fabric for this shawl, test it in front of a full-length mirror with the garment you plan to wear it with, or get a friend's opinion. I learned this the hard way by making a beautiful shawl from a 60-inch (152.4-cm) square of Liberty of London challis that completely overpowered me. Before taking the time to finish the edges, try different sizes of fabric and a variety of prints to find the right size and style for your proportions and for the type of garment you will wear the shawl with.

1. Select a lightweight quality fabric that drapes well and is loosely woven from yarns heavy enough to fringe. (My favorite fabric for this scarf is wool challis!)

2. It is important to cut the scarf on the grainline on all four sides. To mark the grainline on each side, pull a thread the length of the side. Then cut along the marking that is created by the pulled thread.

3. Decide on the size of the fringe. I have found 1 to 2 inches (2.5 to 5.1 cm) to be the best. Anything longer tends to get tangled and caught on things. I pull another thread at the measurement that will end the fringe on all four sides.

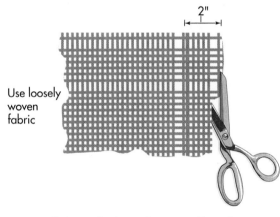

Use loosely woven fabric

Pull thread where fringe will end

4. Fold the edge of the fabric to the wrong side along the line marked by the pulled thread. Set your serger for a flatlock stitch. Experiment on scraps to decide on narrow or wide flatlock and what type of thread to use. A decorative thread in the upper looper for a three-thread flatlock or the lower looper for a two-thread creates added interest. Snap on a blindhem foot or multipurpose foot with a guide.

5. Begin serging at one corner, stitching along the fold. Adjust the guide on the foot so the flatlock stitch jumps off the edge of the fabric slightly, which means that loops will form along the folded edge

I stop at the pulled thread marking for the next side, and turn the corner. Another option is to stitch completely off and tie off the ends later or leave tails of thread at each corner. When all four sides have been flatlock stitched, pull the fabric edge to flatten the stitch.

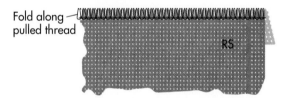

Fold along pulled thread

RS

Serge flatlock on folded edge

6. Pull the fabric threads to create the fringe. Long threads can be tedious to pull, so I snip into the fringe hem edge of the fabric every 12 inches (30.5 cm) or so, cutting all the way from the edge to the flatlock. The smaller sections fringe quickly!

SUE'S FAST FIXES FOR SEWING SLIP-UPS

I first called this chapter "Sewing Disasters." But where others may see disasters, I see design opportunities. Over the years, I've had many more sewing slip-ups than I care to admit. But since I'm not a throw-it-away or "I give up" kind of person, I've tried to learn from every sewing mistake and to make changes so they will not happen again. Some of the slip-ups have "next time" suggestions so you can learn from my mistakes and avoid making them yourself in the future. Just remember to keep smiling and learn from experience!

BUTTON AND BUTTONHOLE BLOOPERS

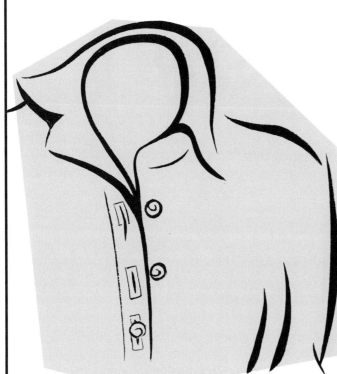

Buttonholing has come a long way. My only fix in those days was to mend the end of the buttonhole carefully. Today I can do something far more creative to fix this and other buttonhole slip-ups.

SLIP-UP
CUTTING PAST THE BUTTONHOLE

Cutting a buttonhole beyond the end or snipping the satin stitching is a common mistake. The garment is finished and ready to wear—what a frustration to have a slip-up during the last step!

fix **Change the Button** Use a larger button and make a larger buttonhole. To do this, baste the area to a piece of tear-away or water-soluble stabilizer behind the buttonhole, and restitch the buttonhole.

fix **Stitch a Decorative Detail** Adding one at the end of the buttonhole covers the slip-up and adds a design detail. Satin diamonds, stars, or flowers perk up any outfit.

I remember once making a black-and-white gingham shirtwaist dress with buttons and buttonholes all the way down the front. As always, I was cutting the buttonholes just before putting on the dress and stepping out the door, and I cut through the end of a buttonhole. I was upset! This was in the days when I had a separate buttonhole attachment for my straight-stitch machine. This made buttonholes quite a project, and it was impossible to go back over a buttonhole to repair it.

Thank goodness today I have a computerized sewing machine with buttonhole functions that measure the size of a buttonhole as it is sewn.

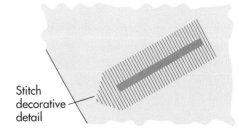

Stitch decorative detail

Cover end of buttonhole with satin stitch triangle

f i x **Camouflage with Fabric**

Perhaps you have suffered a big buttonhole-cutting slip-up and need to take dramatic measures to correct the mishap. You can save the day and add a new design detail to your garment with fabric that camouflages the mistake. Zigzag the buttonhole closed. Cut a shape such as a square or triangle of leather, faux suede or leather, or a complementary fashion fabric, and appliqué the shape over the buttonhole. Then stitch the new buttonhole through the added fabric.

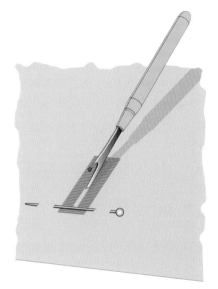

Zigzag buttonhole closed

Try synthetic-suede patch

Restitch buttonhole over patch

Cover buttonhole with appliqué

This is my favorite buttonhole fix! I recently saw a very pricey designer denim jacket with leather squares straight stitched in the buttonhole positions with straight-stitch buttonholes centered in the leather.

Next Time

Use a straight pin as a stopper. If you are cutting the buttonhole with a seam ripper, buttonhole chisel, or scissors, place a straight pin across the end that you are cutting toward. The straight pin prevents you from cutting through the end of the buttonhole. Yes, you may damage the pin and/or dull the ripper or scissors if you cut into the pin, but you've saved your buttonhole!

Use pin as stopper

The best preventive is to invest in a buttonhole chisel and mat or board. They are quite inexpensive. Place the buttonhole over the cutting mat, and push down firmly with the chisel to cut through the buttonhole opening.

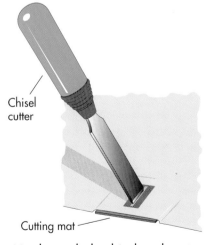

Chisel cutter

Cutting mat

Use buttonhole chisel and mat

SUE'S SNIPPETS

BUTTONHOLE WOES

When Herb and I built our home on family land just outside of Chicago 34 years ago, we did a great deal of the work ourselves to save money. My father lived next door and helped us every step of the way. He is an electrician and helped Herb put all the electrical wiring in the house. I wanted to sew him something special as a way to thank him. This was in the days of the plaid double-knit sport jackets! Do you remember? This was the first men's jacket I ever made.

I carefully matched the plaids and under-lined and lined the jacket. Then I painstakingly stitched, turned, and topstitched the lapels, and finally, I stitched the buttonholes and buttons. Daddy slipped on the jacket and had a strange look on his face as he brought the first button and buttonhole together. "This jacket buttons the wrong way," he said. I was devastated!

SLIP-UP

BUTTONHOLES ON THE WRONG SIDE

I made this mistake on the very first men's suit coat I ever sewed!

fix **Sew Them Closed** Stitch the buttonholes closed, and sew on buttons large enough to cover the closed buttonholes. (Only you will know!) Sew new buttonholes on the opposite side.

fix **Cover Them with Appliqué** Appliqué shapes over the buttonholes and on the opposite side of the garment. Stitch the buttons and new buttonholes over the appliquéd shapes.

Next Time

Take your time. I have made many men's jackets since that first time I put the buttonholes on the wrong side, and I have never made that mistake again! Before I stitch buttonholes on any garment, I whisper to myself, "The woman is always right and the man is left (out)." This little saying has saved me many times from putting the buttonholes on the wrong side.

SLIP-UP

BROKEN BUTTON

Sewing buttons by machine is a tremendous time-saver (see the *Faster* technique in "Buttons" on page 159), but there is always the risk of the needle hitting the button and breaking it. More than once I have been in too much of a hurry and have not tested the swing of the zigzag, only to break a button!

fix **Call in a Substitute** When the garment is a tuck-in blouse, substitute the bottom button for the broken one. Then use a clear, flat plastic backer button at the bottom of the blouse, where it won't show. You'll find this type of button on antique garments anywhere the button does not show. These backer buttons were used to help eliminate bulk in the garment and to save on the cost of more expensive decorative buttons.

fix **Start Over** Purchase another card of buttons, or change all the buttons. Not fun, but it does save the garment.

fix **Glue It** When I've broken a button that was not replaceable, I have actually glued it together and placed it in the least noticeable location.

CUTTING DISASTERS

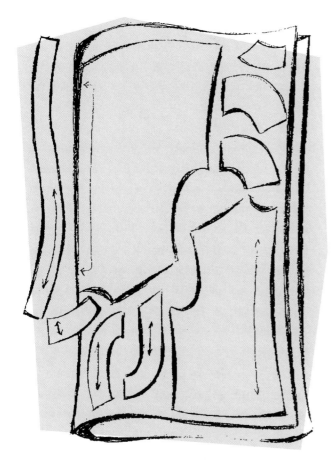

From pattern-cutting mistakes to slips of the scissors (or rotary cutter!), cutting disasters happen to us all.

SLIP-UP

PATTERN MISHAPS

Of all the sewing disasters I have seen over the years, the most frustrating is when you cut out a pattern piece incorrectly, such as cutting on the wrong grainline or nap or running out of fabric before you run out of pattern pieces.

Buy more fabric Sometimes you get lucky and can purchase more fabric to solve the problem. But more often than not, when you have cut the pattern wrong, the solution isn't that easy. Often, cutting disasters happen when you're making something at the last minute, and there isn't time to start over. Or the stores are already closed, so you cannot go out and buy more fabric. In all likelihood, if the stores are open, the fabric you've just cut was an expensive piece off of the end of a bolt, and buying replacement yardage is not an option.

Next Time

Use the buddy system. Anytime you cut out a garment, especially when it's from special fabric, invite a sewing friend over to supervise. For many years I was fortunate to have a next-door neighbor, Dot Snyder, who loved to sew. Even if Dot could not be with me for the layout and pinning process, she would come over and check before I cut into expensive fabrics. It actually made sewing more fun to have a friend help.

Take a class. When working with a new type of fabric, there are so many new sewing tips and tricks to learn that it is well worth the investment in time and dollars to join a class. You will learn about the new fabric, and there will be someone close by in the class to catch pattern slip-ups *before* you cut. Also, while you are learning about new fabrics, consider taking a trip to one of the sewing schools or sewing shows. Sewing techniques and tools are changing so fast that there is always something to learn.

SUE'S SNIPPETS

KEEP A SECRET

Why is it that sewers tell all? So often when I compliment people on their garments, they immediately tell me everything they did wrong while sewing. They think these mistakes are obvious on the finished garments, but they really aren't. I don't get close enough to see a slightly crooked buttonhole or topstitched seam.

Once, at an American Sewing Guild Convention, the creator of a lovely patchwork wool vest promptly told me she made it from a variety of wool fabrics only because she cut two left fronts by mistake. Stop telling people what you did wrong! There is no need to lose sleep over a sewing error. We are too hard on ourselves and take life too seriously. In the big picture, what is really important is family and friends—and our daily walk.

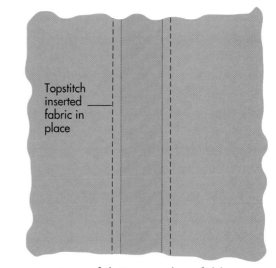

Insert fabric to replace fold

In most cases, the finished insert needs to be ½ inch (1.3 cm) wide to make up for the turned-under seam allowances. For a pleasing design, you might want to make it wider, but be careful that the size of the finished piece ends up the same as the pattern. Additional strips inserted or appliquéd to other areas of the garment will pull the look together.

SLIP-UP

CUTTING ALONG A FOLD

Many pattern pieces have one edge that must be cut on the fold of the fabric. I think every sewer has made the mistake of cutting along the edge of a pattern piece which was to be laid on the fold. Fortunately, it is usually the center front of a garment or other centered seam, which can be perfectly camouflaged with a design detail.

fix **Create a Fabric Insert** Insert a new strip of the same or contrasting fabric between the cut edges. (Contrasting fabric adds a nice design element.) Finish the edges of the strip and the edges of the garment with a serger stitch or three-step zigzag. Press the cut edges ¼ inch (0.6 cm) to the wrong side of the garment, and topstitch the strip insert between the two garment pieces.

Turn cutting slip-up into decorative detail

Add a Flatlock Embell-ished Seam Another option is to place the garment pieces wrong sides together, and serge a flatlock stitch along the raw edge of the fold that you accidentally cut through. Thread the upper looper with decorative thread. Add a flatlock embellishment on other parts of the garment for additional design detail.

Splice Two Pieces Line up the cut raw edges that should have been a fold. Join the butted fabric edges together with a three-step zigzag. Topstitch a ribbon or other decorative trim over the butted seam. The width of the trim isn't important as long as it covers the stitching underneath and ensures a stable seam that won't come apart.

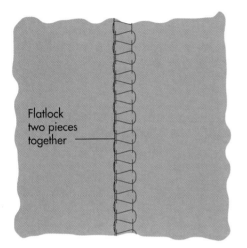

Flatlock two pieces together

Flatlock decorative seam

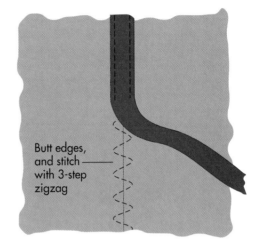

Butt edges, and stitch with 3-step zigzag

Zigzag edges together, and cover with trim

SUE'S SNIPPETS
GIVING GARMENTS A PERSONAL TOUCH

Adding embellishment is a great way to disguise a slip-up and rescue a sewing project. To me, embellishment means adding personal details to our garments that make them ours alone.

Today it is acceptable and desirable to add stitching, fabric, threads, frayed sections, ruffles, tucks, and more to just about any style of garment. I have often said that just a few years ago, if we had tails of thread or fraying fabric on a garment, it would have been considered poorly made or unfinished. Today we call it wearable art!

I love to look for ideas in the fine stores and fashion magazines. What fun to be on the "cutting edge." Have you noticed the trend toward embell-ishment in ready-to-wear? Designers are definitely into fiber and color. What a privilege it was to have a top designer admire my reversible embroidered jacket at the opening reception for the *Dreams on Paper: A History of Pattern Making* exhibit at the Fashion Institute of Technology in New York City. He was very interested in just how I had created it.

Don't misunderstand me—there is a fine line between creative embellishment and overdoing it. That is our challenge: to create classic wearables that make people ask what designer they came from, not overdone originals that just get attention. My general rule with embellishments is, less is better.

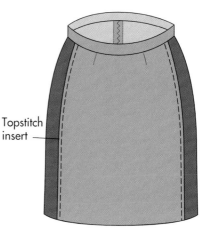

Insert fabric in side seams

CUTTING THE NAP WRONG

One of my first sewing projects when I was in sixth grade was a straight skirt of bright pink corduroy. When completed, the front and back were different colors. This was my first introduction to napped fabrics. Today I cut most fabrics with a one-way layout, so I'm in less danger of a wrong-way nap.

 **Make a Patchwork** When you have cut napped fabrics with the nap running in the wrong direction, think about creating a patchwork of napped scraps for part of the garment. The subtle effect of fabrics pieced together so the nap runs in different directions is one of the most elegant types of tone-on-tone patchwork I have ever seen.

SLIP-UP

CUTTING TOO SMALL

Most sewers have seamed a fitted garment such as a straight skirt or dress only to find that the finished garment is too small. If this happens to you, don't panic.

 Add Fabric Inserts In selected seams, inserts can add needed inches of fabric and design detail. Cut strips of the same fabric or, for more detail, a contrasting fabric. Finish the edges of each strip and the edges of the garment with a serger stitch or three-step zigzag. Press the cut edges ¼ inch (0.6 cm) to the wrong side of the garment, and topstitch the strip insert between the two seam edges.

SLIP-UP

NOT ENOUGH FABRIC

The yardage in my fabric collection was not purchased with any particular pattern in mind. So, often when I'm ready to cut out the garment, I don't have enough fabric for the pattern.

Reduce Seam Allowances It is amazing what a difference it makes to reduce seam allowances to ¼ inch (0.6 cm). Before you start cutting, it is important to know your pattern fits, because there is no way to let out ¼-inch (0.6-cm) seams.

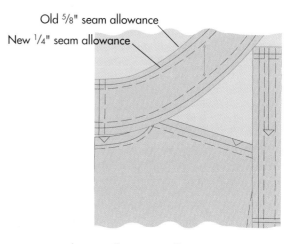

Old ⅝" seam allowance

New ¼" seam allowance

Plan smaller seam allowances

Use a Different Facing

Use a different fabric for the facing and any other pieces that will not show. Many times this can be an advantage if the fashion fabric is bulky. Facing cut from a lighter-weight or lining fabric cuts down on the bulk. Face hems with other fabric or packaged wide hem facing tape.

WS

Use lightweight fabric for hem facing

Face hem with different fabric

Mix Fabrics

This is actually my favorite fix for many sewing disasters because mixing fabrics in the same garment to create wearable art is so popular in ready-to-wear today. Combining fabrics can be fun and easy. Cut the fronts or sleeves from a coordinating fabric, and tie the garment together with trim or stitching.

Next Time

One disaster that usually cannot be fixed is the failure to pretreat your fabric before cutting it out. When you buy fabric, it seldom comes with a care label, so many disasters occur when the finished garment is laundered for the first time. Especially if you buy fabrics from sale tables or flat folds or if you sew from stashes, it is important to prewash washable fabrics and to steam- or dry-clean others before sewing.

SUE'S SNIPPETS

BIRDS ON THEIR HEADS

After years of sewing, I don't make as many sewing mistakes as I used to, but I still remember how upset I used to be when something wasn't right. My favorite story about a cutting disaster dates back to the first time I purchased 5 yards (4.6 m) of Liberty of London fabric. It was the most money I had ever spent on fabric for myself. I prewashed the wool-and-cotton challis so I could wash the garment after wearing it. It shrank from 36 inches (91.4 cm) to 34 inches (86.4 cm) wide! It already posed a cutting challenge. The fabric was an all-over print, and I made note of the one-way design and carefully laid all pattern pieces in the same direction.

When I finished cutting out the pieces, I proudly showed Herb the beautiful fabric and explained my plan for creative tucks on the blouse. He studied the pieces and said, "Did you want the birds upside down?" I could not believe it—the tiny birds were upside down! I had never noticed there were birds in the print. I was sick! But I could not let this investment in Liberty of London fabric go to waste, so I made the skirt and blouse anyway.

I enjoyed this garment for years. It was comfortable, easy to care for, and a style that could be worn anywhere. And in all the years, no one except Herb ever noticed the tiny upside-down birds unless I pointed out the mistake.

FITTING FOUL-UP

Too many times I have completed or purchased a garment only to find that the neckline and/or armholes do not lie flat against my body. Many full-busted people have this problem.

NECK AND ARMHOLE GAPS

When Tracy Helmer came on my "America Sews" television program to teach crazy-patch quilting, she brought a beautiful vest for me to wear. When I put it on, the armholes did not lie flat in the front or back of the vest. The quick elastic trick explained below saved the day. As I travel and teach, this elastic tip has been the favorite of all the tips and techniques I have shared. Students come back months later to tell me how it saved an outfit.

f i x   **Add Clear Elastic**   Stitch ¼-inch (0.6-cm)-wide clear elastic to the seam allowance to keep an armhole (or a scoop neck or V-neck) lying flat against your body.

Usually the garment is completed before you realize the problem. If this is the case, open the facing or lining to access the seam allowance in the gaping area. The seam allowance is usually trimmed, but you do not need a wide edge to sew the elastic to. Place a piece of ¼-inch (0.6-cm)-wide clear elastic on the trimmed seam allowance with one edge of the elastic against the seam stitching line. Zigzag the elastic to the seam allowance, stretching it slightly as you sew.

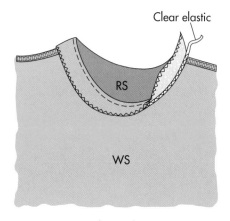

Sew clear elastic to
seam allowance only

SERGER-CUTTER DISASTER

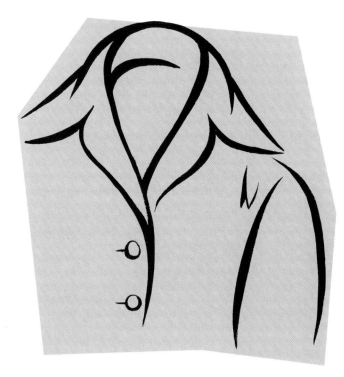

ergers have become a must for home sewers who want professional results. The serger sews very fast and cuts the excess seam allowance fabric away as it goes. Unfortunately, the cutters or knives cut anything that gets in their way. Ask me how I know that!

SLIP-UP

CUTTER SLASHES GARMENT

When you are sewing with limited space or light, it's easy for some part of the garment to get under the cutter, creating a telltale V-shaped slash. Often, sewing in hotels to finish a garment for a specific meeting or class, I find that the space and light are very limited. Once, while serging a knit dress to wear under a pinwoven vest, I got part of the skirt too close to the cutters and nipped a hole in it.

 Patch with Fusible Tricot
Iron a piece of fusible tricot interfacing to the wrong side of the cut fabric to stabilize it and hold it together. The rest of the fix depends on how noticeable the cut is and where it is located on the garment. For small cuts in inconspicuous places, after fusing the interfacing, mend the cut carefully with matching thread. Many sewing machines have special mending stitches that you can use.

Add an Embellishment If the cut is located where an embellishment can be added, stitch an embroidery motif or appliqué to cover the cut, or else topstitch with decorative thread. Add other embellishments as needed to give the garment a pulled-together appearance.

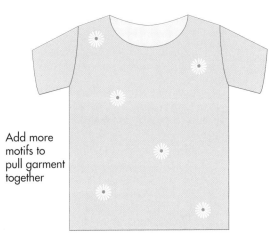

Add more motifs to pull garment together

Cover serger cut with embroidery

WAISTBAND WOES

Generally, I am careful to try on a waistband before sewing it to a garment. But occasionally when I'm in a hurry, I skip this step and later find that the finished waist does not fit. Also, when buying ready-to-wear, waist fit can be a real problem. One of the advantages of being a sewer is that when shopping the sale racks and discount stores, I am not limited to clothing in my size. I can change the size with simple alterations.

WAISTBAND IS TOO LARGE

Yes, believe it or not, sometimes I do find skirts on sale that I just can't resist. If the waistband is too big, no problem!

fix **Add Elastic** A waistband with elastic added fits and is very comfortable to wear. I hate to admit it, but the "grow room" has come in handy on several skirts. Open the waistband just a couple of inches at both ends, select a piece of waistband elastic that is the appropriate width for the waistband, and feed it through. Once the elastic is in place, stitch the ends together, and let the elastic slip into place inside the waistband. Then close the small opening with topstitching or hand stitching.

WAISTBAND IS TOO SMALL

This is usually the case! When a gathered or pleated skirt has a waistband that is too small, it can usually be salvaged. Use one of the following fixes, and then adjust the gathers or pleats to fit.

fix **Splice Some Extra Length** Remove the waistband, and insert fabric scraps to piece the waistband in an inconspicuous spot. Often you can add fabric at the end of the waistband underlap, where it is covered by the other side of the waistband. Or remove the waistband, cut vertically through the center, and add a piece of fabric in the back or front. You can even add a design detail by using a contrasting fabric for the centered piece.

 Piece a Faced Waistband
Remove the waistband, and cut it in two lengthwise. Seam the pieces end to end to make a long, skinny waistband. To face the waistband with other fabric or wide packaged bias hem facing, place the hem facing and fabric with right sides together along the length of the band. Position the pieces so the seam is at the side of the skirt. Sew along the top edge with a ¼-inch (0.6-cm) seam allowance. The waistband will be ¼ inch (0.6 cm) narrower due to the seam allowance along the top, but this usually is not a problem.

on the
FAST TRACK. . .

to Measure Elastic

I have sewn so many of these elastic waistbands that I never measure or cut the elastic anymore. Instead, I simply pull very slightly as I zigzag it to the seam allowances, then cut the elastic at the end.

 SUE'S SNIPPETS

FABRIC "SHORTAGE" NO PROBLEM

Being both short and a sewer gives me a real advantage when it comes to buying ready-to-wear skirts. I can buy an odd size on sale and then adjust it to fit. I always shorten ready-to-wear skirts and can use the fabric that I cut off to make a larger waistband. This is one advantage of being short.

Replace the Waistband
Add a new waistband of contrasting fabric or wide colored elastic.

Add wide elastic waistband

LENGTHY ISSUES

S kirt length is the debate of the century. Fashion tries to dictate what length is "in," but most sewers I meet wear lengths that are the most flattering to their body size and type. I usually measure a favorite skirt, jacket, or pair of slacks for a length guideline.

GARMENT IS TOO LONG

This is easy—shorten it! To avoid the home-sewn look, pay attention to the garment hem. A dead giveaway is leaving too much length in the hem allowance.

Follow the Guideline My rule is no more than a 2-inch (5.1-cm) hem, and many of my hems are 1 to 1½ inches (2.5 to 3.8 cm), especially on slacks.

GARMENT IS TOO SHORT

This can be the tough one. There are not too many things you can do to lengthen a skirt without changing the style or the design details.

Face the Hem If the hem allowance is wide enough, let it down, and face the hem with a lightweight fabric or hem facing tape.

 Add a Border or Ruffle When there is not enough fabric to lengthen the garment, consider adding a border. I like to add a border of contrasting fabric. To carry through the design idea on the rest of the garment, also sew a border on each sleeve. To make a sleeve border, fold a strip of fabric with wrong sides together, and stitch or serge it to the garment edge with right sides together. Press the border band away from the garment.

WHEN DISASTER STRIKES

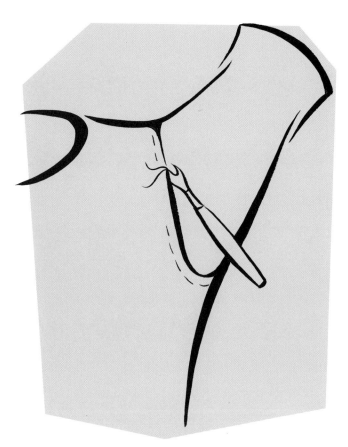

Teaching others to sew has taught me to look for the opportunity in sewing mistakes rather than to focus on the problems they may create. Don't look at these errors as sewing disasters—think of them as design challenges and opportunities to create something unique.

When you have a problem, set it aside for a few hours. Consult with a sewing friend or teacher. Think through the alternatives, and most of all, learn from every mistake, sewing or otherwise.

SLIP-UP
NEED TO RIP STITCHES

I still make mistakes or change my mind about the garment construction as I sew. Everyone has a favorite way to rip. (I like to call it "reverse stitching.")

fix **Buy the Best** Use a quality seam ripper. There is a big difference between the ones on sale in a bargain bin and the ones that come with quality sewing machines. The ripper blade must be small and sharp. Working from one side of the seam, insert the ripper, and cut a stitch every inch or two. Pull the thread on the other side of the seam. Slide transparent tape or a damp cloth along the opened seam to pick up any loose threads.

fix **Lend a Hand** Ask a friend to help you. Have the friend hold the seam on each side and pull firmly to expose the stitching. Carefully slide the seam ripper along the seam, cutting the threads.

fix **Snip and Pull** On serged seams the needle threads are the ones to pull. Snip the needle threads every few inches, then pull them along the way. The looper threads will remain intact and are easy to pull off the fabric.

Next Time

Keep smiling, and learn from experience. There will always be a next time!

GLOSSARY

"America Sews" A PBS television program hosted by Sue Hausmann.

Apex The point, or tip, of a dart, where the dart legs intersect.

Appliqué foot A presser foot designed for use with heavy satin stitching. The design of the bottom of the foot allows the stitching and fabric edge to pass through easily.

Bartack Five to seven zigzag stitches sewn with a very short stitch length and used to secure the ends of buttonholes or garment details such as belt loops in place.

Baste To hold two fabrics in place temporarily until permanent stitching can be completed.

Bent-handle dressmaker's shears Scissors with a bent handle and large finger hole designed for cutting fabrics.

Bias Also called bias grain; refers to any line drawn on the diagonal of the weave of a fabric. True bias refers to the diagonal drawn at exactly 45 degrees to the weave, which is the line of the greatest amount of stretch in a woven fabric.

Bias tape maker A device for folding strips of fabric cut on the bias (or other grainline) to create bias tape.

Blind hem A machine-sewn hem that does not show from the right side of a garment.

Blindhem stitching Machine stitching that combines straight stitches with zigzags to create a blind hem.

Blind stitching Sewn by hand, this stitching is not visible from either the right or wrong side of the garment.

Boiled wool A partially felted wool that lacks drape or grainline.

Breast pocket A patch pocket placed 8 to 9 inches (20.3 to 22.9 cm) below the shoulder line.

Bustline The line drawn around the body parallel to the floor and passing through the bust point.

Bust point The apex of the bust.

Buttonhole chisel and mat A small chisel, usually ½ inch (1.3 cm) wide, designed for cleanly and accurately cutting machine-sewn buttonholes open. Buttonhole chisels are sold with a small mat or wooden board, which is placed under the buttonhole being cut.

Chain stitching Stitching formed on the serger. Thread from the needle passes through the fabric, forming a straight stitch on the top and locking loops that look like a crocheted chain stitch on the bottom.

Computerized sewing machine A sewing machine with computerized sewing functions, such as stitches, stitch lengths, and stitch widths.

Cover stitching Produced on high-end sergers, this stitching is commonly used in ready-to-wear. On the right side of the garment, the cover stitch looks like parallel straight stitches produced on a sewing machine with a twin needle. On the wrong side, the cover stitch looks like a flatlock stitch.

Crimp ease To decrease the length of a seam allowance so it will ease into a shorter seam allowance. This is done by delaying the fabric behind the presser foot while stitching.

Crosswise grain The direction of the weave perpendicular to the straight grain, or selvage edge. The crosswise grain is created by the weft yarns as they are woven in and out of the stretched warp yarns. No matter how slight, the crosswise grain invariably has greater stretch than the straight grain.

Decorative rayon thread Shiny thread made of rayon and intended for machine embroidery. The thread is too delicate to be used for garment construction.

Drape The way a fabric hangs. Drape is affected by the weave and fiber of a fabric, as well as by the direction of the grainline as the fabric hangs.

Edge finish To serge or machine stitch the edges of seam allowances to prevent them from raveling.

Edgestitching A row of straight stitching sewn 1/16 to 1/8 inch (0.2 to 0.3 cm) from a seam or folded edge.

Elastic thread A strand of wrapped elastic that is fine enough to be used in place of thread.

Fabric-glue stick A glue stick made specifically for use on fabric.

Fabric marking pen A pen made specifically for marking fabric. The mark may or may not be perma-

nent, regardless of the manufacturer's instructions. Always test a fabric marking pen on fabric scraps to make sure it won't bleed or stain.

Feed teeth The serrated teeth on the machine bed under the presser foot of a sewing machine or serger. The feed teeth pull the fabric through the machine to advance the fabric as it is stitched.

Finger baste To hold two fabrics in place using only your fingers while stitching.

Flatlock seam Created on a serger, this sturdy seam looks finished on both the right and wrong sides. It is often used in ready-to-wear for decorative effect.

Four-thread stitch The basic serger stitch, sewn using two needle and two looper threads.

Fray-stopping liquid A liquid made for sealing thread tails. This useful sewing aid can create some stiffness in fabrics and may leave wet-looking stains on some fabrics.

Fusible interfacing A woven or knit interfacing infused with adhesives on one side. Heat and moisture activate the adhesives, which bond the interfacing to the fabric.

Fusible thread Thread made from one fine strand of thread and one fine strand of heat-activated adhesive. Fusible thread is appropriate for hand sewing as well as in the sewing machine bobbin or serger loopers.

Fusible tricot A tricot-knit fusible interfacing.

Gingher A manufacturer of fine sewing scissors designed for a variety of uses.

Grabbit A magnetized pin holder.

Grainline The direction of the weave or knit of a fabric.

Hand The feel of a fabric, including its drape, texture, and thickness.

Handwheel Also called a flywheel, the wheel on the right side of a sewing machine or serger that can be rotated by hand to advance a stitch.

Heat-Away stabilizer A temporary woven stabilizer that is removed by pressing it with a warm iron. The stabilizer turns to ash and can be brushed off the fabric.

Heirloom stitching Multistitch decorative stitching that creates the hand-sewn, pulled-thread heirloom effect associated with nineteenth-century garments.

Hemline The line that marks where the fabric is folded to create a hem.

Hipband Usually made from knit ribbing, the hipband is sewn to the bottom edge of a knit garment in place of a hem.

In-the-ditch stitching Stitching sewn from the right side of the garment directly over an existing seamline. The slight indentation where the two fabrics meet in the seam is called the "ditch."

"In the flat" Working a garment part, such as a sleeve cuff, before it is sewn closed into a circle.

"In the round" Working a garment part, such as a sleeve cuff, after it has been sewn closed into a circle.

Invisible-zipper foot A foot made specifically for sewing invisible zippers. This foot is sold in a kit with parts to make it adaptable to any style sewing machine.

Lockstitching Two or three sewing machine stitches sewn in place to secure a line of stitching.

Looper The mechanism in a serger that creates the loops on the underside of the fabric in a serger stitch. All sergers have two loopers, and some have three. Most serger stitches use both loopers.

Machine baste To hold two fabrics in place temporarily with long, sometimes loose machine stitches until permanent stitching can be completed.

Narrow rolled hem A small hem, ⅛ to ¼ inch (0.3 to 0.6 cm) wide, usually sewn with a special presser foot.

Narrow-rolled-hem foot A presser foot designed to roll a fabric edge over as the edge is stitched to create a narrow rolled hem.

Natural fiber A naturally occurring fiber, specifically wool, silk, or cotton, used in fabrics. Rayons, though man-made, are considered natural fibers because fabrics made from them have the handling characteristics of other natural-fiber fabrics and because the fibers are derived directly from wood pulp.

Neckband The ribbing added to the neckline of most knit and some woven garments in place of a collar or facing.

Needle plate Also called the throat plate, this is the removable plate on the machine bed under the presser foot. The needle plate has holes and slots for the needle and feed teeth to pass through.

Notch A V-shaped mark in the seam allowances of commercial patterns to indicate seams that match up. Notches are transferred to the garment pieces in a variety of ways, including with small scissors snips and fabric marking pens.

Nylon tricot A tricot-knit nylon fabric commonly used in ready-to-wear lingerie. Nylon tricot yardage is usually available in widths up to 108 inches (274.3 cm).

Overcast stitching Machine stitching that catches the edges of the fabric to prevent the yarns in the fabric from raveling.

Patch pocket A pocket made from a patch of fabric, usually rectangular, with finished edges, which is sewn with topstitching or blind stitching to the outside of a garment.

Pin baste To hold two fabrics in place temporarily with pins until permanent stitching can be completed.

Pinking shears Scissors with ⅛-inch (0.3-cm) teeth that create a zigzag-cut edge on the fabric. The zigzags create tiny bias cuts that prevent the fabric from raveling (since a bias-cut edge doesn't ravel).

Pintucks Lines of narrow tucks created in a piece of fabric by sewing with a twin needle and a special pintucking presser foot, which helps draw the fabric up into the tuck.

Point presser Made from wood, a point presser has a variety of curves and a point for pressing seams open.

Point turner A small plastic or wooden tool used for turning points in collars and other squared edges. A wooden point turner can be used for pressing the point after it has been turned.

Press cloth A lightweight cotton cloth placed, either dampened or dry, between the iron and the fabric to protect the fabric. When fusing interfacing, a dry press cloth helps to distribute the heat evenly and to create a good bond between the interfacing and the fabric.

Rotary cutter and mat A tool with an extremely sharp, replaceable circular blade used instead of scissors to cut out garment pieces. Rotary cutters make cutting fabric much quicker than with scissors, but care must be taken to prevent potentially serious injury to yourself, children, or pets. A special mat must be used under the rotary cutter to prevent damaging other surfaces and to preserve the sharpness of the blade.

Rotary pinking blade A special circular blade for a rotary cutter. The blade has a wavy cutting edge, which creates a zigzag-cut edge on the fabric.

Schmetz A manufacturer of quality sewing machine needles, available in most catalogs and fabric stores.

Seam/overcast stitching Multistitch sewing machine stitching that creates a seam and a finish along the edge of the fabric in one continuous step.

Seam roll A hot-dog–shaped, tightly packed cloth cylinder about 12 inches (30.5 cm) long, used for pressing open seams. A seam roll is especially helpful when pressing sleeve seams.

Self-fabric The same fabric as that used in the main parts of a garment.

Serger A machine that stitches, trims, and finishes the fabric edge in one step. Sergers use two to five needle and looper threads to create a variety of useful stitches like those used in the ready-to-wear garment industry.

Serger cutters The blades in a serger that trim the fabric as it is sewn.

Shadow tucks Pintucks sewn on a sheer fabric, creating a shadow effect.

Silk-noil A raw silk fabric that has a somewhat coarse weave.

Stabilizer A material used to either permanently or temporarily add body and firmness to a fabric. Interfacings are used to permanently stabilize garment parts, and temporary stabilizers are used to support the fabric during machine embroidery.

Staystitching Stitching sewn inside a curved seam allowance close to the seamline to stabilize the fabric and prevent distortion.

Stitch fingers The small appendages on a serger throat plate that hold the looper threads in place during the last phase of the serger stitch.

Straight grain The direction of the weave parallel to the selvage edge of a woven fabric. Also called the lengthwise grain, the straight grain is created by the warp yarns stretched on the loom and is more stable and less stretchy than the crosswise grain. Garments are cut with the straight grain running vertically to prevent the fabric from sagging and stretching.

Tear-away stabilizer A temporary stabilizer that is removed after sewing by tearing it away from the stitches. Tear-away stabilizer is easiest to remove when used with satin stitching.

Three-thread stitch A serger stitch sewn using one needle and two looper threads.

Topstitching Straight stitching sewn to the right side of a garment, usually ¼ inch (0.6 cm) from the seamline or edge being topstitched.

Twin needle Two sewing machine needles on one needle shank. A twin needle sews two parallel lines.

Two-thread stitch A serger stitch sewn using one needle and one looper thread.

Undercollar The underside, or facing, of a two-piece collar.

Upper collar The top, or outer, side of a two-piece collar.

V-placket A sleeve placket cut in a V-shape.

Water-soluble marking pen A fabric marking pen that marks with ink that stays in the fabric until it is washed out. Even though the ink in the pen is water-soluble, it is always wise to test whether it is washable with every fabric, since the ink leaves a permanent stain on some fabrics.

Water-soluble stabilizer A temporary stabilizer that can be washed off a fabric when stitching is completed.

Weft-insertion interfacing A knit, fusible interfacing with an extra weft yarn woven in for added stability.

Wing needle A sewing machine needle with a wide flange, which cuts a hole in the fabric as it sews. The wing needle is used with multistitch decorative heirloom stitching on delicate fabrics to create the pulled-thread effect associated with nineteenth-century hand-sewn embellishment.

ACKNOWLEDGMENTS

I have many people to thank for helping me shape the vision for this book—first and foremost, the sewers all over the world who have inspired and encouraged me and given me so many ideas to share. I'd also like to thank all the folks at Rodale Press—Nancy Fawley, my first editor, who has since gone back to school to get her master's degree in fashion design; Toni Toomey, the editor who picked up the pieces and carried this book through to the end; Carol Angstadt and Chris Rhoads, the designers of the book; Cheryl Winters-Tetreau, the managing editor of Rodale's sewing books program; and Maggie

Lydic, the editorial director of Rodale Home and Garden books. All of these wonderful people had the faith that I could really do this, and I thank them for their help and encouragement to reach the end. Thanks also to the Education Department at Husqvarna Viking for constant encouragement and support. Thanks to Patti Jo Larson, Husqvarna Viking educator and "America Sews" coordinator, for sewing some of the samples for this book. (I thought I could do it myself and found it was impossible while traveling!) Thanks to Bengt Gerborg, president of Husqvarna Viking USA for giving me the go-ahead on this project in spite of the fact that my plate is already full as senior vice president of education.

Most of all, I want to acknowledge my love and appreciation to Herb, my husband of 38 years, for countless hours of providing encouragement, running errands, creating art orders, and putting up with a tired wife!

SOURCES

Some of the sources below sell by mail order, and others will refer you to the store nearest your home. I encourage you to support your local sewing retailers. Your support and the support of other sewers like you will keep them in business.

The Crowning Touch
3859 S. Stage Road
Medford, OR 97501
800-729-0280
Fasturn tube turner and sewing machine foot

Dos de Tejas Patterns
P.O. Box 1472
Sherman, TX 75091
800-8-TEJAS-8
Sueded rayon used to make Sue's dress on the cover. A swatch card is available for $2.

Fabric Collections
930 Orange Avenue
Winter Park, FL 32789
407-740-7737
Fine fabrics and beautiful buttons. Thanks to owner Louise Cutting for fabrics used in the photography throughout the book.

Handler Textile Corporation (HTC)
450 Seventh Avenue
New York, NY 10123
212-695-0990
Interfacing

Husqvarna Viking Sewing Machine Company
11760 Berea Road
Cleveland, OH 44111
800-358-0001
Quality sewing machines and sergers

June Tailor
2861 Highway 175
Richfield, WI 53076
414-644-5288
Pressing supplies and cutting equipment

Parsons Cabinet Company, Inc.
420 W. Parson Drive
Osceola, AR 72370
800-643-0090
Sewing machine cabinets

The Rain Shed, Inc.
707 N.W. 11th Street
Corvallis, OR 97330
541-753-8900
Sweatshirt knit used for Sue's jacket on the cover

Rowenta
196 Boston Avenue
Medford, MA 02155
781-396-0600
Irons and iron cleaner

Schmetz Needle Company
9960 N.W. 116th Way, Suite 3
Medley, FL 33178
Web Site: www.schmetz.com
Quality sewing machine needles

Sew/Fit
5310 W. 66th Street, Unit A
Bedford Park, IL 60638
708-458-5600
Cutting tables and mats

Stretch & Sew
P.O. Box 25306
Phoenix, AZ 85285
800-547-7717
Pattern for blanket coat shown on page 52

Sulky of America
3113D Broadpoint Drive
Harbor Heights, FL 33983
800-874-4115
Decorative rayon and metallic threads

Warm Company
954 E. Union Street
Seattle, WA 98122
800-234-WARM
Fusible web and cotton batting

INDEX

NOTE: Page numbers in **boldface** indicate photographs; those in *italic* indicate illustrations.

Look for these and other Rodale sewing books wherever books are sold.

Fantastic Fit for Every Body

How to Alter Patterns to Flatter Any Figure

by Gale Grigg Hazen

Learn to create garments that fit and complement your body—no matter what your shape. Nationally known sewing, fitting, and machine expert Gale Grigg Hazen knows what it is like to sew for a less-than-perfect figure, yet her clothes always fit, and she always looks fabulous. Now Gale shares her unique fitting process with you, using real people with real fitting problems.

Hardcover ISBN 0-87596-792-2

High-Fashion Sewing Secrets from the World's Best Designers

A Step-by-Step Guide to Sewing Stylish Seams, Buttonholes, Pockets, Collars, Hems, and More

by Claire B. Shaeffer

Nationally known sewing expert Claire B. Shaeffer reveals the sewing secrets of fashion-industry legends from Ralph Lauren to Yves Saint Laurent. You'll also discover that high-fashion sewing does not have to be difficult!

Hardcover ISBN 0-87596-717-5

No Time to Sew

Fast & Fabulous Patterns & Techniques for Sewing a Figure-Flattering Wardrobe

by Sandra Betzina

Sandra Betzina, star of the television series "Sew Perfect," helps you to sew in record time, offering stylish patterns, step-by-step instructions, timesaving tips, and wardrobe advice. Whatever your skill level, you'll find intriguing techniques for your next garment. Plus, you'll receive a complete set of multisize patterns for several garments when you buy this book.

Hardcover ISBN 0-87596-744-2

Secrets for Successful Sewing

Techniques for Mastering Your Sewing Machine and Serger

by Barbara Weiland

The ultimate owner's manual, full of tips and techniques for mastering a machine—regardless of brand. Includes a comprehensive look at machines and their accessories, plus step-by-step instructions for the most popular and unique serger and sewing machine techniques. Barbara Weiland is a former editor of *Sew News*.

Hardcover ISBN 0-87596-776-0

Serger Secrets

High-Fashion Techniques for Creating Great-Looking Clothes

by Mary Griffin, Pam Hastings, Agnes Mercik, Linda Lee Vivian, and Barbara Weiland

Get the most from your serger, regardless of brand! More than 500 color photographs guide you, step-by-step, through making beautiful serger details for your garments. Choose from more than 80 classy techniques. Learn to select the best threads, needles, and stitches. Master tension settings once and for all.

Hardcover ISBN 0-87596-794-9

Sewing Secrets from the Fashion Industry

Proven Methods to Help You Sew Like the Pros

edited by Susan Huxley

Learn the same tips and techniques that the industry professionals use in their sample rooms and production factories. Over 800 full-color photographs accompany the step-by-step instructions.

Hardcover ISBN 0-87596-719-1

RODALE

For more information or to order, call 1-800-848-4735 or fax us anytime at 1-800-813-6627. Or visit our World Wide Web site at: www.rodalepress.com